MY BATTLE AGAINST HITLER

MY BATTLE AGAINST
HITLER

Faith, Truth, and Defiance
in the Shadow of the Third Reich

Dietrich von Hildebrand

Translated and Edited by
John Henry Crosby with John F. Crosby

IMAGE

NEW YORK

All rights reserved.
Published in the United States by Image, an imprint of the
Crown Publishing Group, a division of Random House LLC,
a Penguin Random House Company, New York.
www.crownpublishing.com

IMAGE is a registered trademark and the "I" colophon is
a trademark of Random House LLC.

Library of Congress Cataloging-in-Publication data is available upon request.

ISBN 978-0-385-34751-8
eBook ISBN 978-0-385-34752-5

PRINTED IN THE UNITED STATES OF AMERICA

Book design by Jennifer Daddio / Bookmark Design & Media Inc.
Jacket design by Jessie Sayward Bright
Jacket photographs: (top) Courtesy of the Dietrich von Hildebrand Legacy Project;
(bottom) Visual Photo

1 3 5 7 9 10 8 6 4 2

First Edition

If God permits evils such as Bolshevism and National Socialism, then of course, as St. Paul says, it is to test us; it is precisely our struggle against evil that God wills, even when we suffer external defeat.

DIETRICH VON HILDEBRAND

That damned Hildebrand is the greatest obstacle for National Socialism in Austria. No one causes more harm.

FRANZ VON PAPEN

NAZI AMBASSADOR TO AUSTRIA

He immunized and protected us from the philosophical waves that swept across Germany in those days. Heidegger's melodies no longer had the power to seduce us, for our ears had become more discerning. Whoever understood von Hildebrand was saved. Despite the many factors at work, I think one can rightly say that history might have been quite different had there been more professors like him.

PAUL STÖCKLEIN

STUDENT OF VON HILDEBRAND AT THE UNIVERSITY OF MUNICH

CONTENTS

PART ONE
THE MEMOIRS

PART TWO
WRITINGS AGAINST THE NAZI IDEOLOGY

A FATEFUL DECISION

Better to be a beggar in freedom than to be forced into compromises against my conscience.

—DIETRICH VON HILDEBRAND

In the early months of 1933, the world watched as Adolf Hitler came to power. On January 30, as election after election saw the Nazi Party gaining seats in the German parliament, he was appointed chancellor of Germany. On February 27 the Reichstag building, the seat of the German parliament, was destroyed in a fire. Hitler quickly exploited the resulting unrest to secure emergency powers and suspend basic rights. Terror ensued and thousands of political opponents were arrested.

One German who followed these developments with deepest indignation and sorrow was the philosopher Dietrich von Hildebrand. His heart bled at the thought that his beloved country had "fallen into the hands of criminals." But Hitler's meteoric rise was more than a source of profound grief for von Hildebrand. It confronted him with a decision. Would he remain in Germany or not? Indeed, *could* he remain? What did his conscience demand? What was God asking of him?

These questions had been on von Hildebrand's mind ever since the Nazi party was born in his hometown of Munich. He was predestined to be an enemy of Nazism, for even before the rise of the movement he had been a vocal opponent of nationalism, militarism, collectivism, and anti-Semitism, the major pillars of the Nazi ideology. Thus the Nazis had already taken note of von Hildebrand in 1921, not because he had attacked them by name, but because he had publicly condemned as an "atrocious crime" the German invasion of neutral Belgium at the start of World War I (1914). His remarks, made at a peace conference in Paris in 1921, created an uproar in the German press. He had violated the nationalist tenet of the Nazi orthodoxy, and for this he was marked for execution and then forced to flee in 1923 when Hitler attempted to seize power in Munich.

By 1933 von Hildebrand had reason to believe that his death sentence of ten years prior had long been forgotten. His decision, then, was based not just on consideration of the dangers he might face but whether he could even remain in the Third Reich. Could he live in a land where the state would legalize countless injustices and where opposition could only lead to arrest and torture?

The answer—or rather, his answer—was no. No, as a philosopher and a Catholic he could no longer stay in Germany. To remain would require a measure of silence and set him on a course of inevitable if gradual acquiescence. This, von Hildebrand believed, was as much at odds with his vocation as philosopher to seek the truth wherever it led, as it was with his Christian vocation to bear witness to the truth no matter the cost.

But von Hildebrand also knew that his decision to "abandon everything" was tied to his unique personal vocation—to "my mission," as he often expressed himself. He knew that not everyone, not even every philosopher, could or should leave Germany. He knew that heroic men like Dietrich Bonhoeffer answered a different call by remaining in Germany and working for the undoing of Nazism from within. He would later support his friends remaining in Germany by encouraging them to nurture a constant "inner rejection" of Nazism and by warning them against the danger of becoming "morally blunted" as a result of living in the midst of an evil regime. But as for himself, he knew that he was called to leave Germany. He knew that he had a particular mission to speak out against Nazism and to help rid Germany and the world of its poison. Where this might lead him he did not know in early March 1933. He abandoned his home, his beloved sisters, his large circle of friends, his rising career at the University of Munich, and his place in the center of a thriving religious and cultural community which gathered for his famous "afternoons" at the family villa on the Maria-Theresia Strasse. In following his conscience and seeking God's guidance, he believed the next step would be revealed to him.

Von Hildebrand's decision was fateful in the deepest sense of the term. It led him to Vienna, where he would establish the premier German-language journal of intellectual resistance to Nazism and Communism. His uncompromising opposition was felt throughout Austria and even deep into Nazi Germany. Hitler repeatedly demanded the Austrian government to suppress von Hildebrand's journal, and by 1937 he had gained so much attention that the Nazi ambassador in Vienna proposed to Hitler a plan to assassinate von Hildebrand and his collaborators.

One can understand von Hildebrand only up to a point if one does not grasp how radically he lived out of his faith. Indeed, in abandoning Germany, he threw himself into the arms of God. Even as he confidently challenged Nazism on the firm basis of philosophical arguments, the real source of his strength and his amazing peace and joy in those darkest of hours lay in his ever-deepening life of faith. "I had the consciousness that what I was doing was right before God," he later wrote, "and this gave me such inner freedom that I was not afraid."

His story might have been forever lost had it not been for his wife, Alice von Hildebrand. His first wife of forty-five years, Gretchen, died in 1957. She was with him during his struggle against Nazism and supported him unreservedly. In 1959, von Hildebrand married Alice Jourdain, with whom he formed a unique intellectual, spiritual, and cultural partnership. One day she said to him, "Being so much younger"—she was over thirty years his junior—"I deeply regret having missed so much of your life." "Then I will write it for you," he answered, and he began already the next day. He produced five-thousand handwritten pages recounting his life in vivid detail, beginning with his childhood, his youth, his life of faith, his education, and finally his battle against Nazism.

The epic scope of the memoirs can lead one to believe that von Hildebrand was writing for a great unseen audience of future readers. For what he reports, especially from his fight against Nazism, transcends the realm of personal recollections by capturing much of the essence of his time. But the original motive for the memoirs, indeed the *original audience,* was his wife, Alice. We owe her a deep debt of gratitude, not only for *instigating* the memoir, but for *inspiring* so much of its intimate and even confessional character.

Dietrich von Hildebrand did not publish his memoirs, nor did he seek to reprint any of his essays against Nazism. In later years he never sought to call attention to his witness in Vienna; he never saw himself as a hero or as someone deserving of special praise. It is a sign of his generous spirit that he left to others the publication of his story. But this volume is truly *by him.* It is a work of autobiography, of self-revelation. In preparing this volume we have sought not to make alterations to his canvas; our aim, rather, was to fashion a well-suited frame, above all in the form of concise historical notes, to enable the reader to relive von Hildebrand's story with all the relevant information at hand.

What might von Hildebrand have called this volume? We can never know, and given his humility he might have suggested a title that honored his collaborators rather than himself. But he did, unwittingly, provide the title. Searching the pages of his memoirs, we discovered that he had entitled an outline for part of his memoirs *"Mein Kampf Gegen Hitler"*—"My Battle Against Hitler." Thus was the present volume christened.

For all the greatness of von Hildebrand's story, his witness remains little known today. May this volume forever change that. And may his voice be heard again and his courage finally be honored, as a memory and a reminder, yes, but also as a warning and a hope.

WHO WAS THIS MAN
WHO FOUGHT HITLER?

Dietrich von Hildebrand left Germany for good on March 12, 1933. He was then forty-three years old, nearly the midpoint of his long life. But he was not unready for the witness he was being called to give. His entire life turns out to have been a preparation for this moment.

Dietrich was born on October 12, 1889, at San Francesco, his family's villa in Florence. His father, Adolf von Hildebrand, was by then one of the most renowned sculptors and architects of Germany. His mother, Irene, was a woman of learning and cultivation, even though she received very little formal schooling. Coming after five elder sisters, Dietrich was the youngest member of the von Hildebrand family and Adolf and Irene's only son. In 1898, Adolf received a commission to create a fountain, the famous Wittelsbacher Brunnen in Munich. Thereafter, the family would spend six months in Florence and six months in Munich, where they lived in a great house built by Adolf in the Maria-Theresia-Strasse.

Where in von Hildebrand's early life do we find the first signs of the future "enemy number one" of the Nazis? An anecdote from his memoirs provides a first clue. He was walking with his elder sister, Nini, who was taken aback by his resistance to her claim that all values are relative. When she appealed to their father, himself an ethical relativist, Adolf said, "but Nini, he is just a boy of fourteen." This greatly upset the young Dietrich who countered, "Your argument is clearly very weak if you have nothing but my age as evidence against me." In the last years of his life, von Hildebrand returned to this episode in the opening paragraphs of an intellectual autobiography he penned. "This episode was quite characteristic of my philosophical outlook," he writes. For not only does it express "my innermost conviction that objective truth exists and can be known," it also shows "my capacity for remaining uninfluenced by my environment and my immunity to ideas that are somehow 'in the air.'"[1]

Something that was not in the air at San Francesco was religion, and yet von Hildebrand, already as a child, showed signs of a deeply religious personality.

Adolf and Irene were nominal Protestants and saw to it that their children were baptized. But their true religion, as it were, was at the altar of beauty. As a result, he grew up living and breathing great art, and especially music, for which he had a great affinity. Religion in the sense of revelation and divine worship was not a part of their world. Churches were expressions of artistic beauty, and religion was a source of aesthetic inspiration.

But the rich culture of San Francesco—this "spiritual island," as von Hildebrand calls it—was fertile ground for more than just a discerning eye and refined ear. This "artistic world of my parents and sisters," he says, was "lofty, noble, and completely free of all triviality, conventionalism, and mediocrity." And it was reverent, not in the full sense of a supernatural reverence before God, but reverent in the recognition that the world is full of mystery and that great things call for wonder.

Even as his family's nominal Christianity all but cut him off from exposure to practice of religion, one can date Dietrich's faith to the age of five or six, if not earlier. "I don't know who first spoke to me about Christ," he writes.

> I do not remember anyone around me who was religious. There was a crucifix in our room, and Vivi [his sister] probably told me about Christ. But the love of Jesus that developed in my soul and my firm belief that Christ is God cannot be traced back to the influence of anyone in my surroundings.

His family was understandably taken aback when they began to notice signs of his religious orientation. His sister Bertele later recounted his response when she repeated what their mother had said at the table, namely that Christ was only the son of God in the sense that everyone is a child of God. She was eight and a half, Dietrich just five. He stood on his bed, solemnly stretching out his hand, and said, "I swear to you, Christ is God!"

Most children would still be heavily under the influence of their parents, but not Dietrich. Speaking of his mother, he writes:

> She probably prayed the Our Father with us, but as she was not herself a believing Christian, she never spoke to us about the divinity of Christ. But my faith in Christ's divinity was such that I was in no way unsettled by the fact that my beloved mother did not believe in it.

But this lack of faith in his mother was not a skeptical agnosticism. In fact, it would be truer to say that faith could take root in Dietrich's soul, *not so much despite* his parents' unbelief, but *rather because* of the climate of reverence and wonder in which they raised their children. Dietrich captures this in another episode that also hightlights his mother's natural religiosity.

> When I was alone [about age five], I sometimes prostrated myself on the ground before a copy of Donatello's *Head of Christ* and would remain in adoration of Christ for perhaps ten minutes. This prayer brought me joy. I remember once how my mother opened the door. Seeing me, she quietly withdrew with tears in her eyes. Though she was not herself a committed Christian, she possessed a deep reverence for all religion. Besides, both my parents had the greatest respect for any impulses in the souls of their children.

Dietrich would not allow his burgeoning religious nature to be stifled. When his elder sister Lisl took an eight-year-old Dietrich to the cathedral in Milan—as an artistic, not a religious outing—he began genuflecting at all the side altars and would not stop thinking that there was something wrong with visiting the church in a merely aesthetic attitude.

A milestone in Dietrich's religious development was reading a book of bible stories. He was six and the experience was overwhelming, for it expanded his sense of the supernatural. "An indescribable joy filled my heart as the world of revelation disclosed itself to me. Even though I did not understand every word, I somehow felt the solemnity of God's world as it enveloped me."

Striking in a different and perhaps subtler way are the signs of a deep ethical sensibility in the young Dietrich. When he was a teenager, his father wanted to show him a nude model. Adolf's reasons were not prurient; he wanted his son to witness the rare instance of a perfectly proportioned body. The boy refused, not out of puritanical shame, but because he already intuited the mysterious self-revelation of the naked body. He said to his father, "I want to save this experience until I have the privilege of seeing my wife in her nudity."

One cannot fail to be struck by von Hildebrand's remarkable independence from his milieu. This is all the more impressive when we remember that he was just a boy of five and six in the earliest instances recounted. In each case, whether intellectual, ethical, or religious, his independence was tied to an uncommon perceptive power. On the occasion with the nude model, for example, it was not just shyness or shame that held him back; rather he intuited a certain mystery of human love connected with the naked human body.

This independence would grow over the course of his intellectual and religious development. Indeed, we will see it again in his immunity to the pervasive anti-Semitism in Germany and Austria and in many other settings as well. Above all, this independence granted him a freedom to see the essence of Nazism and so to recognize that it was beyond redemption, when many of his contemporaries still labored under hopes of shaping Nazism in a Christian direction.

•   •   •

In 1906, von Hildebrand began to study philosophy at the University of Munich. Most of the foundational ideas in his critique of National Socialism were absorbed and articulated during his university years. In Munich, he first came into contact with the philosophical work of Edmund Husserl, who was then teaching in Göttingen. For von Hildebrand and many of Husserl's early students, the extraordinary appeal of "phenomenology"—as Husserl's approach was called—was its radical opposition to empiricism and its restoration of philosophical "realism." This realism attracted von Hildebrand to Göttingen, where he spent several semesters studying with Husserl, under whose direction he would write a dissertation analyzing moral action. From Husserl, von Hildebrand learned to avoid "reductionism" of all kinds, that is, the "nothing but" philosophy expressed, for example, in the idea that morality is nothing but tribal taboo or in the claim that consciousness is nothing but brain function. This commitment to the objectivity of truth made him a particularly keen critic of the Nazi way of reducing the truth of a statement to its agreement with what they believed to be the "Nordic mentality."

During his time in Munich, von Hildebrand also met the German philosopher Max Scheler, who would become a tremendous source of intellectual inspiration. Though Dietrich never formally studied under Scheler, they were for many years close friends and would spend innumerable hours in discussion. Scheler is the main source of von Hildebrand's personalist approach to philosophy. Actually, von Hildebrand never refers to himself as a "personalist," but his thought has all the hallmarks of a philosophy that seeks to answer the crucial questions of human existence by looking first to the nature and dignity of the human person. From Scheler he learned a deep reverence for the mystery and inviolability of each person. This made him especially alert to the depersonalizing tendencies of National Socialism, as shown in its idea that the individual exists only as a part (dispensable at that) of the nation.

While in Göttingen, von Hildebrand met a young woman named Margarete Denck with whom he soon fell in love. By 1910, he wanted to marry "Gretchen," as she was called, but his parents refused to give their consent, without which he could not legally marry. While they found Gretchen attractive, they relished neither her north German background nor her relatively undistinguished family pedigree. They also felt that her age (she was over four years older than Dietrich) would push him toward marriage at a moment when he was still unready. At the time, not yet being a Catholic, Dietrich and Gretchen entered a relation of sexual intimacy which both of them understood as a life-long commitment. In early 1911, Gretchen discovered she was pregnant. Dietrich's parents still would not grant him permission to marry but offered to support them financially while he finished his dissertation. The young couple moved to Vienna in the spring of 1911, where they lived until the birth of their son Franz in February 1912. Only after the arrival of their grandson did Adolf and Irene finally consent to their son's marriage, though they did not attend the Protestant ceremony which took place in May 1912. While in Vienna, von Hildebrand completed his dissertation under the direction of Husserl, who gave it a distinction of *opus eximium* (highest honors).

A decisive role in preparing the ground for von Hildebrand's conversion to the Catholic Church was played by Scheler, who made the surprising and arresting claim, "The Catholic Church is the true Church because she produces saints." Scheler spoke to von Hildebrand about St. Francis of Assisi and helped him to understand that the splendor emanating from this saint was not like any natural virtue but pointed to a new and higher source. It was the unearthly beauty shining in the saints that, more than anything else, drew von Hildebrand to Christianity and to Catholicism, to which he and Gretchen converted in 1914.

But if the beauty of Christ and the saints drew von Hildebrand to Christianity, it was his philosophical commitment, honed in his studies with Husserl and Reinach and enriched by his friendship with Scheler, that allowed his faith to mature. "It was not faith that determined my fundamental philosophical orientation," he later wrote; "rather it was my philosophical orientation that leveled the path for my reception into the Catholic Church."[2] Fideism, in which faith is understood without any dependence on reason, was always foreign to von Hildebrand.

• • •

Part of the fascination we experience with Dietrich von Hildebrand's life comes from the degree to which he remained immune to the siren song of the great ideologies of his time. Just as he showed a striking independence from the milieu of his upbringing, so he showed an unusual independence from the currents of the age.

The First World War broke out on July 28, 1914. As a married man with a son, von Hildebrand was not called to fight and was able to fulfill his military obligation for most of the war by serving as assistant to a surgeon in a Munich hospital. Only in 1918, when Germany was losing the war, was he called up for active duty. He narrowly escaped deployment in the final days of the war when he was diagnosed with chronic appendicitis.

It is difficult for most of us today to imagine a world in which Germany's hatred for its neighbors, notably for France, could stir up frenzied popular support for the war. Von Hildebrand hated this sort of militaristic nationalism, which he thought emanated from the Prussian military culture embodied by the Iron Chancellor, Otto von Bismarck. While he initially sympathized with Austria, which had been attacked in the assassination of Archduke Franz Ferdinand, he came increasingly to hate the war. He even secretly began to hope, as he says in his memoirs, that the Allies would win.

Dietrich's characteristic independence also manifested itself in another way: his absolute freedom from anti-Semitism. Like countless others, he was appalled by the violent racism of the Third Reich. But what really sets him apart from many of his contemporaries was his total freedom from the comparatively moderate anti-Semitism widespread during the 1920s and 1930s. Thriving on stereotypes—the liberal, wealthy, exploitative, amoral, and, invariably, socialist Jew—this more moderate anti-Semitism was pervasive. And it had enough currency that even Catholics who spoke out against Nazism—and personally protected Jews—could simultaneously harbor antipathy for the supposed liberalism and moral degeneracy of Jews.

In his memoirs, von Hildebrand describes one of his earliest encounters with anti-Semitism. The year 1920 saw the premiere of the orchestral *Fantastic Apparitions on a Theme by Berlioz* by his brother-in-law Walter Braunfels, by then one of Germany's leading composers. During the final applause, a man stood up in the concert hall and shouted, "I object to this Jewish music." (Though a convert to Catholicism, Braunfels was half Jewish through his father.) Approaching the man on the stairway outside the hall, von Hildebrand challenged him, "What is the meaning of this nonsense?" The man repeated his charge. When von Hildebrand pointed out, "Braunfels is not even Jewish but Catholic," the man shot back, "By race he is Jewish." All this took place in the presence of the departing concertgoers who stood silently as they waited in line at the cloakroom. "I cannot describe how much the man's outburst upset and outraged me," writes von Hildebrand. "This was the first time I experienced this rubbish which became so widespread: the notion of 'bourgeois' and 'proletarian art' in Bolshevism, and the notion of 'Aryan' and 'Jewish art and mathematics' in Nazism."

In 1919, von Hildebrand became adjunct professor for philosophy of religion at the University of Munich. Throughout his career in Munich he became increasingly outspoken in his critique of National Socialism, using the classroom and his frequent public lectures to speak against its ideological foundations. Many of von Hildebrand's students have commented on his intuitive power. Balduin Schwarz, his leading student in Munich, captures this well: "He had a great talent for detecting what was 'in the air,' almost as if he had a kind of barometer for whatever was ominously brewing in the atmosphere."[3] While his comments could be blunt—"I tell you the Nazis are the most vicious animals,"[4] he said in 1924—he was also enormously persuasive. "He immunized and protected us from the philosophical waves that swept across Germany in those days," remembers his student Paul Stöcklein. "Heidegger's melodies no longer had the power to seduce us, for our ears had become more discerning. Whoever understood von Hildebrand was saved. Despite the many factors at work, I think one can rightly say that history might have been quite different had there been more professors like him."[5]

One German professor who helped history turn out as it did was

Martin Heidegger. Even though Heidegger is probably the best-known German philosopher of the twentieth century, he was notoriously a zealous Nazi, and in fact in later years he never recanted his Nazi allegiance. It is true that von Hildebrand and Heidegger had the same teacher in philosophy, namely Edmund Husserl, but on the question of Nazism, they were as opposed as two thinkers can possibly be. To the scandal of Heidegger's Nazism we oppose the heroic witness of von Hildebrand.

In keeping with his own public stance, von Hildebrand also challenged his students to take action. But this action was distinctly philosophical in nature. Rather than urging direct political involvement, let alone violent agitation, "he sent them to attend gatherings of National Socialists where through pointed questions they could expose the inhumanity and intellectual incoherence of Nazism."[6]

In 1930, von Hildebrand published *The Metaphysics of Community*,[7] his major work in social philosophy. The book can be seen as the culmination of his reflections on the nature of community, a subject that he thought was badly misunderstood, even by fellow Catholic thinkers. But this book, while a work of fundamental philosophy, was full of implications for the crisis of the day, especially the collectivism of National Socialism. It had prepared him in a unique way to think clearly and outside of the conventional political paradigms and the usual false alternatives, especially the widely held view that one had to choose between collectivism or individualism.

Indeed, he understood why collectivism appealed so strongly to ordinary Germans. He saw that people experienced the bankruptcy of what he called "liberal individualism," which made them feel isolated from one another. National Socialism seemed to offer relief; as a dynamic movement it exploited this deep craving for community and offered a powerful feeling of togetherness. Mingled with the nationalism to which Germany was ever vulnerable, collectivism had something irresistibly appealing about it. But von Hildebrand saw that the intoxication of mass rallies and marches created only a pseudocommunity. It played on a need, but did not offer the real thing. Nazism could produce elation and a sense of national purpose, but it also paved the way for a state in which an individual who opposed its ends was simply eliminated.

We can see other key ideas in von Hildebrand's philosophy at work in his critique of Nazism. Striking is the degree to which he opposed Nazism aside from any harm it might do to him or to his family or to the Catholic Church. Here he was prepared philosophically by the seminal concept of "value," which he had developed in his dissertation and which would form the golden thread throughout his entire body of thought. To see "value" in something in von Hildebrand's sense is to recognize its goodness "in itself" and not only to recognize it as something beneficial for me or others close to me. The same logic carries over to "disvalue," which is badness, not in virtue of any harm it might bring to me, but simply bad in itself.

If abstract in theory, "value" and "disvalue" become concrete in von Hildebrand's anti-Nazism. Take an episode from early 1933. Speaking to a friend who was vice president of the Catholic Academic Association, von Hildebrand expressed his surprise that the Association would hold a previously planned symposium on the grounds that the true work of the Association was surely impossible under the Hitler regime. His friend responded by jubilantly producing a cordial telegram he had received from Franz von Papen, then-vice chancellor of Germany. Von Hildebrand was dismayed:

> How could a vice president of the Catholic Academic Association, founded to imbue everything with the spirit of Catholicism, base his judgment of a regime on whether it was courteous toward the Association, rather than looking to the regime's spirit and its first principles?"

Here von Hildebrand speaks out of his value philosophy. While his friend still appraised Nazism in terms of how Hitler would treat the Association, von Hildebrand was looking only at who Hitler really was.

The turbulent years in German public life that coincided with von Hildebrand's tenure at the University in Munich gave him great reason for concern; nevertheless they were exceptionally fruitful for him in terms of new philosophical insights. In 1922, he gave a series of lectures on the virtue of purity at the Catholic Academic Association, of which he was a leading member. These lectures, published in German in 1927 and in English a few years later as *In Defense of Purity* (1931),[8] created a stir in Catholic circles, which received them in the awareness that they marked a sea change in the Christian approach to sexuality. Not a few people who read his work on purity in the 1930s and 1940s describe a sudden awakening to a sense of the depth and beauty of conjugal love that was totally unlike what had been presented to them in their religious education. He would expand his reflections in his pathbreaking book *Die Ehe*, published in 1929 (and in English as *Marriage* in 1942). One cannot understand the seismic shift in von Hildebrand's thought on love and sexuality without grasping that for nearly two thousand years Christian teaching had defined the conjugal act almost exclusively in terms of its power to bring about new life. According to historian John Noonan, von Hildebrand was the first Catholic thinker to argue thematically that sexual union was oriented not just to procreation but also to expressing the love between spouses.[9]

The ideas on marriage that von Hildebrand was pioneering during the 1920s would find expression in the Second Vatican Council's teaching on the dual meaning of the conjugal act, namely to generate new life and also to enact the love between spouses.[10]

The depth and reverence with which he approached married love empowered him to think with clarity about the attacks on marriage embodied in the Nazi race laws prohibiting intermarriage between Germans and Jews. He saw with particular keenness not just the overreaching of the state but the invasion of this most intimate and sacred of human spheres.

The Nazi crisis led von Hildebrand to address questions that might otherwise not have caught his attention. One of these was the rise of anti-Semitism. He opposed, as already noted, not just the anti-Semitism that aimed at extermination but also the more moderate anti-Semitism found in pervasive stereotypes and antipathies. But anti-Semitism also led him to think deeply on the meaning of the Jewish people. In his writing the "Jewish question" took on an entirely different meaning than it generally did in German and Austrian political and intellectual life at the time.

The German race laws and even many Catholic thinkers approached the question from a purely racial and ethnic basis. By contrast, von Hildebrand wrote that the Jews are the "only people whose inner point of unity lay not at a racial or cultural level but on the religious level. True belief in the one God," he says, "and the awaiting of the Messiah constituted the 'form' of Israel's unity."[11] The historian John Connelly, in his book *From Enemy to Brother*, marvels how von Hildebrand could emerge so completely unaffected by the anti-Semitism under which so many other Catholics labored.[12]

The relentlessness of von Hildebrand's anti-Nazi critique might suggest a stern, even severe, disposition. Nothing could be further from the truth. All who knew him say he radiated a contagious joy and mirth. "He was happy and grateful for all great things that call for reverence," remembers his student Paul Stöcklein. "His inner happiness made itself felt in the way he spoke. This happiness struck me as free of any self-deception. I had never realized it was possible for someone to be so happy."[13] His philosophical genius and extraordinary culture did not make him inaccessible; rather, his "inner wealth" was integrated into a lively concern for the well-being of his friends, his family, and especially his students.

He was spontaneous and effusive, but not in a way that was reducible to natural disposition. It was an expression of how deeply he lived by his own "value philosophy," with its emphasis on the "due response" to values and disvalues. It was also, for anyone who knew him, an expression of joy that flowed from the deep faith in which he lived moment to moment.

Von Hildebrand's rich contact with "the world of values" challenges us to think of his political witness not just in terms of resistance and opposition. He was not merely *opposed* to Nazism. Or rather, his opposition was *rooted in his devotion to* the West, which to him above all meant the Judeo-Christian West with its commitment to truth, its respect for the dignity of the individual person, and its great cultural inheritance.

It is now high time that we open the pages of von Hildebrand's memoirs. The stage has been set. We join him, in Paris, as a youthful professor of thirty-one.

The year is just 1921, yet already battle with Hitler looms on the horizon.

A NOTE ON THE TEXT

Most of the texts presented in this volume are drawn from a German edition of von Hildebrand's anti-Nazi papers edited by Austrian historian Ernst Wenisch and published under the title *Memoiren und Aufsätze gegen den Nationalsozialismus (Memoirs and Essays Against National Socialism)*.[1] Not only did Wenisch have privileged access to the manuscript of the memoirs, from which he made selections for this volume, he also produced a first-rate set of scholarly notes, which form the basis of many of the notes in this volume. Wenisch's volume also includes about a third of von Hildebrand's essays from *Der christliche Ständestaat*, of which we have selected twelve (in many cases just excerpts). Wenisch features two important remembrances of von Hildebrand by Balduin Schwarz and Paul Stöcklein, students of von Hildebrand at the University of Munich. We cite their personal testimonies in "Who Was This Man Who Fought Hitler?"

Our edition also features new material never before published. Of greatest importance are new passages taken directly from the handwritten manuscript of the memoirs, as well as extensive passages, featured in the chapter, "Escape from Vienna," derived from unpublished outlines and sketches by von Hildebrand. One particularly precious source we present is a previously unpublished letter of Michael Braunfels, von Hildebrand's nephew, to Alice von Hildebrand describing his role in helping his uncle and aunt leave Vienna on the night of March 11, 1938.

John Henry Crosby is translator of the memoirs as well as author of "A Fateful Decision," "Who Was This Man Who Fought Hitler?," and

"Escape from Vienna." William Doino and David Mills helped in crafting the many passages that introduce and strengthen the narrative flow of the memoirs. John F. Crosby is the principal translator of von Hildebrand's essays (with help from the team of translators mentioned in the acknowledgments), author of the brief introductions that accompany each of the essays, and his son John Henry Crosby's indispensable intellectual and editorial partner.

PART I

THE MEMOIRS

1921

In early December 1921, von Hildebrand went to Paris, "with high expectations," to attend a convention organized by the philosopher and politician Marc Sangnier (1873–1950). Sangnier had become famous for seeking to reconcile Catholicism with the French Republic, and more broadly Christianity and Democracy, in part as a counter to working-class movements that were overtly anticlerical. Sangnier hoped to reevangelize young men by proving Catholicism was sympathetic to their social and economic needs. He also sought common ground with non-Catholics.

At first, the Christian-Democratic movement he started, Le Sillon (The Furrow), won many devoted followers, including numerous bishops. But when it began to advocate new ideas, not yet approved by the Church, Pope Pius X intervened to close the movement in 1910.

Sangnier's response to "the destruction of his life's work" is described by von Hildebrand in great detail. Despite the suppression of Le Sillon, many of Sangnier's ideals about the laity, social justice, ecumenism, and society were fulfilled by Vatican II's teaching. One of his greatest admirers was Pope John XXIII, who called the Council.

Arriving in Paris, von Hildebrand was met at the train station and brought to the headquarters of the Young Republic League, the political party Sangnier had founded. There he met Sangnier, "this great and noble Catholic"—words similar to those Pius X had used, even as he closed down Le Sillon—and several of his followers at breakfast.

· · ·

The spirit of love of neighbor and of Christian warmth, which suffused the milieu, made an overwhelming impression on me. Everything was very simple—typically French coffee, served in a bowl and strongly flavored with chicory, along with a piece of bread—yet I was received as an old friend. The spirit was one of simple togetherness and collaboration. I was delighted.

Marc Sangnier had founded a movement which was the first Catholic movement in France to be established on the footing of the Republic. French Catholics and all of the French bishops were Royalists of a decidedly conservative stripe. Drawing on an encyclical of Pope Leo XIII,[1] in which the Holy Father declared that the Church took a neutral stance toward questions of monarchy and republic, he had founded a religious movement which he called "Le Sillon," meaning "Furrow." The purpose of the movement was to bring about a deep religious renewal, and with it a truly Christian spirit.

"Sillon" was the very antithesis of the "Action française." A predominantly conservative and nationalist movement, the "Action française" valued the Church primarily as a cultural entity, viewing "Catholic" as equivalent to "Latin," whereby the "Esprit Latin" was naturally equated above all with the spirit of France. The anti-Semitism which had manifested itself in such a dreadful way in the Dreyfus Affair[*] continued to exist in the "Action française." In contrast to all of this, "Sillon" was filled with a supranational spirit, free of all anti-Semitism, concerned with social issues, seeing the Catholic Church as the mystical body of Christ, filled with a truly deep Catholic spirit and an obedient and loyal love of the Church.

Late in the evening, Sangnier often went to the basilica of Montmartre with his followers where they spent the night in prayer and religious song. Along the way, he gave them talks on religious subjects. A spirit of boundless readiness to be of service to each other, a joyful, loving, selfless collaboration filled this movement, which quickly spread all over France and soon numbered many young priests and seminarians.

---

[*] A reference to Alfred Dreyfus (1859–1935), a French Jewish officer unjustly convicted in 1894 on alleged charges of treason.

"Sillon" represented a real religious springtime and as such became a great and profound center of formation in true Christian living. Sangnier, who came from a very affluent family, had given a great portion of his fortune to this movement.

The bishops—who were all conservative and royalists at the time—took a suspicious, not to say hostile, stance toward "Sillon." Added to this was the occasional silly and exaggerated statement made by a young and enthusiastic seminarian. The bishops turned to Pope Pius X, to whom they painted an unfavorable image of "Sillon." Being the time of the struggle against modernism, it was not difficult to portray a movement as dangerous. Pius X wrote a letter to Marc Sangnier in which he called upon him to subordinate his movement to the respective local bishops.

This would have been the end of "Sillon," since the bishops would have wanted to reshape everything. Pius' letter was a terrible blow for Sangnier, yet he offered a wonderful and unique example. A quarter of an hour after he had received the letter which destroyed his life's work, he dissolved "Sillon" and wrote a letter to the Holy Father in which he said, "This is the most beautiful hour of my life, for now I can show how much I love the Church and that I do not want to serve her as I wish but as she wishes."

He proceeded to found a political movement called the Young Republic League, which, since officially it was purely political, did not need to be placed under the bishops' control. Yet the deeply Catholic and profoundly Christian spirit continued to exist in this political movement. Everything in the League's house in the Boulevard Raspail gave evidence of this.

Out of this supranational Catholic spirit, Sangnier had called for a peace congress to which for the first time he had also included Germans as warmly invited guests. He was a great and noble personality. In his presence one felt the tremendous warmth of his heart, the fire of his spirit, his unwavering faith in his ideals. And he also had the immense charm of a Frenchman, a delightful wittiness. He was an orator of exceptional ability, one of the best I ever heard. I was deeply impressed by him, especially after I had heard his entire story, which made the image of his personality emerge with greater liveliness and clarity. He was a

great and devoted son of the Church, a heroic crusader against nationalism and all prejudice, a generous and captivating human being. I felt a
real love for him and we were entirely of one mind.

Among the Germans who had been invited were two priests. One
was Fr. Metzger from Graz, where he led a religious, pacifist movement
called the "White Cross."* He was originally from Swabia. The other
priest was the founder of the German Catholic Association for Peace, a
vicar from Ehingen an der Donau.†

Fr. Metzger was a striking personality. Someone later said to me of
him that he was a mixture of saint and extraordinarily talented businessman. What predominantly struck me was that, while filled with
a heroic religious fervor, he had something of the sectarian in his veg-
etarianism and his radical opposition to alcoholism. He was very kind
and friendly, addressed me with the familiar "Du"‡ a little too quickly,
and amazed me by his enormous talent for organization.

During the congress I was utterly appalled to read in a German
newspaper an incredibly tactless article about Marc Sangnier. At the
very moment when, burdened by great difficulties and attacked from all
sides, he dared to invite Germans to Paris and to make this extraordinary friendly gesture to Germany, there appears in a German Catholic
newspaper an article in which he is portrayed as a dubious Catholic,
having been recently censured by Rome.

I was beside myself with rage and when I met a German journalist
by the name of Alfred Nobel,§ I said to him, "which tactless blockhead
wrote this article?" Unfortunately he was himself the author and naturally I had made in him a mortal enemy. It was not long before I would
feel this directly.

There were many sessions—smaller gatherings as well as public

---

* Max Josef Metzger (1887–1944), priest who later founded Una Sancta and was executed by the
Nazis as an opponent of National Socialism.

† Probably Fr. Franziskus Stratmann, OP (1883–1971), cofounder with Fr. Metzger of the German Catholic Association for Peace.

‡ The form of "you" reserved for family and friends.

§ Probably Alphons Nobel, later chief editor of the *Augsburger Postzeitung*.

presentations—at which lectures were delivered by well-known French personalities. During one of the smaller discussions—even so, all of the delegates and many French attendees were present, in all a group of perhaps fifty—a lady from Berlin called out to me in a side room where I was engaged in a private conversation, "Please come. The situation is getting very tense. Perhaps you can be of some help."

As I approached the table, I heard a Frenchman attacking Sangnier for having invited Germans, saying, "These Germans are not really anti-nationalists and pacifists. I have only to ask them whether they will admit that Germany is responsible for the war and then you will see how their nationalism prevents them from making this admission." At this I stood up and said, speaking in French, "It would not be sincere on my part to answer this question, for I do not know the Russian archives, I do not know the historical antecedents of the war, and I am not in a position to find out about these things. Besides, the question itself can have different meanings. But if I had the opportunity to get informed and if I saw that Germany was at fault, I would not for a moment hesitate to say so. I am not a nationalist in any sense of the word and so I would feel no inner resistance to admitting it."

Thereupon the man arose and said, "Very well, then I will put another question to you. Your answer will clearly demonstrate whether you are honest. If you say that you are not a nationalist, then what do you think about the German invasion of Belgium?"[*] I stood up again and said, "That was an atrocious crime." Thunderous applause greeted my words. I continued, "I have no problem in admitting that it was a dreadful crime. For I am first a Catholic, then a Catholic, and yet again a Catholic, and so on and on." Again, thunderous applause.[†]

Afterwards people congratulated me and a senator from Brussels said to me, "You are a good young man from a family of bad reputation"

---

[*] On August 4, 1914, at the very beginning of World War I.

[†] Belgian neutrality was protected under the Treaty of London (1839), to which England, Austria, France, Prussia, Russia, and the Netherlands were signatories. Von Hildebrand's repeated profession of his Catholic identity would have been an obvious and poignant allusion to the fact that this treaty was signed "In the name of the Most Holy and Indivisible Trinity."

("*Brave jeune hommo d'une famille de mauvaise réputation*"). But above all I was surrounded by the followers of Marc Sangnier, all of whom congratulated me. Sangnier was very happy about what I had said, yet I saw in Nobel's face how outraged he was. I was soon to experience his revenge. Metzger, who was murdered by the Nazis in 1944, as well as the chaplain from Ehingen, however, were entirely in agreement.

As I returned to Munich the next morning and reached our house in the Maria-Theresia Strasse, I found Gretchen in a state of great agitation, for my name was mentioned throughout the German press as one who had committed a kind of high treason for having announced in Paris that Germany alone was guilty of the war. An inquiry had also come from the university: I was immediately to clarify the truth of this charge. The faculty was largely composed of German nationalists who would have preferred to drive me away from the university.

All this had been brought upon me by Nobel through his deliberately false report—I had, after all, explained that I could not take a stance toward this question since I was not educated on the prior history of the situation. For condemning the invasion of Belgium no one could reproach me; after all, Cardinal Faulhaber* had done so too. But of course, as a sworn enemy of nationalism, the nationalists were from their perspective right to hate me.

In any case, I was completely occupied with composing for the press and, in a separate document, for the university, an exact account of the facts and with refuting Nobel's misrepresentation. I also received a letter from the president of the Catholic Academic Association, Wilhelm Bergmann, in which he wrote to me, "Since to date you have been the chairman of the commission for relations with foreign countries, I would ask that you send me an exact account of the events in Paris."[2] This was clearly disavowal of me and a kind of implied removal from the commission. I sent him my statement to the press with a note that this should settle the affair. I did not in any way go into the possibility of being removed from the commission.

---

* Michael von Faulhaber (1869–1952), archbishop and later cardinal of Munich and Freising.

1922

In the years following World War I, Germany experienced enormous political and economic turbulence. In June 1922, the German foreign minister, Walter Rathenau (1867–1922), was assassinated. "Words cannot express," says von Hildebrand, "how deeply this latest political assassination upset me."

Once again the devilish countenance of German ultranationalism smirked at me, which had already so deeply shaken me at the time of Erzberger's[*] murder. Once again I felt the increasing barbarization of morals. I remember crying out to Gretchen, "I no longer want to remain in this awful country! I want to leave Germany!" Almost as bad as the awful deed, not to mention the attitude of the murderer, was the perception of the murder by broad segments of the public.

On the occasion of Eisner's[†] murder by Count Arco,[‡] it was still possible to find mitigating factors, namely the fact that Eisner was a usurper who had toppled the Bavarian monarchy through a revolution and made himself head of state. Even though he did not create a dictatorship, he did permit dangerous elements to take root and systematically pursued his aim—against the will of the people—of attacking the

---

[*] Matthias Erzberger (1875–1920), German politician and finance minister.

[†] Kurt Eisner (1867–1919), German journalist who led the socialist revolution that brought down the Bavarian monarchy.

[‡] Count Anton von Arco auf Valley (1897–1945).

Church and imposing a radically socialist spirit. Arco could in good faith view himself as murdering a tyrant, as carrying out the people's will. Of course, his action was morally questionable and problematic, yet it was not a typical case of criminal political murder.

But the case of Erzberger was different. He had done nothing to harm anyone, had for years served as a legitimately elected member of the Reichstag, and had become minister in a constitutionally legitimate manner, governing without even the faintest hint of a dictatorship. He had done much to his credit and was a noble man of conscience. It was thus impossible to find any mitigating factors for his murder. And those who killed him, Tillesen and Schulz, embodied a spirit totally unlike that of the pious and conscientious Arco. Their words, "The pig must be slaughtered" betrayed the depth of the awful, base, petty, and criminal spirit that animated them. The fact that they were motivated by an ugly nationalism and that they viewed themselves as heroes only made their dreadful act of murder all the worse.

I was terribly upset by what even Catholics said to me, at the time. "The ordinary man on the street is not upset by this murder," I would hear, "for he sees how many people died in the war. How can one more death really matter?" As if the decisive factor was not the murder itself! On one occasion a Catholic—a priest, I fear—said to me, "This won't stir up the people. They'll say, 'one Jew more or less is of no consequence.'" I was deeply upset by this moral value blindness and the loss of any sense for the horror of murder, which had permeated German public opinion.

The response of Chancellor Wirth[*] to the death of his friend and colleague in the Federal Ministry was quite forceful. Expressing his indignation at a session of the Reichstag, which had immediately been convened, he uttered his famous words: "The enemy stands to our right." Wirth was correct inasmuch as the murderous spirit that had led to the assignation reigned above all in ultranationalistic circles. But one could reasonably question whether the term "right" could be ap-

---

[*] Joseph Wirth (1879–1946), German politician of the Catholic Center Party.

plied to these circles without qualification. In any case, the problem did not stem from the monarchists and from circles who were conservative in the best sense of the term. Rather, it came from those animated by the spirit of Ludendorff[*] and by a wild anarchism tainted with strong sympathies for a Greater Germany.[†] It came from the forerunners of National Socialism who could hardly be called "right" in the traditional sense of the term.

On the other hand, the tremendous danger of Socialism and Communism had not yet been overcome. Just three years before we had had the Socialist Republic in Munich, and in 1922 there had been heavy fighting against the Communists in Essen. Wirth's articulation thus perhaps oversimplified the situation too much. But I was still happy because he took a strong stance against the murderous spirit of these assassinations and expressed an attitude so different from the one I often encountered in the public.

I still remember walking with my beloved and revered Nuncio Pacelli[‡] and Don Mario. This took place shortly after the murder of Rathenau and I spoke with him about what Wirth had said. He was very unhappy about Wirth's statement because he found the notion of "right" far too vague. He rightly emphasized that one could not allow one or more political murders perpetrated by those on the far right to diminish the danger of Communism and to allow us to forget all the atrocities being committed from that side.

---

[*] Erich Ludendorff (1865–1937), German general who was then widely viewed as a hero for his victories in World War I.

[†] The unification of all German-speaking peoples in a single German nation.

[‡] Eugenio Pacelli (1876–1958) nuncio in Munich (1917) and Berlin (1920–29), Vatican secretary of state in 1930, elected Pope Pius XII (1939–58).

1923

Von Hildebrand's denunciation of nationalism at the convention in Paris in April 1921 earned him the hatred of the Nazis. "The political situation was taking on an increasingly threatening character," he writes, while "the Nazi demonstrations were becoming ever more brazen." Von Hildebrand would have his first real brush with danger two and a half years after Paris, when Hitler attempted to seize power in Bavaria in the famous Beer Hall Putsch of November 8 and 9, 1923. Arriving with six hundred Storm Troopers—the paramilitary of the Nazi Party—Hitler entered the Bürgerbräukeller in Munich where Gustav von Kahr (1862–1934), the state commissioner of Bavaria, was holding a rally with a crowd of several thousand supporters.

As Hitler and his henchmen entered the hall that night, a shot was fired at the ceiling, and Hitler took the floor, yelling, "The national revolution has broken out!" Hitler's aim was to depose the Bavarian government and then topple the Weimar Republic government with a "March on Berlin," similar to Mussolini's "March on Rome" the year before. Hitler had Kahr and his associates detained at gunpoint and ordered them to cooperate. A feverish Hitler returned to the podium to declare, "I can say this to you. Either the German revolution begins tonight or we will all be dead by dawn!"

A cheer then went up as General Erich von Ludendorff (1865–1937), a national hero from World War I, appeared to offer the revolutionaries his support. As the chaotic evening unfolded, the putsch rapidly came apart, as Kahr escaped (or was allowed to flee) and the mutiny was soon put down by the Bavarian police. But none of this was known to von Hildebrand when the news first reached him the next morning.

. . .

Thus came November 9, 1923. I attended 7:00 a.m. mass in Bogen-hausen. My class was to begin at 9:15 a.m. As I left the church, I met Prince Clemens, the son of Prince Alfons, whose brother was Prince Ludwig Ferdinand.* He asked me if I already knew what had happened last night. I said I hadn't heard anything, and so he told me that, at the Bürgerbräukeller, Ludendorff had been proclaimed President of Germany and Hitler Chancellor. Kahr had acquiesced, while other members of the Bavarian cabinet had been taken captive.

By his account it sounded as if the Nazis in association with Ludendorff were in control, at least in Munich, and as if the army in Bavaria would not offer any resistance. The extent to which this putsch would succeed throughout all of Germany was naturally the question. One could hope that the army would remain faithful to the Reich government.

But I had no time for any of these considerations. I was completely distressed and horrified by this turn of events, about the fact that Bavaria had fallen into the hands of criminals, about the triumph of this horrid ultra-nationalism and this deeply anti-Christian spirit. At the same time, National Socialism and Hitler as its leader represented the epitome of kitsch—a flat, gloomy, and incredibly trivial world, a barren and ignorant mindset. But aside from all these reasons to be distressed, the putsch presented a great and immediate danger for me. I had after all just learned from Marguerite Solbrig†, my future secretary, who had it from a reliable source, that I was on the Nazi blacklist.

Marguerite told me at the time about an exchange she had with an injured soldier, who had previously been under her care for some time. He was an officer who had lost both his arms and legs. He spoke to her enthusiastically about Hitler, to which she responded that he should discuss this with me as I would clearly show him how false and

---

* Members of the House of Wittelsbach, the royal family of Bavaria until 1918.
† Marguerite Solbrig (1890–1969), close lifelong friend of von Hildebrand.

un-Christian the ideas of Hitler were. He answered, "What, should I speak with Dietrich von Hildebrand, that traitor? He has long been on our blacklist of those we will execute immediately when we come to power." This information would prove very important for me. The designation "traitor" was naturally due to my critical statement about the German invasion of neutral Belgium at the congress of Marc Sangnier.

I hastened home on my bicycle. I needed to be at the university by 9:00 a.m. for my class. Could I still risk teaching or should I flee without delay? I immediately telephoned Fr. Alois Mager* and asked him what I should do. He recommended that I go to my class since the entire city was not yet in the hands of the Nazis. Kahr had retracted his consent, which he had given under duress.† The Nazis only controlled the city to the right of the Isar River, and of course the university lay to the left.

Fr. Mager was to come to the university after my class to tell me whether I must flee and to advise me in my next steps. So I got onto my bicycle and road across the Bogenhausen bridge right past the SA‡ checkpoint and into the side of the city to the left of the Isar. There was no barricade for civilians. I passed through without being noticed and so, crossing the English Garden, I arrived at the university on time. There, to a reduced class, I gave my lecture on the idea of being and on the difference between essence and existence. All the while, one could hear the sounds of demonstrations around the university, and the entire situation was filled with great tension.

I no longer remember how much I knew that morning about the actual unfolding of the putsch. How much had Prince Clemens told me, how much did he know himself, how much had Fr. Alois told me by telephone?

Having concluded my lecture, I found Fr. Alois standing at the door of my classroom. He said to me, "I inquired and read a placard an-

---

* Alois Mager, OSB (1885-1946), a prominent Benedictine monk of the Abbey of Beuron and also von Hildebrand's confessor.

† Hitler would take his revenge on Kahr, having him murdered in the so-called "Night of the Long Knives" on June 30, 1934.

‡ Short for "Sturmabteilung," often called "Brownshirts," the original paramilitary of the Nazi Party.

nouncing the establishment of a popular tribunal, where there is only acquittal or the death penalty. The death sentence must be carried out within an hour of being handed down. Even if the Nazis only maintain power for a few hours, this means that your life is at risk. You must leave until order is reestablished or, at least, until the Nazi putsch is quelled. Obviously you cannot go to your home, where you could quickly be found, especially since your house is in the part of Munich occupied by the SA. Come with me to Beuron College.'"[*]

Expressing my thanks, I went with him to the College. From there I spoke with my wife Gretchen[†] by telephone. I told her I wanted to flee with her to Württemberg.[‡] I asked her to pack the necessities and told her that a student of mine, Balduin Schwarz,[§] would come over to carry the suitcase to the train station. Balduin, who was in my course, had naturally heard of all this and had come with me and Fr. Alois to Beuron College. From there he went to the Maria-Theresia Strasse, probably riding his bicycle through the English Garden.

Fr. Alois advised that I ride the streetcar to Pasing and there board the train to Ulm, since a checkpoint for travelers might already have been set up at the central train station in Munich. He thought that my wife Gretchen and our son Franzi[¶] could risk boarding at the central station. Beuron College was close to the Barer Strasse. So I rode with Fr. Alois on the streetcar along the Augustenstrasse to Pasing. This naturally took some time so that we arrived in Pasing around noon.

A friend, Elizabeth Kaufmann, whom—if memory serves—I had met at Beuron College, lent me some money, as I did not have enough with me for the trip. I met Gretchen and Franzi on the train and we rode to Ulm. Already in Augsburg I learned that a battle had broken out between the SA and the army on the Odeonsplatz. Ludendorff stood at

---

[*] A Benedictine residence.

[†] Margarete (née Denck) von Hildebrand (1885–1957) married Dietrich in 1912.

[‡] Württemberg was the German state to the east of Bavaria.

[§] Balduin Schwarz (1902–93), leading student and close friend of von Hildebrand, taught in Germany, Switzerland, and New York.

[¶] Franz von Hildebrand (1912–77), von Hildebrand's son and only child, who would have been just eleven in 1923.

the front of the Nazis assuming that his presence would be sufficient to deter the army from shooting. Yet this is not what happened. The army opened fire, several Nazis fell, Ludendorff was taken captive, and Hitler fled.

I no longer recall how many details I already knew in Augsburg. In any case, I was aware of the armed confrontation and that Ludendorff had been taken captive, for I still recall getting into a discussion about Ludendorff with another passenger. He was lamenting that this "great man" had been captured, whereas I did not hesitate to say that through his participation in the putsch he had forfeited his life, and that I hoped he would receive the appropriate punishment.

From the rumors I realized that the battle had taken place just as I was riding to Pasing with Fr. Alois. Had we known this, it would no longer have been necessary to flee. Nevertheless, we rode to Ulm where we stayed at a very good hotel well known to us. The next morning, when it was clear that the Nazi putsch had been completely subdued, we rode back to Munich in high spirits. Hitler had been found hiding under Fräulein Hanfstaengl's bed, and was now under lock and key.[*]

Our return to Munich was especially joyful. Not only is it remarkable how much more we appreciated public peace and security, having just been in great danger, but also the pathetic failure of the Nazi putsch had a wonderful cleansing effect on the oppressive milieu which had been building up for years. The uncanny feeling that the Nazi movement was becoming an increasing menace, the fact that growing numbers of people saw it as inevitable, even if they did not explicitly welcome it, had been poisoning the political atmosphere for a long time. The government of Kahr had only served to heighten this concern.

Now this danger had suddenly collapsed. Ludendorff was being tried in court. Hitler had made a laughingstock of himself through his Buffalo Bill entrance, his ignominious flight, and discovery under Fräulein Hanfstaengl's bed. One had the impression that the Nazi nightmare had been definitively averted. Unfortunately this later turned out to be

---

[*] In fact, Hitler had been found hiding in a closet in the country home of Ernst (Putzi) Hanfstaengl, who was later head of the Nazi Foreign Press Bureau.

mistaken, but in November 1923 it seemed that way. It was possible to breathe a sigh of relief, and I more than most was overjoyed.

To my great regret Ludendorff was acquitted.* It was unbelievable that one did not dare to punish him because of his status as a World War I hero. The truth is that he should have been punished for his role in the World War, where aside from many war crimes he was also to blame that a truce was not reached in 1917. The Bavarian judges at that time were deeply infected by nationalism. Ludendorff's participation in the Hitler putsch was clearly a crime. Had a leftist done the same thing, he would undoubtedly have been shot.

Even worse was the fact that Hitler, who lacked even the appearance of a national hero, was condemned to a respectable imprisonment rather than at least being sentenced to life in prison. Even so, it seemed that Hitler was finished once and for all. A year later, *Simplicissimus*† ran a caricature depicting Hitler in a restaurant selling his book *Mein Kampf* for two marks. Hitler had written this book during his imprisonment, which had become public knowledge even though it had not yet been published.‡

---

* The Hitler-Ludendorff trial took place between February 26 and March 27, 1924. In the verdict of April 1, 1924, Ludendorff was acquitted and Hitler was sentenced to five years' imprisonment.

† A satirical German magazine.

‡ Hitler had worked on the book until October 1924. It appeared in two volumes in 1925 and 1926.

1932

Though sentenced for five years, Hitler was released after just nine months. As he began to rebuild the Nazi Party, von Hildebrand's concern, only briefly assuaged by the failure of the Beer Hall Putsch, once more began to grow. "I tell you," he said to one of his students in 1924, "the Nazis are the most vicious animals." By early 1932, the German political situation was "increasingly poisoned by the growth of the Nazi movement."

On April 10, Paul von Hindenburg (1847–1934) was reelected president of Germany with over nineteen million votes, but Hitler received over thirteen million. In early May, von Hildebrand gave a talk at the Special Conference on Sociology offered by the Catholic Academic Association, which at the time boasted a membership of over 10,000. It was held at the Abbey of Maria Laach, a Benedictine monastery in western Germany. There he met several theologians advancing "Reichstheologie," which led them to seek common ground with National Socialism. Franz von Papen (1879–1969), a Catholic and the German chancellor in the latter part of 1932 who would play a role in Hitler's rise to power, also attended the conference.

Two days later, after the elections, Wilhelm Groener, Minister of Defense and the Interior, banned the private National Socialist militias,* which

---

* Both the "Sturmabteilung," or SA, and the "Schutzstaffel," known as the SS.

seemed like a very positive development and which I saw as a stroke of very good fortune. As I found out much later (in 1945) from Brüning personally,[*] this was a great a mistake since Hitler was bankrupt and no longer capable of paying his units. Had they not been banned, Hitler would have had to send them packing for financial reasons, which might have been a fatal loss of prestige for him. Thus Hitler was spared a great disgrace and he was able to play the role of the loyal citizen by declaring that if the state forbade his militias, then there was no alternative but to disband them—albeit with a heavy heart. In reality this prohibition was very convenient for him.

No one knew about this at the time, that is, neither I nor surely many others knew it. Opponents of Nazism therefore welcomed the ban which they perceived as an awakening on the part of the government, as a long-awaited intervention to end the intolerable situation of the militias, which of course only the state has a right to maintain (such as an army or a police force).

Yet Groener was soon forced out of office, a very bad omen followed in short order by Brüning's resignation on May 30. The symposium at Maria Laach probably took place at the end of April or in the first days of May. It thus occurred in the midst of this politically turbulent period, lending a particular timeliness to my lecture on "The Individual and the State."

I was terribly upset by a talk of the Franciscan priest Soiron,[†] whom Münch[‡] greatly esteemed and who so far had made a very good impression. Soiron's talk was completely infected by the poison of collectivism and showed that, under the intoxicating influence of the Zeitgeist, he was completely blinded. He overemphasized the notion of community at the expense of the individual. His talk was not only philosophically false but also heretical and politically dangerous, particularly at that

---

[*] Heinrich Brüning (1885–1970), German chancellor from 1930 to 1932.

[†] Fr. Thaddäus Soiron, OFM (1881–1957), well-known theologian and homilist.

[‡] Franz Xaver Münch (1883–1940), priest, theologian, and general secretary of the Catholic Academic Association.

moment. Several others spoke in the same vein. Landmesser* of course was also completely infected by this collectivistic tendency.

My talk naturally had an explosive effect. The excellent pacifist and federalist, Schmidt[†] was so enthusiastic that he proposed that my text should immediately be reproduced and sent to all members of the Reichstag. This of course aroused the vehement protest of Fr. Soiron and many others. It was decided that Schmidt's proposal could only be pursued if a committee reviewed my talk and made appropriate revisions.

The committee was made up of Fr. Soiron, the young Fr. Damasus Winzen,[‡] myself, and two others whose names I have forgotten. But I did not want my talk to be censored by these people, who had not even understood it and who were infected by collectivism. We would never have been able to come to an agreement and so it was a waste of time. Meeting as a committee in the cell of Fr. Damasus, I quickly saw the futility of the attempt and declared that it seemed better to drop Schmidt's proposal and to abandon the idea of sending the talk to members of the Reichstag, rather than to spend time in pointless discussion.

My talk was the fruit of all the investigations that formed the subject of my book *The Metaphysics of Community*, which had been published two years before.[1] In the talk I sought to make clear that every attempt to establish a community at the expense of the individual person is not only in itself false but necessarily leads to a misconception of the true nature of community. I pointed out the horror of antipersonalism and totalitarianism, showing their absolute incompatibility with Christian revelation, and I criticized the false thesis of Hegel who held that the state is a higher entity than the individual. Only the indi-

---

* Franz Xaver Landmesser (1890–1940), priest, theologian, and general secretary of the Catholic Academic Association.

[†] Probably Fr. Expeditus Schmidt, OFM (1868–1939), historian of theater and literature.

[‡] Damasus Winzen, OSB (1901–71), monk at Maria Laach, he sought to establish common ground with the National Socialist concept of the Reich. He abandoned these efforts after 1933, emigrating to the USA in 1938.

vidual person is a substance in the full sense, while the state is only a quasi-substance.

At the same time, I stressed the reality and dignity of true community in contrast to every kind of false liberal individualism. All of this was philosophically grounded with great care, yet there was no chance of convincing the other members of the committee, who were not very acute philosophically and who had allowed themselves to be swept away by the Zeitgeist.

There were also heated discussions in the public sessions of the symposium. My position was defended by a Dutch Dominican priest (he was half-Jewish) whom I had already come to know in Fribourg, but the strongest support came from a very intelligent friend of Hedwig Conrad-Martius[*] who worked in a government ministry under Ferdinand Kirnberger, who was then president of the Catholic Academic Association. I remember how well he responded to Fr. Soiron who accused my position of not being Catholic because I was denying that all natural beings are in the image of God, whereas Soiron claimed that as God is a trinity it follows in the natural realm that community must be superior to the individual person. He responded to Fr. Soiron, "Yes, but in the Trinity the three persons form one substance."

Just after my talk, Abbot Ildefons[†] and I were strolling up and down along the cloister walk of the monastery. He said to me, "When you speak, I always learn something new. Your remarks have opened new dimensions for me." This made me very happy since Abbot Ildefons, because of his opposition to a nineteenth century misconception of community and its intrinsic value, was in fact rather prone to falling into collectivist errors. I was thus all the more touched by his open-mindedness toward ideas that were foreign to him. I think he was primarily struck by the way I showed that one could never arrive at a true

---

[*] Conrad-Martius (1888–1966) belonged to the Göttingen circle of philosophers around Edmund Husserl and was a close friend of Edith Stein.

[†] Abbot Ildefons Herwegen (1874–1946), abbot of Maria Laach and a key figure in the liturgical movement.

conception of community without acknowledging the full ontological dignity of the individual person. This had made sense to him.

Not everyone was as receptive as the abbot—who later would still fall for Nazism, and try to do exactly what von Hildebrand warned against—reconcile Christianity with nationalism—before he was persecuted by the Nazis himself.

One participant at the conference was Fritz Thyssen (1873–1951), a Catholic and early major donor to the Nazi Party. He later grew to oppose Hitler and was sent to a concentration camp for several years.

The most negative moment of the symposium occurred when the industrialist Fritz Thyssen requested the floor and made a short speech. It was horrible in every respect, yet in places so grotesque that it had a comical effect. He began by attacking Catholics who were critical of Fascism—he avoided the word National Socialism—especially those who were infected by pacifist ideas. He expressed all of this in a totally primitive way, both in the formulation of his sentences as well as in his use of foreign expressions. As a result, he came across as completely naïve. It was pure propaganda for National Socialism, above all for the militarism of National Socialism.

The pinnacle of the grotesque came when he remarked, "I find myself in good company with this thesis of mine, namely with St. Teresa of Avila. After all, it is she who says, 'Take care, be ready, the enemy is near at hand.'" Already the imprecision of the quotation was problematic, because St. Teresa is quoting from the Gospel, not to mention that the passage clearly refers to the devil and to a preparation of self in the sense of being spiritually alert. The quotation thus had an extremely comical effect as an argument for militarism and for the ideology of violence promoted by the Fascists and National Socialists.

Later I was riding to Cologne in a car with several industrialists who worked for Thyssen and they all expressed regret that he had spoken and embarrassed himself in such a way. It was so apparent that even his employees saw it clearly. Franz von Papen was also present at this symposium. In those days he did not yet play an important role. Still, his sympathies for the *Stahlhelm** and for Fascism were known.

In the fall of 1932 I spoke in Giessen, where I was invited by Professor Theodor Steinbüchel. This lecture was significant for me in many respects. First of all, Steinbüchel and I had an excellent mutual understanding, both philosophically and politically. It was a joy to encounter a person of real philosophical talent who was so open-minded and so free of any narrow Thomism.† He wanted to publish a "Handbook of Philosophy" in multiple volumes, and I believe it was on this occasion that he invited me to collaborate by writing the first volume on "The Nature of Philosophical Questioning and Knowing."[2] The theme of my lecture must have been individual and community since I remember being sharply critical of collectivism in all forms, of the deification of the state, and above all of National Socialism.

Afterwards I also met Ernst von Aster, who was a professor of philosophy in Giessen and whom I knew well from the time of my studies at the University of Munich. I had met him already in 1906 and had also taken one of his courses. Regrettably he was a follower of the philosopher Hans Cornelius and a total positivist. In those days we discussed issues at the Academic Psychological Association and always arrived at completely opposing views. But now we did not speak of philosophy but of the political situation and were very much in agreement. This is why he was enthusiastic about my lecture, and we spent a beautiful evening together. It is always a joy to meet someone who brings back vivid memories of earlier times and with whom one gets along better than before. Even if the new rapport now lies in another sphere, still it is a joy to be able to make common cause in an important and pressing matter.

A very different response came from a friend of Ernst Kamnitzer.‡

---

* A paramilitary associated with the conservative German National People's Party.

† Meaning doctrinaire followers of St. Thomas Aquinas.

‡ Ernst Kamnitzer (1885–1946), writer and friend of von Hildebrand's, who later emigrated to Paris where he belonged to the circle surrounding philosopher Jacques Maritain.

I had heard a great deal about this friend, who was a specialist in German studies and professor in Giessen. He disagreed with my lecture because he was already infected by the rising Nazi movement, even though he was half Jewish.

Most people, especially the intellectuals, were not attracted to Nazism because of its anti-Semitism, let alone its racism. They were drawn by the dynamism of a powerful movement, by the celebration of blood and soil in the face of a mechanized world, and primarily of course by nationalism. But of all factors, perhaps the most contagious for the more sophisticated intellectuals was the collectivism, the Hegelian influence, which manifested itself in a great variety of ways during this time, whether in Communism, in Fascism, or in National Socialism.

But Communism had discredited itself by the awful terrorism, the horrid crimes, and the rivers of blood. As bloody as National Socialism would become, most did not see or even sense it coming the way I did. There was a great deal of sympathy for Fascism and also for National Socialism. The intellectual who typified this collectivist mentality was Othmar Spann.* Yet there were many professors at the German universities who were drawn to Nazism in this way, and I am not speaking of those who were then already Nazi Party members.

Around this time there was the possibility of a professorship at the German university in Prague. There was a vacancy in the position that I believe Fr. Johannes Lindworski had previously occupied. I pursued the position as financial reasons made it necessary for me to have a paid professorship. Sad as it would be to leave Munich, Prague naturally offered a much more attractive atmosphere than the university towns in Germany.

I no longer recall why nothing came of this opportunity. I only remember being severely reproached for my antinationalistic statements: one said that I risked throwing away the possibility of a professorship. Being the bulwark of the Sudeten Germans† against Czech nationalism,

---

* Othmar Spann (1878–1950), influential Austrian Catholic philosopher and political theorist who, despite his support for National Socialism, would later be imprisoned by the Nazis.

† The ethnic German population living within Czechoslovakia, who numbered over three million.

the German university in Prague was of course dominated by German nationalists. I no longer remember what I had said publicly that caused me to be scolded. But I responded, "The battle against nationalism belongs to my mission. I cannot make any compromises in order to secure my career."

1933

In late 1932, the Catholic Association for Peace in Munich asked von Hildebrand to address a meeting of pacifists representing a range of political parties. Realizing there would be a preponderance of socialist and communist groups, he initially declined, then accepted when told that Cardinal Michael von Faulhaber, the archbishop of Munich and Freising, wanted him to speak. The Nazis tried to disrupt the meeting, which took place January 10, 1933, but the police cleared their protesters and let people enter the hall. Many journalists were there, including one from the Völkischer Beobachter, *the Nazi newspaper.*

I was the first speaker. Among other things, I said, "The deification of the state is an old error—found already in Sparta—while nationalism is a product of the modern era, above all a creation of the French Revolution. Both rest on classical dangers in human nature. Racism, by contrast, is a completely artificial, far-fetched, stupid theory with no organic basis in human nature."

My talk dealt primarily with the Catholic conception of peace, the meaning of the supranational, and the moral obligation to oppose both nationalism and militarism. I was followed by several speakers who attacked the Church and who pushed what was plainly Communist propaganda. I was outraged, and Dr. Quidde,* the chairman and a friend of

---

* Ludwig Quidde (1858–1941), German historian, politician, and Nobel laureate.

my parents, attempted in a very dignified manner to suppress these outbursts, which had nothing to do with our theme. But the Communists were not to be deterred, whereupon I stood up and publicly declared that I was not willing to listen to this nonsense any longer; I had not come to hear Communist propaganda and mendacious attacks on the Catholic Church. Having said this, I left, to the great disappointment of Dr. Quidde.

Arriving at home, I found my wife Gretchen in a state of great agitation. She had received phone calls from several of the people who had attempted to prevent the gathering. They had called to say that my presence was scandalous, and that they would deal with me soon enough. This was very galling for me, since I had only attended and agreed to speak at the urgent request of the Cardinal. After all, I hated both sides equally: the Nazis who wanted to sabotage the gathering, and the Communists who wanted to exploit it to disseminate their propaganda. Give me clear battle lines and even persecution for standing on the side of the good, for defending justice and truth—this is much more to my taste. My speech was indeed given very much in this vein, yet the overall spirit of the gathering, which the Nazis opposed for dishonest reasons, was in the end very unsatisfactory. For this reason, my participation did not succeed in contributing to the cause of justice against injustice.

On January 30 came the terrible news that Hitler had been appointed Chancellor by [German president] Paul Hindenburg. I was terribly distressed by this political development. Until the very end, I had firmly hoped that Hindenburg would never take this step. To be sure, I had reckoned with a putsch, but then it would have come to civil war, and the armed organization of the Social Democrats—the so-called "*Reichsbanner*"—together with the completely dependable police force would not have been easily overcome. I quite realized that I would probably not be able to remain in Germany. I still had a faint hope that Hugenberg* had perhaps tricked Hitler and then, as much as I hated

---

* Alfred Hugenberg (1865–1961), industrialist, nationalist, and leader of the German National People's Party.

Hugenberg, Germany would remain a constitutional state under the rule of law, where one could freely speak one's mind and not be forced into compromises. This is why I only say that I "probably" would have to leave Germany, since this faint hope still existed. I wanted to wait to see if it might be realized, and I assumed the coming weeks would likely make this clear.

As long as Hitler did not abolish the Constitution, the government led by the Bavarian People's Party still remained in power in Bavaria, and it was still possible to live on as before, even if with the greatest apprehension and with the awareness that the clock might soon strike for me.

February 13 marked the fiftieth anniversary of Richard Wagner's death in 1883. I took this occasion to speak about Wagner's genius and his artistic work for the entire hour of my aesthetics class. I knew that real understanding for Wagner had declined since the First World War. The official Nazi admiration for Wagner rested on a complete misunderstanding of his work. For to approach the music of Wagner in search of overarching philosophical themes is to find the denunciation of power, the glorification of love and compassion, the rejection of the merely conventional, and the exaltation of the individual in contrast to all collectivism. There was therefore no basis for the Nazis to have such enthusiasm for Wagner.

I spoke about the true greatness of Wagner and also about how deeply his music had come to be misunderstood. I spoke with deep emotion and out of my great love for Wagner, mindful of all that he had revealed to me and of everything his art meant to me. Today I would speak with even greater enthusiasm and with much greater clarity. Yet at that time, I was oppressed by the overall situation.

One evening I returned home to find my wife in a frantic state over a speech Hitler had given in Munich. His words had been full of threats against the Bavarian monarchists and full of warnings that any attempt to restore the Bavarian monarchy under Crown Prince Rupprecht would immediately be squelched.[*]

---

[*] Crown Prince Rupprecht of Bavaria (1869–1955) stood at the center of efforts to restore the Bavarian monarchy.

. . .

The next day von Hildebrand and his wife were invited to lunch by the Archduchess Maria Josepha, mother of the Emperor Charles I and a friend who "had been the most faithful and regular attendee of my afternoon discussions between 1924 and 1931." Among the other people there were his "very dear friend" Infanta Maria de la Paz (1862–1946), daughter of Queen Isabella II of Spain, and Count Konrad von Preysing (1880–1950), then bishop of Eichstätt, who would become bishop of Berlin in 1935 and a fierce and unbending foe of the Nazis.

Also at the luncheon was a friend and Catholic industrialist named Theodor von Cramer-Klett (1874–1938), who said, to von Hildebrand's horror, that he liked Hitler's speech very much. Von Hildebrand comments, "How could Cramer-Klett, the great Catholic and Bavarian monarchist, say such a thing?" The luncheon was especially significant in hindsight because, "though I did not realize it at the time, this was the real moment of farewell for me." He never again saw the Infanta Maria or the Archduchess Maria Josepha.

On February 28, news came that the Reichstag had been burned, and on the evening of the same day, the arrest of many Communists and the ban of the socialist press. Not even for a moment did I doubt that all of this was a farce being put on by the National Socialists to gain emergency powers to clear the way for a dictatorship. With this, the die had been cast for me. I neither could nor wanted to remain in a National Socialist Germany—in the "Third Reich." New elections to the Reichstag were set for March 5. I decided to go to Salzburg [Austria] on February 28 to await the outcome of the coming days.

But I was already firm in my resolve to leave Germany once and for all. I simply could not make compromises, and it was clear to me that I was in the greatest danger of forfeiting my freedom. On the afternoon of February 28, Gretchen packed my bags and I rode to Salzburg. While this was not to be the last parting from the house on the Maria-Theresia Strasse, from Munich, and from Germany, I cannot say that I felt any certainty about returning to Munich for a final farewell.

The Catholic Academic Association had scheduled a conference in Munich on social questions that was to take place on March 11. I had agreed to give a lecture at this conference. Curiously enough, I felt a kind of obligation to deliver my talk as long as the situation in Munich did not deteriorate to the extent that my departure could no longer be postponed. It really is quite striking how formal obligations continue to play a role, even in such a decisive moment when entirely different goods are at stake. In any case, I wanted to be outside of Germany when it came time to decide whether to speak at the conference, and in Salzburg I was certainly free to make this decision.

My reasons were various. In the first place, it seemed likely that the conference would be cancelled given the current political situation. Second, in Salzburg the door could not close on me and prevent my flight. Finally, I did not want to be in Munich for the elections to the Reichstag scheduled for March 5. I was well aware of the elections in Soviet Russia, of how elections in totalitarian and terrorist states took place, and I did not want to put myself at risk of being violently forced to vote for the Nazis. Of course, it was possible that the election would still proceed normally, yet who could guarantee this in a moment of upheaval when even a deceitful farce like the burning of the Reichstag no longer shocked anyone? My time in Salzburg passed in great tension.

Meanwhile, the government in Berlin issued an official declaration that it would recognize the Bavarian government and—for the time being at least—that it would not insist on any changes. In light of this, I felt I could return to Munich for a few days to give my lecture and then to leave for good. As long as the Bavarian government remained in power, I assumed that I did not have to worry about being prevented from leaving, that it would be too late, and I would be trapped. So, I decided to travel back to Munich. In the election of March 5, the Nazis had only received 44% of the vote. This was not hugely successful given how many people, especially in Germany, fall prey to the idea that history unfolds inexorably—and will then swim with the current. Considering how many Germans already realized that the election would no longer alter the situation and that it was safer not to take a contrary stance—one cannot forget that people's votes were somewhat influenced by the oppressive air of terrorism—the outcome of less than half the vote was really quite poor.

Upon arriving in Munich, I immediately went to the Maria-Theresia Strasse, where I was greeted with great rejoicing. Yet it was not long before the situation fundamentally changed. On the night of March 8, the Bavarian government was overthrown in a putsch. SA men burst into the home of the Interior Minister and arrested him in his nightshirt.

The remaining senior officials fared similarly, and the government was taken over by the Nazis. The way in which the government was toppled was typical of the Nazis in that they did not even bother to put on the show of a legal proceeding. In the days following the burning of the Reichstag, it became very clear that the constitutional state and the rule of law in Germany were a thing of the past. A "popular uprising" was staged—the government was forcibly toppled, the "voice of the people" had spoken—whereas in reality it was a measure that had been carefully planned in advance, organized in Berlin, and commanded from there.

One can indeed ask: why did no one resist? Where were the police, which after all were under the control of the Interior Minister? Where was the portion of the army stationed in Bavaria and under the command of Bavarian officers? What had become of the militias of young Bavarian patriots who were monarchists?

The cause of this passivity was fear, which had taken hold of the leading elements, beginning with the burning of the Reichstag, and then with the abrogation of the constitutional state. Already in February the gruesome speeches of Hitler had had a crippling effect—on President Held,* on the leadership of the Bavarian patriots—like the gaze of a serpent on its victim. There is a moment when intimidation and paralysis set in to such a degree that one becomes passive in the face of something harmful, no longer actively resisting, even though the possibility of resistance still exists.

It is not difficult to imagine my feelings when I heard about this

---

* Heinrich Held (1868–1938), minister president of Bavaria from 1924 to 1933.

in the morning. The die had now been definitively cast for me. The decision to leave Munich was in every respect inexpressibly painful for me. The parting from my sisters, from the beloved, beautiful house for which I had sacrificed my fortune, from my teaching, and from the place of my roots—all this meant a very great sacrifice. At the same time, I had to face a completely uncertain future, without a position and with just fifty marks in my pocket!

Yet it was clear to me that I could no longer teach in a National Socialist country because I was convinced that I would be forced to make compromises, and that I would either have to keep silent about the injustices that would come or else risk the concentration camp.

Better to be a beggar in freedom than to be forced into making compromises against my conscience! This was reason enough for my decision to leave Germany.

Beyond this, I realized that I might have to reckon with immediate pursuit, since my hostility toward National Socialism was of course very well known. The death sentence for my high treason in 1923 had been completely forgotten in the meantime.* Yet my membership on the board of the Association for Opposition to Anti-Semitism engendered the hatred of the Nazis, and it was unlikely that my attack on National Socialism at the gathering of pacifists on January 10 had been forgotten. I had to assume I was at risk of ending up in a concentration camp and, even if this did not materialize, on a degree of surveillance that would interfere with my ability to leave the country.

I think I can honestly say that I would have left Germany even without all of the peril of these various reasons. I had the conviction that this was right before God and thus, despite all the uncertainty of my future livelihood, I felt myself to be completely secure in the love of God. *Deus providebit!*—God will provide!

I decided to give my talk at the conference of the Catholic Academic Association on Saturday, March 11, and then to depart. I was actually supposed to give lectures in Holland on Monday, March 13, but I was

---

* Just prior to Hitler's Beer Hall Putsch in November 1923, von Hildebrand had learned that his name was on the Nazi blacklist.

so preoccupied with the political catastrophe that I did not feel I was in a state to do so. On March 10, I went to see Beck* at the student center where the conference was to be held on March 11. I told him I thought it rather unlikely the conference would even take place under these circumstances, yet he answered that he had not heard anything of a cancelation. I shared with him my resolve to leave Germany and not to return as long as the National Socialists were at the helm. He said, "You're completely right. Without question, you must leave without delay."

"Why don't you leave as well?" I asked. "No, I must remain here, like a captain who cannot leave his ship." I said to him, "The notion that the Reichstag was burned by the Communists is plain nonsense, don't you think?" Beck replied, "Indeed, in strictest confidence I can tell you that the fire was staged by the Nazis themselves. I know this." I tried once more to urge him to leave Germany as well, yet he clung to his point of view that he must stay. "But you must go," he said, "there is no longer a place for you here. What has begun will continue inexorably until all of Germany is consumed in flames." We parted with heavy hearts. I would never see Beck again.

When I came home, Fedja† told me that sixty affluent Jews had suddenly been arrested without cause. I was completely beside myself. Justice was already being trampled on! A Jewish lawyer by the name of Dr. Siegel, who was known for his brashness, had protested the arrests and spoken harshly about Hitler. As punishment he was dragged through the city the next day with a sign around his neck bearing the words of his "slanders," now directed back at himself.

I was infuriated, but when I expressed my outrage to Borissowsky,‡ he replied, "It serves him right. Why did he berate Hitler? After all, he is the Chancellor." Hearing Borissowsky speak in this way, I lost all of my trust in him. My retort was very sharp and I decided not to tell him

---

* Fritz Beck (1889–1934), pacifist who directed the Student Welfare Fund in Munich.

† Theodor Georgii (1883–1963), sculptor married to von Hildebrand's sister, Irene.

‡ An aristicratic Russian emigrant in Munich whom von Hildebrand befriended and supported financially.

about my plan to leave immediately after my lecture on Saturday evening. I did not trust him anymore.

D'Ormesson* had invited us during this time. Sadly I had to decline. Much as I would have liked to see him, much as I knew we would have been of one mind, it was simply too risky for me to visit the French ambassador, since the Nazis were surely spying to see who visited him, and I wanted to draw as little attention as possible. Besides, I did not have the time. After all, I had to prepare my lecture, which was not easy given the agitation and outrage that filled me.

On Saturday morning, I attended the opening of the conference. Münch had not come, but Landmesser, the Vice President of the Association, was there. Seeing him before the opening, I expressed my surprise that the Association had decided to hold the conference under these circumstances. After all, the Hitler regime made the ongoing work of the Association impossible. He replied, "On the contrary, look at the telegram for the Association I received today from Vice Chancellor von Papen. Brüning would never have bothered to do the same." I was horrified. How could a Vice President of the Catholic Academic Association, founded to imbue everything with the spirit of Catholicism, base his judgment of a regime on whether it was courteous toward the Association, rather than looking to the regime's spirit and its first principles?

This kind of egotism would be catastrophic for any kind of organization. To ask only whether one's own organization would suffer under the Nazis, while failing to consider what the Third Reich meant for Germany and for the entire world, would have been disgraceful even for an association with the interests of, say, the Masons. Yet for an organization whose very *raison d'être* was to suffuse all things with the spirit of Christ, one would be hard-pressed to conceive of anything more grotesque than to judge the Antichrist's rise to power by whether the Association was treated cordially by the government. Add to this the fact that von Papen, after the burning of the Reichstag, was a very insignificant, uninfluential background character, and that a friendly

---

* Probably André d'Ormesson (1877–1957), French diplomat stationed in Munich in 1933.

telegram from him did not in the slightest represent the government's stance toward the Academic Association.

Landmesser's attitude was therefore not only a betrayal of the spirit of the Association—and, indeed, a betrayal of the Catholic Church, which was naturally far worse—it was in addition an expression of great stupidity. I was horrified and did not continue speaking with him since I realized that he was totally blind and that I would not be able to open his eyes, regardless of what I might say. Moreover, there was no longer any time for extended discussion.

Franz Xaver Landmesser delivered a lecture which provoked the eminent Catholic social theorist, Fr. Oswald Nell-Breuning (1890–1991), into harshly criticizing phenomenology, the philosophical tradition in which von Hildebrand had been educated. The charge was that phenomenology did not show respect for reality but remained too subjective. Unfortunately, Nell-Breuning "took Landmesser to be a phenomenologist," writes von Hildebrand, "and so he assumed I was fundamentally in agreement with Landmesser." Both Landmesser's lecture and Nell-Breuning's response "in a sense challenged me directly, and so my task had become something other than I initially had planned on." Von Hildebrand wanted to show that phenomenology, rightly understood, is distinguished by its unconditional respect for reality.

The main issue for me now was to fend off the errors in regard to phenomenology, and also to distance myself from Landmesser's thesis, since I found what Nell-Breuning had said about social questions to be much more correct than Landmesser. I decided to present a different lecture than I had planned, which meant I had to prepare a new text quickly during the lunch recess which I would then present sometime after 4 p.m., once the conference had resumed.

It was 12:30 p.m., and I hurried home to eat a hasty lunch, and then to draft the new lecture with my response to Fr. Nell-Breuning during the two hours at my disposal. Of course, it could at most be a very detailed outline, and I would have to speak freely. I had initially expected the lectures of Landmesser and Nell-Breuning to be shorter and, indeed, my own talk had originally been scheduled for before noon. Under the circumstances, I decided to postpone my departure from Germany until Sunday evening, since the time after my lecture would not suffice for making final preparations.

I had just finished eating and was still sitting at the table when Marguerite Solbrig arrived in a state of great agitation. She said to me, "You must leave immediately. This morning, SA officers came to the office and arrested many of my colleagues. You cannot imagine the horrible expression in their faces, and how cruel and brutal they were." Though what she said made a strong impression on me, I replied, "Please tell me more after I have prepared my lecture, which I have to focus on now. We can discuss everything afterward."

I drank a strong cup of coffee and turned to my preparation. Within an hour and a half, my outline was complete. It was a refutation of Nell-Breuning's attack on phenomenology as well as a short exposition of my position on the sociological questions which had been at issue. Yet the primary emphasis lay in my exposition of the true nature of phenomenology. Marguerite and I still spoke briefly, and she told me in greater detail about her awful experience with the Nazis who had come to her office. We spoke of my departure on Sunday evening, and then I said goodbye and left to go to the student center for my lecture. I think I succeeded in speaking with great precision and liveliness, and in so doing to enter into the depth of the problem. It was my last lecture in Germany. Not until 1948, fifteen years later, would I again speak in Germany. Nell-Breuning was very impressed and said to me, "I am 99% in agreement with what you said." I did not remain for the conclusion of the conference, but went home immediately.

As I walked to the streetcar with my wife, I think Rintelen* was also there. It is true that we weren't on the best of terms, yet at that moment I felt solidarity with him in opposing the Nazis. From his remarks I

---

* Fritz-Joachim von Rintelen (1898–1979), a professor of philosophy in Munich.

could see how upset he was at the persecution of the Jews in the last few days. I began to speak about the Nazis so sharply and in such a loud voice that Gretchen begged me to be cautious since my words could easily be heard.

I still remember the following details about the time just before my departure. It must have been on Sunday afternoon that d'Ormesson came to visit me. He was very serious and he said, "I understand fully why you did not accept my invitation. Even now, I did not come in my car so as to avoid drawing attention to my visit. But since I assume you are abandoning Germany, I wanted to bid you farewell." I said to him, "You are indeed right. I have decided to give up everything and to leave Germany." I explained my reasons and how as a Catholic and as a Catholic philosopher I could not in good conscience witness all these horrors and remain silent. Such a violent regime presented only one alternative, namely to make compromises or to end up in the concentration camp. Only by emigrating could one escape this alternative.

D'Ormesson, of course, understood me completely, and he said, "We are heading for a war, but I want you to know that I do not consider this to be the only Germany. I am happy to have come to know you, and in you, a different Germany. May God protect you!" I was very moved by the nobility of this outstanding human being, and moreover that he had come to say goodbye. We parted with great warmth. My last full day in Munich was filled with the solemnity of a farewell. I was fully aware of the sacrifice I was making, and expressly made a conscious farewell to the beloved house, indeed to every single room. It was clear to me that I was unlikely ever to see it again. I told Stonner[*] about my plan to leave, and he strongly urged me to carry through with my decision. "For God's sake," he said, "you must leave. You cannot remain here."

At midday on Sunday, I decided it was after all better if Gretchen joined me in leaving Munich. Initially, I had wanted to depart for Florence alone. She was in far less danger than I was, and it was unlikely that her departure would be obstructed, especially since she, like I,

---

[*] Anton Stonner (1895–1973), an Austrian theologian.

possessed a Swiss passport. She could always follow me later. Yet at the last moment, I decided I would rather she travel with me. After all, our future was so completely uncertain. Everything lay in total darkness for us. We did not know where and how we would live, and on what basis, for I had no money, and what I could bring over the border was very limited. I had surely picked up my monthly stipend for March—300 marks—to which I was entitled as an adjunct professor. Yet after settling various debts and buying our train tickets to Florence, I had only about 150 marks left.

There was so much to consider together with Gretchen that it was better if she traveled with me. Yet I think the main reason I asked her to come with me was that I did not want to be alone during this time of such difficulty and sadness. On Sunday evening we sat in complete silence for the entire train ride to Florence. Strangely enough, our passports were not even inspected by the German border control as we passed out of Germany, an oversight, naturally, yet something that struck me as strange at a moment I perceived as one of flight.

They arrived in Florence at San Francesco, the villa that von Hildebrand's father, Adolf, had bought, and at which von Hildebrand had been born. It was now owned by his sister Elizabeth (Lisl) Brewster. The Ethics *he mentions was not written until the 1940s and not published until 1953 in New York under the title* Christian Ethics *and not in Germany until 1959.*

We reached San Francesco in the afternoon, and while Lisl was very happy to see us, she was also surprised by the suddenness of our unexpected arrival. I did not initially tell her that we had fled and what my arrival signified. I now find it incomprehensible that I did not immediately explain everything to her. I was so caught up in my own rule of not discussing anything, which I had already observed in Salzburg, that I felt everything must be kept in the dark, at least for the time being. Yet Lisl was not to be fooled and said, "Your arrival, of course, means that you have fled," to which I said, "Yes, if that is how you wish to describe it." Being extraordinarily generous, she did not hesitate to receive us with great warmth.

I lost no time writing to Otto Müller in Salzburg to propose that he pay me an advance of 100 marks per month for my *Ethics*, which I would deliver to him in the foreseeable future. With this came, of course, the understanding that Müller would publish the *Ethics*, which he was eager to do, while for my part I hoped in this way to have at least enough money to live. After all, for the moment we were Lisl's guests, depending on her even for our daily bread. Yet it was clear from the start that we could not burden her over the long run, as her financial situation was not the best.

At the beginning of the year, the French Catholic philosopher Étienne Gilson (1884–1978) had invited von Hildebrand to speak at a celebration at the Sorbonne honoring St. Albert the Great's elevation to Doctor of the Church, to be held for several days in early April. The celebration of the German saint was in part a friendly gesture toward Germany, and the German ambassador was chairman of the celebration. An attaché at the German embassy in Paris also wrote von Hildebrand with a warm personal invitation. Von Hildebrand was to be one of the three main speakers, with Gilson and the French education minister, and had been asked to speak on "the unity of the West as it had existed during the Middle Ages, and how this unity could be restored." He had also been invited to give lectures in Leiden and Utrecht (Holland) in the middle of March.

One of the first things I did upon arriving in Florence was to send a letter to the attaché at the embassy in Paris. In it, I told him that in light of the situation in Germany and my departure from there, I realized that surely they were no longer counting on me as I could hardly still speak as a representative of Germany. After all, the original invitation had invited me as a German, as a friendly gesture toward Germany, and the German ambassador was chairman of the celebration. Being set for the beginning of April, I had to write immediately to give them enough time to invite another German. Yet to my great amazement, I received a reply from the attaché at the German embassy telling me that my assumption was wrong, that I was still the speaker as before and that they were definitely counting on my presence. He also hinted of his hope that this invitation might open the door for an academic position for me in Paris.

Not long after, I received a letter from Gilson asking me to send my manuscript in German so that he would have time to translate it into French. Gilson also told me, "You cannot say anything against National Socialism in the lecture. Otherwise the ambassador will get in trouble." I also could not say that the spiritual unity of Europe could only be restored through the Catholic Church since this would cause considerable embarrassment for the Minister of Culture, de Monzie,* a Freemason, who was to speak after me. None of this made the lecture any easier, since I did not in any way want to make compromises.

I immediately sat down and worked intensely on the lecture. I could ignore National Socialism without any compromises and speak only of the danger of nationalism. I could also point to the role of the Church in the earlier unity of the West without saying that the spiritual unity of the West could only be revived if everyone became Catholic. I succeeded in bringing everything into the lecture that was burning in my soul without failing to meet the two conditions given me by Gilson. Within about ten days, the lecture was finished. Hamburger,† whom I found in Florence, once again helped me in the most wonderful way. It was a great gift for me to be together with him at this moment.

Leaving Florence, von Hildebrand traveled to Paris by way of Basel, Strasbourg, Metz, Brussels, and Leiden, where he was a guest in the home of Johannes Barge, a Catholic doctor and professor.

· · ·

---

* Anatole de Monzie (1876–1946), was in fact French Minister of Education.
† Siegfried Johannes Hamburger (1891–1975), philosopher and von Hildebrand's closest friend.

It was a strange feeling for me to pass through Alsace, so near the German border, which I no longer wanted to cross at any cost—the Germany from which I had been separated so suddenly, the Germany which now lay before me as enemy territory.

Barge was a very nice person and we had a very good time together. I asked him whether as a Catholic he did not feel a closer bond with the Flemish of Catholic Belgium than with the Protestant Dutch. After all, the Flemish and the Dutch derive from the same racial group and speak almost the same language. As a Catholic I thought he would feel a greater connection to the Belgians than to the Protestant Dutch. He answered, "No, because we Dutch, whether Catholic or Protestant, are a Renaissance people, whereas the Belgians are medieval. The Belgians remain in their cities with their narrow streets, while we are sailors who have circumnavigated the world. Among us there is a different overall sense of life."

I found this remark intriguing and I understood what he meant. As I looked upon the charming old furniture with its ornate metal fittings, with the afternoon sun streaming into the room, I breathed the very particular air of the Dutch world. I reflected on the incredibly enterprising spirit of the Dutch, on their deep bond with ships and with the sea, and on their mercantilism, which Swedenborg claimed they would not give up even in eternity. I thought of the paintings and frescos of the elder Sattler,[*] in which he painted Holland with its coastlines and its ships. Of course, I have a special love for the particular cultural character of different nations, and I always enjoy the opportunity to experience in a potent way the atmosphere and genius of a country.

Following dinner, my lecture took place at the university, where I was received by Huizinga,[†] who was the rector there at the time. Huizinga was, of course, a very significant man who had achieved great renown in Europe through his various books. Though he was not a Catholic, he

---

[*] Johann Ernst Sattler (1840–1923), painter and father-in-law of von Hildebrand's sister, Eva, called "Nini" (1877–1962), who was married to architect Carl Sattler (1877–1966).

[†] Johan Huizinga (1872–1945), eminent medieval historian, best known for his book *The Waning of the Middle Ages*.

showed a great degree of receptivity to, and also understanding for, the world of the Middle Ages, and indirectly also for the Catholic Church. He was a very attractive personality and impressed me as being a significant mind.

After the lecture, some of us sat together and Huizinga asked me what I thought of the burning of the Reichstag and whether I knew who had set the fire. He added, "Please don't feel you must answer, if it would be awkward for you. We would entirely understand." I had not explained that my departure from Germany was for good, so in their eyes, I was still the professor from Munich. My first response was to say that the fire had been caused by the man who had been arrested on this charge (a Communist, whose name I have forgotten*). Everyone laughed and had the impression I would prefer not to answer for understandable reasons. I no longer remember why I spoke like this. After all, I knew it was the Nazis themselves who had set the fire, and as I no longer wished to return to Germany, I had no reason not to speak openly. Perhaps I was joking, and I assume I must then have said that I suspected the Nazis had set fire. It was in any case an interesting, stimulating evening.

From Leiden, von Hildebrand traveled to Paris for the celebration of St. Albert the Great.

My first visit in Paris, I think, was to Count d'Harcourt,† who lived on the Rue de Grenelle. It was a beautiful spring day. The trees were already green, but still with that new green of spring. It was uncharacteristically warm. Paris lay before me in all of its unbelievable charm. I told him that I had left Munich and why I no longer wished to return. He said, "I admire you for being so resolute and so filled with an enter-

---

* Marinus van der Lubbe, executed in 1934.
† Robert d'Harcourt (1881–1965), French literary historian and journalist.

prising spirit at a moment when you have given up everything and are facing such a completely uncertain future." I remember how I paced back and forth in the room and spoke about the situation in Germany.

It was probably on the same day that I visited the attaché at the embassy, or perhaps he came to me at the hotel and invited me to dinner. In any case, I quickly established a very warm rapport with this fine person. He had previously been an officer and then become a diplomat. I think he was a convert. He was certainly very pious. He shared my political views completely and was an ardent anti-nationalist. Our mutual understanding was excellent.

He hoped that Gilson would arrange a professorship for me at the Sorbonne or at the Collège de France. He told me that there was a strong atmosphere in France at the time in favor of bettering relations with Germany. The celebration in honor of St. Albert the Great was proof of this. Having chosen the German ambassador to preside over the celebration, and having invited a German keynote speaker (namely myself), it would be entirely consistent to nominate a German professor who would act as a living link between these two countries.

This was all very attractive, yet I did not see how this role could be given to me, for I had left Germany and could never represent a "link" between France and the Germany of National Socialism. At best, I could hope that I would be given a professorship in France as an act of protest against National Socialism—that I, the German who had fled his homeland for reasons of conscience, would be welcomed warmly and with honor by the French, and as the symbol of "another" Germany. I did not place a great deal of hope in this prospect, since I did not really know how Gilson stood toward me philosophically.

I had already planned to ask Foerster* not to talk to me at the solemn celebration where I was to give my speech. I could hardly greet Foerster except in the warmest way, yet since he was now *persona non grata* in Germany it would be highly embarrassing for the ambassador if the speaker from Germany (in this case, myself) were to approach Foer-

---

* Friedrich Wilhelm Foerster (1869–1966), philosopher, educational theorist, and pacifist then living in France.

ster as a friend in such a public setting. So I had sent word to Foerster through d'Harcourt asking him not greet me publicly that evening. It is possible the attaché at the embassy had also suggested I do this.

I lost no time in going to the home of Reynald, to see if I might still find Wolfgang,* who had lived there while studying in Paris. Upon arriving, the concierge told me that Wolfgang had quite suddenly left for Cologne, as he had received very bad news from home. What this news consisted of she did not know, but her words shook me and filled me with great concern. I also visited the German ambassador.† He was a very cultivated and congenial man, and he received me with great warmth. He seemed very worried about the course of events in Germany. He looked sad. Of course, he chose his words carefully, yet from his demeanor I saw he was under no illusions about the Nazis. His own leaning, I think, was *Deutschnational*.

Gilson had invited me to supper. This was the first time I met him. He made a very congenial impression on me. He had an attractive face expressive of real inner life and he impressed me as a very cultivated personality. We sat first in his study to discuss my lecture, of which he handed me a French translation. At the end, he said, "There is just one change you ought to make. You speak of Berlioz as the greatest French composer, when you should really say this of Debussy. Berlioz can hardly rival Debussy!" Naturally, I objected and we had a lengthy discussion about music. He had great reverence for Mozart, yet he lacked sufficient enthusiasm for Beethoven, while his opinion of Wagner was downright dismissive. But of course that attitude was quite typical at that time.

Gilson's wife was very likeable and friendly. One of his daughters—I think her name was Claude—was very beautiful. I told him so, which pleased him immensely, and I could see how much he loved her. The food, and especially the wine, was excellent.

We had a lovely time together, yet Gilson avoided entering into a

---

* Wolfgang Braunfels (1911–87), art historian and son of composer Walter Braunfels (1882–1954), who was married to von Hildebrand's sister Berta, nicknamed "Bertele" (1886–1963).

† Roland Köster (1883–1935), diplomat and German ambassador to France (1932–35).

philosophical discussion. When I sought to raise a philosophical question with him, he immediately said, "You will find something very interesting on this in St. Thomas." And that was the end of that.

The next evening the German ambassador hosted an elegant dinner that was part of the celebration for St. Albert the Great. As the speaker representing Germany at the celebration, I was naturally one of the principal guests. To my great joy, I was seated next to Count d'Harcourt for the meal. We had a wonderful conversation, and I was edified by the way he observed the Lenten fast, truly a sacrifice as the meal was excellent. With charming simplicity, he remarked, "Sadly, I cannot eat any more of this delicious food as it is Lent." I felt myself somewhat dispensed from fasting, as I was traveling.

After dinner there was a musical performance. A choir of young men from the music conservatory in Cologne sang a variety of selections. During the intermission I introduced myself to them and asked whether anything had changed at the conservatory in Cologne. They were amazed. "What, don't you know that your brother-in-law [Walter Braunfels] was dismissed and how this came about?" This was how I learned that my dear Walter had already lost his position as a victim of anti-Semitism. I was deeply affected and distressed. To learn indirectly of the heavy misfortunes of close and beloved friends is a very unique experience, especially when their misfortunes are part of a larger catastrophe. It is an experience in which we are able to "feel" the rhythm of historic events in what befalls those we love, and it is not entirely unlike actually living through these historic events ourselves.

Either on this trip or his December visit to Paris—von Hildebrand is not sure which—he met Charles Du Bos (1882–1939), a Catholic writer and philosopher of religion. Through Du Bos, he met the Catholic philosopher Gabriel Marcel (1889–1973). Du Bos invited von Hildebrand to lunch at his home on the Île Saint-Louis.

. . .

Upon arriving, I met a very dignified and cultivated looking person—much more delicate in appearance than Gilson. By comparison, Gilson was imposing and possessed a certain potent vitality. There was something very English about Du Bos and he reminded me much more of certain English rather than French types. He received me with great friendliness and warmth, telling me that he had known my father and that he had been at San Francesco many years before. He told me that he had converted only recently, though I don't know whether he had been a Protestant before or just a lapsed Catholic. He was a great friend of André Gide.[*] In any case, he had lived in a milieu that was completely areligious although intellectually very refined.

We had a very good conversation. There was something deeply spiritual and also incredibly kind about Du Bos. He told me that a friend of his by the name of Gabriel Marcel, a very gifted philosopher and writer, had also recently converted. Du Bos had invited Marcel because he wanted me to meet him. At lunch, we were joined by a man of small stature and very unusual appearance. He was neither physically attractive, nor did he possess the spirituality and nobility so evident in the face of Du Bos, yet I found him to be very likeable. As we spoke, Marcel immediately made clear that he was not a Thomist and that in philosophical matters he was not in accord with Maritain.[†] He gave me a copy of one of his plays, *La Soif.*

Marcel certainly awakened my interest, yet I did not realize sufficiently that I was in the presence of a great and significant philosopher, nor did I adequately appreciate the wealth of thought and culture embodied by Charles Du Bos. It is remarkable how deeply we can become trapped in our own inner world and how much this diminishes our ability, if we are not sufficiently prepared, to open ourselves to significant encounters, which are a gift from God. We focus on what lies immediately ahead, on our plans, and on those people we already know and will see tomorrow. As a result, we fail to approach those we do not

---

[*] André Gide (1869–1951), French novelist, playwright, and poet.

[†] Jacques Maritain (1882–1973), major French philosopher known for developing a new Christian humanism rooted in Thomism.

yet know well with sufficient attentiveness to be able to grasp their importance fully.

The next morning there was a solemn liturgy at Notre-Dame, a votive mass in honor of St. Albert the Great. The mass was celebrated by a Dominican priest and the singers were also Dominicans. The music was a special type of chorale, i.e., it was a Gregorian chant with certain specifically Dominican elements. I was greatly impressed by the beauty of the celebration, which was enhanced by the magnificent space of Notre-Dame.

Upon leaving the church, I met the priest who was then the provincial of the German Dominicans. I think this must have been the first time I met him. When I praised the beauty of the celebration and of the singing, he declared, "In Germany we also sing beautifully." His words struck me uncomfortably as being extremely nationalistic. After all, I hadn't said anything to imply that the German Dominicans would have sung any less well. Having just heard something beautiful, why should he be defensive rather than happy, as if my praise had implied a reproach of the German Dominicans? Besides, I very much doubted that the German Dominicans cultivated the liturgy, especially Gregorian chant, in the same way as the French Dominicans. The French Dominicans are unique and the level of their spiritual culture surpasses that of Dominicans in all other countries, including those of Italy and Spain, and even those of England, whose level is very high. Of all these, the German province was the least prominent. With a few exceptions it was engaged only in pastoral care at this time and stamped by popular piety. All this only served to make the provincial's remark more disagreeable.

At midday there was a formal luncheon at the Dominicans on Rue St. Honoré. I was seated next to Cardinal Baudrillart,* the Rector of the Institut Catholique. This in fact was a seat of honor, though not necessarily very comfortable for me, since I knew the Cardinal had a bitter hatred of Germans and saw in me a representative of Germany; after all, I was the speaker who had been formally invited to represent

---

* Alfred Baudrillart (1859–1942), French theologian, historian, and bishop, would only become cardinal in 1935.

Germany. It was quite impossible to explain to him my attitude toward National Socialism and toward German nationalism: he would hardly have believed me and, moreover, out of respect for the German ambassador, I could not openly criticize Germany. The entire dinner long, I could feel how the poor Cardinal struggled not to show too much of his antipathy for all things German, how he tried to hide from me the sacrifice he had to endure by being seated next to me.

After the meal, I again met the German provincial in the hallway. The dinner had been excellent, a rich demonstration of the great culinary culture of France. I said to him, "Was that not a wonderful meal?" to which he responded immediately, "Indeed, in Germany we also know how to cook." This was just too much for me, and I said to him, "No, when it comes to cooking, no connoisseur can doubt that France is superior to Germany."

The major event of the celebration for St. Albert took place later that evening at the Panthéon of the Sorbonne. Gilson spoke first. He gave a very entertaining lecture portraying the history of the Sorbonne during the time of St. Albert. He spoke much longer than the forty-five minutes he had previously indicated to me. I was to speak for an hour, followed by the Minister of Culture, who was to speak for about half an hour. There were to be musical performances between the talks.

Gilson spoke for an hour. The most significant dimension of his lecture was his strong emphasis on the antinationalism that marked the two highpoints of the Sorbonne, namely the thirteenth and seventeenth centuries, during which there were more foreign professors at the Sorbonne than French. During the time of St. Albert, then, the glory of the Sorbonne was primarily the contribution of foreign professors: Alexander of Hales and Roger Bacon from England, St. Albert from Germany, and St. Thomas and St. Bonaventure from Italy.

The music performed following his lecture was very long. I was very worried how I would still fit my lecture into the remaining time. I began, but after just a quarter of an hour, Gilson said to me, "You have to shorten your talk as the Minister of Culture is already getting impatient." There is nothing more disruptive for a speaker than to be forced to abbreviate in the middle of a talk, especially when one is not speaking freely but bound to a manuscript as I was. I did my best, but regrettably I had focused on the difficult philosophical parts at some length so that I was unable to do justice to the issues of present concern, except in abbreviated form, which would have interested most of the audience of 2,700 people.

As a result, my lecture obviously did not have the impact I had hoped for. This really was too bad. The applause as I concluded was merely friendly and polite. I no longer remember what the Minister had to say. After the lecture, I still spent a little time talking with Gilson and the embassy attaché at a café. After a little while, Gilson said, "You've exerted yourself. Speaking in a foreign language at length is draining. Go and get some rest." And so we parted.

It was at this time that many terrible things happened in the world. April 1 saw the first large boycott against the Jews in Germany. The response of Cardinal Verdier,* the archbishop of Paris, was very beautiful and edifying, namely to call for prayer in all the churches of Paris that the suffering of the German Jews would be alleviated. This was particularly uplifting as, to my great sorrow, just fourteen days after Hitler's seizure of power, the German bishops had lifted the excommunication that previously had been attached to membership in the National Socialist Party, including both the SA and the SS. Moreover, Franz von Papen† was working zealously for a Concordat between Germany and the Holy See. The conclusion of the Concordat was imminent, and it must have given Catholics throughout Germany the impression that the Vatican was withdrawing its rejection of National Socialism and of racism—as if it were possible to be a Catholic and a Nazi at the same time.

Yet by then, a great number of awful things had already taken place. Many people had been dragged into the terrible concentration camp in Dachau, among them Gerlich, the noble publisher of *Der Gerade Weg* (*The Straight Path*).‡ Having previously been a very nationalistic editor

---

* Jean Cardinal Verdier (1864–1940).

† Then vice chancellor under Hitler.

‡ Fritz Gerlich (1883–1934), fierce Catholic journalist and opponent of the Nazis who had been arrested the previous year.

of the *Münchner Neuesten Nachrichten*, Gerlich had converted through Therese von Konnersreuth.* He became an ardent Catholic and a passionate follower of hers. He drew all the consequences of his conversion, completely abandoning his former nationalism and attacking the Nazis from the Catholic standpoint in the most courageous of ways. *Der Gerade Weg* was excellent. He was mistreated terribly; I think he lost an eye and was then dragged off to Dachau. I cannot express how much it pained me that the Catholic hierarchy did not take a definitive stance against the Antichrist, who raised his head in Nazism.

I visited Marc Sangnier during my stay in Paris, and we spoke about the appalling developments in Germany. He said to me, "Does it suffice to be in power to be recognized by the Church?" What a disappointment it was for him who had labored so much on behalf of peace and the reconciliation between Germany and France, and who had fought so hard against nationalism. He had believed in a better Germany, and yet now everything had turned so completely in the opposite direction. It was a painful time together, yet we were deeply united in our outlook.

On the last evening before my return to Florence from Paris I was invited by the friendly attaché at the German embassy, but unfortunately the Provincial of the German Dominicans and the Prior of the Dominican monastery in Berlin were also invited. At the table there arose a very disagreeable discussion. The Provincial began by saying, "But we have no reason at all to reject Hitler when he stresses the idea of authority and the value of the nation. Above all, he keeps speaking about God." I answered, "Hitler is so stupid that he does not even know what the word, 'God,' means; when he uses the word, in no way does it mean that he is professing the true God."

The poor attaché looked at me in desperation and made a pleading gesture—I ought not to say such things openly in his presence. He was right, since if this had become known, he would immediately have lost his position. Perhaps he even said, "My dear Professor, please bear in

---

* Also known as Therese Neumann.

mind that I will immediately be fired when it becomes known that the Führer was described as stupid in my home!"

The Provincial continued, "We Catholics have to put ourselves in the front ranks of National Socialism and in this way give everything a Catholic turn." I answered, "National Socialism and Christianity are absolutely incompatible, and besides it is a terrible illusion to think that Catholics would be able to influence this movement by means of compromises." I mentioned the awful speech of Esser,* who had said at a belated Goethe celebration (the hundredth anniversary of Goethe's death had been in 1932), "I'm glad these festivities are coming to a close, since I prefer every poet of freedom a thousand times over the internationalist Goethe." The Prior responded, "I also greatly prefer Schiller to Goethe; there is nothing wrong with this opinion."

I was beside myself. These two unfortunate friars showed me the entire tragedy of the situation of Catholics in Germany, the terrible temptation of being drawn into compromises, and I saw more than ever before how right it was that I had left Germany. In the attitude of the two friars, I saw so clearly the danger of compromise by German Catholics. After dinner the Prior even began laughingly to sing the *Horst Wessel Lied*,† at which I declared, "I have to go to the train station in twenty minutes, but I will leave here immediately if you continue to sing this song, for I have no intention of listening to it for even a moment." At that they stopped with their singing.

The German attaché accompanied me a few steps, probably to my hotel, which was quite close to his residence. He said to me, "You must know that I am one hundred percent in agreement with you, and that I was very unhappy about the behavior of the friars. But I cannot, after all, take a public stance; otherwise I will lose my position tomorrow morning." The poor fellow apparently still hoped to outlast the regime at his post and did not realize that he would anyway soon be replaced by

---

* Hermann Esser (1900–81), Nazi politician and minister of economics.
† A popular Nazi song.

a Nazi, and that a critical statement on his part would not cost him his position but his freedom. He was a very nice person whose heart was in the right place. I felt tremendous pity for him. I never saw him again and do not know whether he survived the Nazi regime. We parted in great warmth.

I think he had spoken with Gilson about whether I might be given a professorship at the Sorbonne or at the Collège de France. He hoped that the aspiration for the spiritual unity of Europe, which the celebration in honor of St. Albert was meant to symbolize, would lead to the creation of a chair for a German philosopher in Paris to renew the ancient tradition of the Sorbonne, and he hoped that I would be appointed to this chair.

But Gilson had clearly said no, and I can easily imagine why. To begin with, it was hardly possible to build this bridge to Germany at a moment when Germany was betraying all of its own great traditions and had fallen not only into the hands of criminals but into the clutches of radical philistinism, ignorance, and kitsch. Second, while I could perhaps act as a representative of an earlier Germany, my appointment would have been anything but a bridge to the Germany of Hitler. Third, Gilson probably did not think too highly of me, for he was first and foremost a scholar and a strict Thomist, for whom phenomenology was a dubious form of philosophy.

Von Hildebrand returned to Florence, where he saw his brother-in-law Walter Braunfels. This was their first meeting since Braunfels, who was of Jewish descent, had been dismissed as director of the music conservatory in Cologne.

It was a significant reunion with Walter. He had immediately traveled to Florence upon being dismissed. I was now able to get a firsthand account of the terrible events that had occurred, how he had been let down by those he had especially helped to advance and whose friendship he had counted on. Sadly, it was above all a Catholic who had treated him so badly. But I was happy to see that Walter was in complete agreement with me in the radical rejection of Nazism.

I received a letter from Gretchen who was in Munich in which she wrote that it had been announced on German radio that a celebration had taken place in Paris for the German thinker St. Albert the Great and that this was intended to honor Germany. The German ambassador had attended the celebration and Dietrich von Hildebrand had spoken as a representative of Germany. This was quite amazing to me. As a mortal enemy of the Nazis who would not have crossed the border at any cost, it was almost comical that they should mention me in this way. It shows how little everything had yet been forcibly coordinated under the Nazi policy of *Gleichschaltung*. Had not the foreign office also approved of my speech?

During a stay in Rome, von Hildebrand and his wife met two of his colleagues from the University of Munich. One reported on the situation the Nazis had created there.

In particular, they told us about the dismissal of all professors who were "non-Aryan"—according to the official definition of Aryan. A person was considered non-Aryan if he was fully or even half Jewish. Having a Jewish grandmother or grandfather sufficed to make one non-Aryan, unless the grandparent had been baptized as a child and raised as a non-Jew.

I no longer remember whether it was already before my trip to Rome that I received the questionnaire about Aryan status, which was sent to all the professors and instructors at the University. Most likely, it arrived only after I returned to Florence. In any case, I decided to identify myself as non-Aryan. There was, of course, a certain basis for this as my father's mother's, whose maiden name was Guttentag, was Jewish, though as a child she had been baptized as a Protestant. But the questionnaire stated that whoever declared themselves "Aryan" had to give proof of this under oath, while those who designated themselves as "non-Aryan" were not required to do so. I was fundamentally opposed to the very question itself, and in any case I had resolved never again to return to Germany. I could have written "Aryan," according to the official definition. Yet I was loath even to recognize the distinction and to join the ranks of the non-persecuted "Aryans." Moreover, I absolutely did not want to supply evidence why, in spite of my Jewish grandmother, I could call myself "Aryan." For in this, I already saw myself as "dealing" with the Nazis, which I wanted to avoid at all costs. Finally, it was perhaps less dangerous for my sisters if I were dismissed for being non-Aryan rather than leaving the University of my own accord for reasons of fundamental philosophical opposition. Thus I submitted the questionnaire marking myself as "non-Aryan." I was proud at this moment to belong to the non-Aryans.

This open act of solidarity with the persecuted Jews was a radical act of defiance. In response, the Nazis dismissed von Hildebrand from the University of Munich on June 27, 1933. He had taught philosophy there for fourteen years. Back in Florence, he began work on a book about epistemology—a "grand and beautiful task"—he had long wanted to write. His only source of regular income for the time being was the advance of 100 marks a month from the publisher Otto Müller for the Ethics *he would be writing.*

In the meantime, many unfortunate things had again come to pass. Monsignor Kaas,* who played a leading role in the German Center Party, sent a telegram to Hitler in April offering best wishes on his birthday and speaking of the good he had done. What a disastrous and undignified way to ingratiate himself with Hitler, and besides, this gesture was in no way expected of him. While there is no moral justification whatsoever for a priest to congratulate an Antichrist and to speak of his

---

* Ludwig Kaas (1881–1952), theologian, politician, member of the Reichstag, and longtime chairman of the Center Party, the major Catholic political party in Germany at the time.

good deeds, not even in the hope of securing something of decisive importance, such an ignominious compromise was in any case completely senseless. There was no reason to hope that a congratulatory telegram would alter Hitler's stance toward the Church or secure greater freedom for Catholics, or that one could somehow convince him not to encroach on the life of the Church, on Catholic schools, etc., let alone to gain for the Church an exemption from the Nazi policy of *Gleichschaltung*.

I saw with horror the path that some leading Catholics were taking, and I saw how terribly the soon-to-be concluded Concordat with Hitler was bound to affect the spirit of Catholics, how their inner resistance would be paralyzed by it. Hitler had given an address in the Reichstag in which he uttered many expressions about peace and his love for peace. The duplicity and dishonesty of these phrases were as clear as day to me. But unfortunately, not for many other Catholics in Germany, who were eager to shelter themselves in an illusion. Münch saw this speech as a hopeful sign that Hitler is really much better than one had thought. He even influenced Nini* for a moment, so that she also took this speech as a good omen and thought that I was too peremptory in my rejection of Hitler. All this saddened me deeply and I realized ever more clearly how great the danger was for German Catholics to fall into "wishful thinking," to allow themselves to fall for illusions, and thus to falter in their inner resistance.

For my part, I threw myself completely into the writing of my new book, laboring uninterruptedly and with greatest intensity from dawn till dusk. Rarely in my life have I worked with such philosophical intensity as I did then. Of course, I had experienced such consuming work in the past, as in completing *In Defense of Purity*, when the intense rhythm spanned three to four days, though well into the night. Now, by comparison, the work rhythm stretched over two and a half or three months. Certainly, the twenty-three days during which I wrote *Liturgy and Personality*[1] were in their own way a pinnacle of intense work. Yet then it had been more like harvesting ripe fruit, while this time I was engaged

---

* Nickname of von Hildebrand's eldest sister, Eva.

in arduous philosophical work in which I was not just deepening and developing previously acquired ideas but conquering new territory. Hamburger worked with me a great deal and his help was crucial.

One afternoon Carlo Placci[*] invited me to tea. I went mainly for the chance to see my old friend Placci again. It is quite remarkable how preoccupation with personal concerns can cut one off from one's surroundings and from present events. I was oppressed by the tragedy of Germany falling into the hands of criminals and by the fact that my life in Munich had been irretrievably lost. I was full of indignation at all the injustice daily taking place in Germany, and so I felt very alien in Florence, surrounded as I was by people who saw the things happening in Germany more in the light of a historic event that did not concern them personally in an immediate way. For Placci and many others, the Maggio Musicale[†] was more important at the moment. For Lisl it was also not a matter that concerned her daily. Other concrete things of the present moment stood in the foreground. With Hamburger it was of course different—he shared my concerns and my pain, but he was not as preoccupied by them as I was.

But above all I had the feeling when I met other people or came into a room that I was present there as a stranger, not because they did not greet me in a friendly and interested way, but because I was completely preoccupied by something that did not directly and personally touch them and so was cut off from them. This is a very particular phenomenon, which I have experienced in various situations in life. It brings out another dimension of Ovid's words, *Donec eris felix multos numerabis amicos; tempora si fuerunt nubila solus eris* ("As long as you are lucky, you will have many friends; if cloudy times appear, you will be alone"). Ovid is pointing to the attitude of others toward us when we have hit on hard times. But what I have in mind is a form of *solus eris* ("you will be alone") which is not the fault of others but the consequence of our own state of mind, which does not entail any fault on our part either. I

---

[*] Writer and cosmopolite in Florence.

[†] A spring music festival in Florence.

am also not thinking of a condition of "being abandoned" in an outward manner, but rather a state of "feeling alone" due to an objective situation for which we are not to blame.

I remember only one conversation from my visit with Placci. I told him about the letter from the Nazis sent to all university professors, requiring one to state whether one was Aryan or non-Aryan, and also about the decree that any non-Aryans were to lose their professorships. Placci was horrified by the whole situation. He said, "While I know that my ancestors were Catholics, I would be unable to offer any details about their race. Until now, this question has not interested anyone. I could not prove that there had never been a non-Aryan among my ancestors." Placci's statement made me happy. I fear this was the last time I ever saw him. Dear, congenial Placci. His presence was a constant in my life from the earliest years of childhood until 1933. Ever delightful, Carlo Placci would reliably turn up from time to time.

It must have been during this same May that the Catholic Academic Association once again held a conference at the Abbey of Maria Laach. To my great distress, Papen had been invited to give a lecture. The whole conference turned out to be an ignominious affair. A priest from Maria Laach praised the Third Reich as the realization of the Body of Christ in the secular world. All sorts of speeches were given in praise of National Socialism and the Third Reich. Landmesser also gave a disastrous talk. I was completely beside myself as I heard the details of the conference. I decided to withdraw immediately from the Association, above all, to resign as a member of the board and as chairman of the Association's foreign commission.

I had already heard about statements by Münch and Kirnberger which I thought were appalling. Both of them had said to Gretchen (or to someone in Munich who told Gretchen) that the only thing still necessary was for Hitler to find his way to the faith and to convert. If that happened, the new situation in Germany would in fact be tremendously fortunate. Thus, we had to storm heaven for Hitler's conversion; we had to pray for him. This was a horrid blend of equivocation and an attempt at self-deception. To begin with, there was far more to be decried in Hitler than his personal lack of faith, namely his entire gruesome doctrine, the totalitarian state he had created, and the spirit of all his collaborators.

This remark would have been meaningful in the case of a great and enlightened monarch, whose only shortcoming lay in not being a believing Catholic. Yet in the case of Hitler, everything was permeated by the spirit of the Antichrist, and so everything had to be rejected— nationalism in its entirety, from top to bottom. Even Franz von Papen, who at least in his private life gave the impression of being a fervent Catholic, had taken part in the abolition of every liberty and in the use of terror. Had Hitler actually converted, he would in consequence have had to dismiss all of his subordinates, dissolve the Third Reich, and immediately turn himself over to a court for his many crimes. It was therefore total nonsense to believe that Hitler was only lacking faith and nothing more. Certainly one should pray for him, as one should pray for every criminal, for the eternal good of his soul, but one should simultaneously pray that he be removed from his position as soon as possible, that Germany and the entire world be freed of him.

Much as I was saddened by the remarks of two such close friends who had always stood against National Socialism and even against German nationalism, what I heard about the conference went far beyond this. I was terribly upset by this shameful betrayal, this miserable compromise. I wrote to Kirnberger, though in very cautious terms, since already then it could be compromising with the censors to receive a letter attacking the regime. Thus I only wrote, "I cannot accept the direction taken by the Catholic Academic Association at its recent conference. For this reason, I am resigning from the board. I am also giving up my place as chairman of the foreign commission, since in any event I will no longer be living in Germany." In his response, Kirnberger expressed his great regret about my resignation, saying that he did not understand what I had said about the direction of the Catholic Academic Association; at Maria Laach, the intention had simply been to incorporate the Catholic intellectual heritage into the new historical situation.

Münch was naturally at fault for this intellectual confusion in my dear friend Kirnberger, who was himself deeply pious and antinationalistic.

Münch was so superior to Kirnberger intellectually and in force of personality that it was not difficult to induce Kirnberger to join his own "wishful thinking." There were many unconscious motives at work in Münch. First, he was terribly anxious about his own well-being. Second, he feared that the Association might be banned, thus leading to the destruction of his life's work. Third, he labored under a tendency toward self-deception and of falling into "wishful thinking." He frantically sought an interpretation of the circumstances in Germany which would not confront him with the alternative of either giving up everything or making compromises—this would have weighed heavily on his conscience.

So he tried desperately to talk himself into believing that he was taking a much more hopeful path and that everything could suddenly take a turn for the good, as for example through the "conversion" of Hitler. He did not want to see that it would be far more horrifying if Hitler committed all manner of awful deeds while at the same time adopting a positive and friendly stance toward the Church, thus bringing about a friendly coexistence between National Socialism and the Catholic Church in Germany.

The Concordat reached between the Third Reich and the Vatican naturally contributed to this intellectual confusion.[*] Von Papen had personally gone to Rome for this purpose and to my greatest sorrow the Concordat was solemnly ratified. From the perspective of the Church, of course, a concordat does not in any way signify an endorsement of the regime with which the concordat is agreed. It is a treaty to secure the rights of the Church: to dispense the sacraments and so forth. After all, following the Concordat with Mussolini, Pope Pius XI had said, "I would have concluded a concordat with the devil if I could thereby save a single immortal soul."

Yet the impact on the minds of believers is completely different in a country where those who represent the most pernicious and false

---

[*] The Concordat was signed July 20, 1933.

doctrine are capable of exerting terrible pressure. This danger was very great in Germany, as soon became evident. Fr. Leiber* grasped the situation correctly when he said at the time, "The only remaining hope is that von Papen (who was on his way to Rome for the ratification of the Concordat) will perish in a plane crash; otherwise there will no longer be any escape from the disaster of the Concordat." A year or two later one frequently heard the witticism, "Papen Papam fefellit" ("von Papen tricked the Pope"). This was at the time when the Concordat was already being violated and the open battle for the annihilation of Christendom, and with it the persecution of the Church, had already begun.

Critics hold that in signing the Concordat the Church sought to preserve its own interests rather than speak out against Nazism with uncompromising force, pointing to ambiguous statements by the German Catholic bishops that von Hildebrand deplored. Defenders counter that the agreement was a defense mechanism against an increasingly dangerous regime, citing, for example, an article in the Vatican newspaper L'Osservatore Romano *by Cardinal Secretary of State Eugenio Pacelli published a week after the Concordat was signed. The article stressed that the Concordat in no way implied Church tolerance for Nazism's moral and religious errors.*

The Holy See thought that the Concordat would at least secure continuing religious liberty, including the right of the Church to operate its schools and charities. Only unusually prescient individuals like von Hildebrand remained immune to the notion that the Church could find a modus vivendi *with the Third Reich.*

In later years, von Hildebrand would write, "I personally regretted the Concordat for its psychological effect on the Catholics in Germany, and so did many others." But then he adds, "The Concordat itself did not contain any yielding to Nazism—and Germany was at that time still a militarily weak country. It was not yet the dangerous aggressive power that it became

---

* Robert Leiber SJ (1887–1967), private secretary to Eugenio Cardinal Pacelli, the later Pope Pius XII.

in 1938; Hitler was not yet at the head of a strong and powerful state. Germany was still tolerated as a member of the 'League of Nations' in Geneva."

He continues, "But as soon as Pope Pius XI saw that Hitler was not respecting the terms of the Concordat, but was trying to enslave the Church in Germany, he raised his voice in the magnificent encyclical Mit brennender Sorge (With Burning Anxiety). *He did not speak in a conciliatory spirit, but he condemned with holy authority, like a St. Gregory VII. Hitler's response was a terrible persecution of the Church."*[2]

Fr. Leiber later echoed von Hildebrand, "At that time, in the early months of the Third Reich, the Holy See would have preferred a modus vivendi *in the form of an extended validation of the individual Länder concordats [with the individual German states] rather than the Reich concordat. But the government exerted pressure and offered extensive concessions. The Holy See would have been wrong to refuse and thereby to have exposed Catholics in Germany to the gravest dangers. This was the considered opinion of all those who were consulted for responsible advice, even of those who had little liking for the Concordat."*[3]

Around Pentecost, relatives came to visit in Florence. I was told I could not be too strict in judging National Socialism since the young people with whom they were coming were all more or less enthusiastic about Hitler. They were not ideological disciples of National Socialism, but were enthused for the new, for "upheaval" and for "breakthrough," for national self-consciousness, for Hitler's "forceful" emergence and entry into the fray. They were young people caught up in National Socialism while it was at the present moment in the air. Some of them were Catholics.

In general, the directive from German bishops and priests was this: one may participate in everything that does not violate the faith and the commandments of God. In other words, one can join the SA, continue teaching at the school that has conformed itself to National Socialism, one ought not to give up one's position where one can at least prevent what is "worst" in small things, continue to do good, and so forth. With the bishops and priests adopting this stance, it is hardly surprising that young, naïve Catholics, particularly those who were only Catholic out of tradition, should merrily sing the *Horst-Wessel Lied* and be filled with enthusiasm for the *Führer*. I was of course horrified by such a friendly and benign attitude toward the Nazi regime, and I expressed my total rejection of National Socialism and my disdain for Hitler in very clear terms.

But I was much more upset when I noticed that anti-Semitism was being somewhat excused, "Of course, it is terrible to persecute the Jews—but really they are often very provocative and disagreeable, there is something about them that engenders the antipathy of so many people in so many countries; one can't deny this if one wants to be objective." I answered, "I will not tolerate a word against the Jews at the present moment. This kind of argumentation means that you give the devil your little finger—it means opening a door for infection by a dreadful heresy."

At a time when a heresy was rampant, the Catholic Church would forbid all debate of the issues, even when such debate was in itself justifiable, as long as believers might thereby be infected by this heresy. Thus, in the time of Luther, every stress on the apostolate of the laity was forbidden because of the heresy of the priesthood of the laity. Just when a racism absolutely incompatible with Christianity is spreading, when Jews are being persecuted in a horrible way because of their "race" and independently of their religion and their convictions, when human beings are treated not as persons but as horses or dogs, when the individual no longer counts but only one's membership in a race—at such a moment one simply cannot entertain any kind of discussion about whether Jews are really agreeable or disagreeable. The very idea of such a sweeping question is stupid and immoral; such a question can and should only be asked with respect to individuals.

But even if one can meaningfully speak about the agreeable quality of a national identity (and that, of course, is by no means a question of race!), one should not do it at this moment, since it represents, if only slightly, an "understanding" and to some extent excusing gesture toward National Socialism and thus it opens a trap door for the evil enemy. In the face of such dreadful movements and heresies as Bolshevism and Nazism, in which the Antichrist raises his head, every attempt to "understand," every attempt at a certain neutral objectivity, is entirely impermissible. Here we are required to pronounce nothing other than an unconditional *anathema sit.*

For this reason, at Pentecost 1933, I wrote a letter to close friends in Munich in which I attempted to describe the stance which to my mind was the only one possible for Catholics living in Nazi Germany. I called attention to the terrible danger of allowing oneself to be pressed into compromises and above all of inwardly adopting a neutral or even friendly stance toward National Socialism. I explained that they were being confronted by the Antichrist and that, if they were forced to live with him—indeed, even to be exposed to his force—it was absolutely necessary to bear the concealed "dagger," as it were, of absolute and irreconcilable enmity, ready to make use of it at the first opportunity, without thereby risking the concentration camp.

I further wrote that it is completely immaterial if the Antichrist refrains from attacking the Church for political reasons, or if he concludes a Concordat with the Vatican. What is decisive is the spirit that animates him, the heresy he represents, the crimes committed at his behest. God is offended regardless of whether the victim of a murder is a Jew, a Socialist, or a bishop. Innocent blood cries out to heaven. The absolute, unbridgeable antithesis toward the Church lies in the racism, the totalitarian system, and in the anti-Christian ideology, none of which is mitigated by the fact that Hitler for political reasons concludes a Concordat with the Vatican—which, on top of everything else, he has no intention of observing in any real way.

I think the letter succeeded in expressing all my love and concern for my friends, and in articulating why I thought it necessary to make them aware of a dangerous attitude growing among many Catholics in Germany, and from which I wanted to protect them, namely of inwardly "making peace" with the Nazis. At the very least, these friends ought to adopt the stance, which from the Catholic standpoint was the right and only possible one, even if all around them many Catholics and a portion of the hierarchy in Germany did not do so themselves.

• • •

Von Hildebrand was visited by Fr. Max Josef Metzger, who after serving as a chaplain in World War I had become a pacifist and founded the German Catholic Association for Peace. As described above, von Hildebrand had met him in Paris at a convention in 1921 and the two had become friends.

Fr. Metzger spoke with us about the situation in Germany, and he and I were in complete agreement. He was just as unhappy as I about the stance of the bishops and of many Catholics. He recognized the Antichrist in National Socialism and wanted to avoid falling into any compromises whatsoever. I was terribly concerned for his safety in Germany, yet he believed that he must persevere there. I had the impression that he had grown a great deal since 1923. Back then, he was a deeply religious person, with a touch of the zealot and a genius for business. Now it appeared that the purely religious element had become completely dominant; he was much gentler and humbler than before.

I can hardly express how encouraging and consoling it was for me to meet a German priest who saw everything in a true light, who was completely free of all confusion, and who understood that there was only one possible stance for Catholics, namely the relentless battle against National Socialism—waged secretly when it would be futile to act publicly, yet never with even the slightest acquiescence or tolerance.

Metzger was murdered by the Nazis in 1933 or 1934.* He died as a martyr in the broad sense, by which I do not mean the completely meaningless and illegitimate use of the term to describe those who would rather die than change their convictions. This use would apply to every idolater who would rather perish than recant, to anyone who is executed for clinging to their evil idols. Giordano Bruno was clearly not a martyr. In speaking of a martyr in the broad sense, I mean those who because of their uncompromising repudiation of the enemies of Christ

---

* Actually in 1944.

and the Catholic Church are murdered by these enemies, in contrast to those who, given the choice to reject Christ or face death, choose death.

I forgot to mention that, upon returning from Germany, Gretchen told me that her old friend Jacobsohn had thrown himself under a moving train. He could not bear the thought that his children, being Jewish, would no longer count as full Germans, as full citizens. I had just seen Jacobsohn in the summer of 1931, barely two years before, when he came to visit me at home at the Maria-Theresia Strasse with his son, who was an extremely talented student of mine. Gretchen was completely beside herself as she told me about his death. She said, "Even if the Nazis had done nothing besides driving this noble and deeply gracious person to his death, it would suffice to qualify them as criminals."

It was truly symptomatic of the ugly face of National Socialism that such a pious and noble man was driven to suicide by the "Third Reich." What must a man like Jacobsohn have endured that he, a pious Protestant, would decide to take his own life! I was profoundly shaken, and yet at the same time it showed me how deeply these Protestant Jews were rooted in Germany—so much so that Jacobsohn never even considered leaving Germany with his family. The thought that his children could no longer be full citizens drove him to despair.

Around this time, I came across a copy of the *Summa* of St. Thomas Aquinas, which the Dominicans had newly translated and published in collaboration with the Catholic Academic Association. To my horror, there on the first page I read, "In the Holy Year of the Germans." When I inquired through others about the meaning of this very ambiguous and misleading choice of words, I was told that since this was a Holy Year it was also a Holy Year for the Germans. Of course, this was a very stupid response; adding "the Germans" would inevitably cause people to make a connection with the Third Reich. This Holy Year was equally for Catholics everywhere, yet by this emphasis the impression was given that this Holy Year had some special relation to Germany. There was absolutely no basis for this link to Germany, and so one could only have seen an allusion to the Third Reich.

One day, Hamburger visited me with a friend from a previous chapter in his life, a very likeable and intelligent Jew. We had a very beautiful and interesting conversation. He was so deeply dejected by the persecution of the Jews that it was difficult to encourage him and to offer him consolation. Though I surely advised him to abandon Germany, like many Jews, he could not bring himself to do so since he was still deeply attached to Germany. I think his name was Bloch. To my great sorrow, I later heard that he had taken his life.

News again arrived from Germany that cast an increasingly stark light on the terrible unfolding of events. I heard that a schoolteacher who had been fired for drinking but who was a fervent member of the Nazi Party had been appointed Minister of Culture in Bavaria. His name was Schemm.[*] In an address to professors of the University, he said, among other things, "From now on, you no longer need to ask in your research, 'Is this true?' but only 'Does it correspond to the spirit of National Socialism?'" These words from the Minister of Culture, let alone the fact that Schemm had become the Minister, spoke volumes about the "spirit" of National Socialism—to the extent that one can even speak of spirit. Coming out of the lecture, Professor Vossler[†] said humorously to his colleagues, "I am 'aschemmed.'"

But much sadder and incomparably worse than this radical intellectual and cultural decline was the letter of the Catholic bishops gathered in the town of Fulda. Contrary to all tradition, the bishops took a position toward the government. They began by listing all the things within National Socialism to which they spoke a full, approving "yes." We affirm the spirit of authority, we affirm the commitment to the German Nation, we affirm, etc., etc. All this affirmation was a shameful betrayal, quite apart from the fact that the bishops after World War I did not take a similar position toward the Weimar Republic, so that taking an official position in the present context was unnecessary. Terms such as "authority," "nation," and the like were used equivocally, when it was clear to everyone that what the National Socialists understood by these terms was something the bishops could never affirm. Besides, the fact that

---

[*] Hans Schemm (1891–1935).

[†] Karl Vossler (1872–1949), professor of Romance studies.

the affirmation of many points was very much in the foreground created the impression of a primarily affirmative stance toward National Socialism as such. It is true that the bishops in an appendix stated that they could not accept racism in certain forms, yet the impression remained that the overall tenor was one of joyous affirmation, so that the faithful could only take it as an approval of National Socialism. No word about the heresy of the totalitarian system, no protest against the innumerable crimes and the terrorism, no real condemnation of racism and of the whole ideology of National Socialism! Two weeks before Hitler seized power, membership in the Nazi Party still entailed excommunication, and now this affirmation!

Words cannot describe how this failure of the German episcopacy grieved me. To my sorrow, I saw how right I was to fear that Catholics in Germany would allow themselves to be carried away by a shameful spirit of compromise and accommodation toward the Antichrist. Later I found out who the "evil spirits" were among the German bishops. Above all, it was Bishop Berning of Osnabrück, who really was infected and later was appointed a member of the *Staatsrat*,[*] as well as Bishop Gröber of Freiburg,[†] who went along primarily out of fear. Many bishops did not have clear positions of their own, and so allowed themselves to be determined by these two. Bishop Bares[‡] and Bishop Preysing[§] were naturally completely outstanding. It is thanks to Preysing that the restriction about racism was at least added to the end of the letter.

Having publicly opposed Hitler and Nazism until his appointment as chancellor on January 30, 1933, the German bishops were faced with a situation in which this very man and movement were now the official rulers

---

[*] Wilhelm Berning (1877–1955). By the time Berning joined the *Staatsrat*, the former upper chamber of the Prussian legislature had been reduced to an advisory capacity.

[†] Conrad Gröber (1872–1948).

[‡] Nikolaus Bares (1871–1935), bishop of Berlin.

[§] Count Konrad von Preysing (1890–1950), bishop of Eichstätt until 1935 when he became bishop of Berlin.

of Germany. On March 23, in a speech to the Reichstag, Hitler promised to respect the Christian churches and work with them. He had no intention of keeping that promise, of course, but many Christians, including influential bishops, took him at his word.

And so, despite their past warnings, and against all misgivings, the bishops released a joint pastoral on March 28 and then another on June 3. Both letters noted their past condemnations of Nazism, but also contained the affirmations and equivocations von Hildebrand found so deplorable.

In Florence, which would serve as his base for seven and a half months, von Hildebrand began to take note of the leadership of the Austrian chancellor, Engelbert Dollfuss (1892–1934), a conservative politician and devout Catholic who opposed Nazism and resisted the notion of Anschluss, the fusion of Austria into the Third Reich. He has come down in history as a highly controversial figure, for reasons that form part of von Hildebrand's story.

Dollfuss became Austrian chancellor in 1932. He was a member of the conservative Christian Social Party, faced on the left by revolutionary agitation from the Austrian Social Democratic Party, and on the right by terrorist activity from the small but vocal Austrian Nazi Party. In March 1933, Dollfuss suspended the Austrian parliament, while curtailing civil liberties and free speech. He banned the Nazi and Communist Parties, which went underground, as well as the Republican Protection League, the paramilitary of the Social Democrats. Two months later, he founded the Patriotic Front to gather together those who supported his policies.

The primary goal of the Patriotic Front was the independence of Austria and the battle against National Socialism. The Patriotic Front, however, was at odds with the Social Democrats who were then very radical and who did not at all understand that the urgent task now lay in saving Austria from *Gleichschaltung*, from Nazification, which in turn would automatically have led to the Anschluss of Austria to the Third Reich. At this moment, Austria could only be saved by an authoritarian government, which at the same time would be able to call forth a new Austrian patriotism. The Social Democrats, whose party platform had always endorsed the *Anschluss*, had completely suppressed the sense for the entirely distinctive national character of Austria. The Social Democrats, therefore, could not form a stronghold against the Anschluss which the Nazi regime in Germany was promoting in all variety of ways, and which was being demanded by those in favor of the "Greater Germany" and by the Nazis within Austria.

Only a government that would unreservedly stand for the autonomy of Austria could stem the tide of the German Nazi wave that threatened to inundate all of Austria. Indeed, only a man, like Dollfuss, who opposed the Antichrist with the spirit of Christ and who rejected National Socialism on the basis of his Catholic conviction, could take up the nearly hopeless battle against National Socialism.

I was jubilant when I read what had happened to Nazi Justice Minister Frank[*] who had come to Austria to spread Nazi propaganda. Frank was met by an Austrian official who courteously conveyed the undesirability of his visit; he had even been escorted back to the border. Finally someone was willing to confront the Nazis without compromise; indeed, here was a Catholic government with the courage to take up the battle against Nazi Germany. Like David against Goliath, entrusting itself fully to God, Austria took up arms against the Third Reich. As I thought of the embarrassing and yielding stance which the great political powers and the League of Nations took toward Nazi Germany, the courage of Austria was all the more admirable. That it was my beloved Austria which had found the courage for resistance gave me special joy.

During this time, I followed the events in Austria with greatest interest and full of hope. Nazi Germany immediately responded to the "expulsion" of Minister Frank with a penalty of 1,000 marks for all Germans who wished to travel to Austria, i.e., only those who paid the State 1,000 marks were allowed to visit Austria. This was a significant economic blow to Austria. Tyrol, Salzburg, Vorarlberg, and also to a large

---

[*] Hans Frank (1900–46).

extent Carinthia and Styria all drew German tourists in the summer, while in the winter they were major areas for skiing. Of the tourists who came to Austria, at least 60% had been German. The loss of this tourism created great economic distress, which in turn is particularly effective for awakening ill-feeling toward the government. With this measure, Nazi Germany hoped not only to strike at Austria economically but above all to engender propaganda against the government, indeed, even indirectly to awaken sympathies for Nazi Germany.

Discontent of any kind makes for fertile ground for infection by powerful historic currents, not to mention that it causes people to adopt an attitude of blame. They say, "The stupid government brought about our economic woes by treating Minister Frank the way it did. Was it really necessary? As a result, those of us who rely on German tourists are being sacrificed recklessly." Thank God Dollfuss did not allow himself to be swayed from continuing in his struggle against Hitler.

One very welcome development around this time was that Mussolini had made a toast to an independent and sovereign Austria on a visit by Dollfuss to Rome. Dollfuss was on very good terms with Mussolini, who in turn took a clear stance in favor of Dollfuss and his policy of resistance against Germany.

Toward the end of June, Otto Klemperer* called me by telephone—or perhaps he visited me. At that time, I only knew him by reputation. Münch had often spoken about him and his conversion. Scheler† had also known him well, for Klemperer had been conducting in Cologne in the years 1920–21, prior to being appointed in Berlin. He called to tell me that he had lost his post in Berlin for being Jewish and that he had left Germany. He said he would like to meet me and invited us to Fiesole, where he was then living. I was very interested to get to know him. I had heard much about his great talent as a conductor. Soon thereafter

---

* Otto Klemperer (1885–1973), renowned German conductor.
† Max Scheler (1874–1928), major German philosopher and close friend of von Hildebrand.

we went to Fiesole to have tea with him. He was a handsome man, very tall, a sort of Maccabean Jewish type, with a large, chiseled, and well-defined face. He made the impression of being a strong personality.

Regrettably, I had the feeling that he primarily hated the Nazis because they had dismissed him; a further reason was perhaps their anti-Semitism. It was not primarily their terrible doctrine, their glorification of violence, or their idolatrous nationalism which upset him. I rather doubt he would ever have left Germany had he not been sent away. Nevertheless, we found common ground in the radical rejection of National Socialism which, however motivated, now predominated in him. He lived in a magnificent house with a wonderful view. The widow of Busoni* was also present. We had a very interesting and stimulating conversation. He struck me as tempestuous, incredibly passionate, and ambitious, yet he was, quite aside from his great quality as a conductor, a cultivated human being and an interesting personality. Sadly I soon discovered that he lacked any understanding for Wagner, and we had a fierce dispute about *Tristan*† (not at this first encounter but later, when he was invited for supper at San Francesco by my sister).

This visit with Klemperer in Fiesole is a very beautiful memory. The entire experience made a very strong impression on me. I will still tell of various other occasions on which Klemperer and I were together. The summer of 1933 was colored by his presence.

During this time, [Theodor] Cramer-Klett passed through Florence on the journey to Rome (or perhaps from Rome) and paid me a visit. It was very gracious of him, but I feared that we might have unpleasant conversations about Nazism. We went together into the Campo and thankfully Cramer-Klett said nothing positive about the Nazis. He was considerate of the fact that I had left Germany, which he realized was tied to many great sacrifices for me. This is surely why he tactfully avoided saying anything friendly about the Nazis. In any case, I was glad we were able to avoid an uncomfortable discussion. He also made

---

* Ferruccio Busoni (1866–1924), Italian composer and pianist.
† *Tristan und Isolde*, an opera by the German composer Richard Wagner (1813–83).

an observation about Austria which, though a bit ambiguous, did express the hope that Austria would not be Nazified. Our time together was relaxed, human, and warmhearted.

It was the last time that I saw Cramer-Klett. Having been bound in real friendship since 1921, I am happy that our last encounter was harmonious. In later years, I am sure he will often have thought of how right I was in my rejection of National Socialism. He would have realized this in 1936, when the persecution of the Church was in full swing, and also later when his house in the Otto-Strasse was set on fire, when his passport was stolen, and when he was intermittently imprisoned.

One day I ran into Hopfen on the street, a German who had lived in Florence for many years. Being a member of the German National People's Party,* I was all the more delighted by his complete rejection of Hitler. He told me about the suicide of a leader in the party (I think by the name of Oberfohren) whose conscience tormented him over the fact that his party had participated in Hitler's first cabinet as Chancellor. As he realized what criminal hands Germany had fallen into, and seeing that there was no longer anything that could be done to free Germany of Hitler, he was seized by such despair that he took his own life.

This made a great impression on me and filled me with deep sympathy for this poor man whose grasp of the situation was far more honest and morally clear-sighted than that of most people. Hopfen told me about someone who had said that Germany seemed like a ship whose captain had gone mad and who in a blind rapture was now running the ship at full steam toward the rocks on which it would be shipwrecked. I thought it a very good comparison, though the only thing missing was that the captain was not just a madman but a criminal as well.

I received a letter from Fedja Georgii [his brother-in-law] urgently seeking my consent for the sale of the house on the Maria-Theresia Strasse. This filled me with great sorrow. I was still hoping that the Nazi regime would not last for too much longer in Germany and that we could perhaps still move back into the beloved house after three or four years.

---

* A conservative nationalist German party.

All this was still quite vague, but the sale of the house, for whose maintenance I had sacrificed so much—everything valuable I possessed—was nevertheless a final break with the past. I felt in a very poignant way the loss even of any future existence in Munich. But I could not refuse Fedja's wish. He said that he could not keep the house by himself and feared that under the circumstances my share of the house would be confiscated by the state, making the house unsalable. What he was urging made sense, yet this did not make it any less painful for me. After some hesitation I sent him the statement he was requesting.

In July, I received a visit from Klaus.* We were both total opponents of Nazism, and the seriousness of our common fate, to which both of us had been brought by Nazism, set our relationship on a fundamentally new basis. We had an important discussion about politics on the rooftop terrace of San Francesco. We spoke about the wonderful resistance by the Dollfuss government, about the awakening of Austria, and the possibility of doing intellectual battle from there against National Socialism. We discussed the necessity of providing philosophical support for the resistance of Dollfuss, which we so welcomed, and of the possibility of offering our services to Dollfuss as intellectual officers in this battle. We had the idea of establishing a Catholic, antiracist, and anti-totalitarian journal, and we made a plan to travel to Vienna in June to try to found such a publication. Before going, I was supposed to write for the *Reichspost*, the leading publication of the Christian Social Party, an article about Austria's great mission at this moment.

Upon Klaus' return to Rome, I soon began the composition of the article. It flowed from my pen, or rather, from my heart and soul, since I was compelled to write both by my enmity toward Nazism as well as my great and lifelong love for Austria. I welcomed the chance to speak openly, indeed to present publicly in writing, everything that had

---

* Klaus Dohrn (1909–79), German journalist and relative of von Hildebrand's sister, Eva, by marriage.

become clear to me about the dreadful ideology of Nazism and its betrayal of the whole great culture of Germany.

At the same time, I wanted to express my admiration and enthusiasm for the stance taken by Austria, for Dollfuss' resistance to Nazism, and for the great mission which had been entrusted to Austria at this moment, a mission surpassing any that Austria had ever had, a mission to be the protector of all the great cultural values of Germany in the hour of its deepest degradation, when Nazism was trampling all that was great and noble in its tradition. I still remember how this betrayal of Germany's spirit and culture once struck me when Gretchen in Florence played on the piano the magnificent cantata of Bach, *Vergnügte Ruh, beliebte Seelenlust*. In light of this noble music I realized in particularly stark terms the egregious betrayal of the spirit of Germany by Nazism.

I think it was around the beginning of August that I sent my article to the *Reichspost* with the title "Austria's Great German Hour."[4] Meanwhile, I received a letter from Balduin Schwarz in which he told me of his intention to leave Germany. He underscored the impossibility of remaining in this atmosphere, though he expressed this very obliquely in light of the censors. He also told me that he was coming to Florence to visit me in September. That Balduin felt the moral impossibility of remaining in Nazi Germany with such clarity made me immensely happy.

Von Hildebrand left Florence for Vienna around August 10. Passing through Salzburg, he wanted to keep his presence there quiet because he feared being forcibly taken across the border into nearby Germany, having heard about priests and other opponents of the Nazis to whom this had happened. "Because of my radical anti-Nazi stance, my article for the Reichspost, *and my many statements in Florence, I mistakenly thought that I was much better known to the Nazis than I actually was at this moment." In Hallein, very near Salzburg, he saw his friend and confessor, Fr. Alois Mager, OSB. He then went to the train station in Salzburg for a meeting with Wilhelm Wolf (1897–1939), an official in the Austrian Ministry of Education in Vienna.*

• • •

Wolf had a great interest in my books and was always hoping that I would get a professorship in Vienna. For this reason I assumed he could give me valuable suggestions for my plans in Vienna; after all, he held an important position in the Ministry of Education. I thought I could trust him completely, which later turned out to be a great mistake.

The reunion with Fr. Alois was very happy and beautiful. He was an ardent opponent of Nazism and we were completely of one mind. He thought my plans for Vienna were very good and he listened to everything I had to say with the greatest interest. He completely shared my enthusiasm for the government of Dollfuss and spoke encouragingly of my plans.

It was a joyful reunion with Gretchen who came over from Berchtesgaden. She took part fully in all my plans, and it was admirable how little she worried about our future and how little she complained about leaving Munich, which was a terrible blow for her. But it was more than just that: the parting from the house, which she loved dearly, and from home, which Munich had become for her in the fullest sense of the word. Once again she revealed her greatness and her capacity for heroism. In ultimate matters of conscience and first principles, no sacrifice was too great for her. We agreed that she would return to Munich and the house on the Maria-Theresia Strasse until I had reached Vienna and begun realizing my plans.

I met Wilhelm Wolf for an hour in the restaurant of the Salzburg train station until my train departed. Wolf was in Salzburg for the Hochschulwochen.[*] He was very kind and listened closely, yet he neither gave me any valuable advice, nor did he fill me with much courage. He was rather passive and empathized primarily with my difficult situation, my dismissal from the University of Munich, etc. I told him I also intended to pay a visit to Kurt von Schuschnigg,[†] who

---

[*] A gathering focused broadly on Catholic thought and culture held annually each summer at the University of Salzburg.

[†] Kurt von Schuschnigg (1897–1977), politician and later chancellor of Austria.

was then Minister of Culture. At this Wolf asked me to put in a good word for him with Schuschnigg, saying that Fr. Alois, on the basis of some misunderstanding, had presented him (Wolf) in a false light to Schuschnigg as being politically unreliable, etc. I promised I would try to clear this up if at all possible. Having said our farewell, I rode to Vienna where I went to the Hotel Kummer. Later I picked up Klaus Dohrn at the train station, who arrived that evening from Rome. I was very happy to see him again and we spent the next few days discussing our battle plan.

Unfortunately, I no longer recall the exact sequence of events during these days in Vienna. I will simply recount everything without worrying about the order. Klaus introduced me to an acquaintance of his from Hellerau now living in Vienna with whom he had already corresponded about our plans. The acquaintance was a Jewish man by the name of Brüll, who was interested in the creation of a journal such as ours and who was also ready to contribute some money.

He was very nice, but he did not inspire great confidence. I was not particularly happy about the thought of collaborating with him and even being somewhat financially dependent on him. It was for me of paramount importance that the journal should be deeply Catholic, and in this respect I had some doubt whether Brüll was really a suitable donor. On the other hand, I was of course very grateful for any source of money that facilitated our plans. A friend of Brüll, a lawyer named Marcuse, also wanted to provide 10,000 schillings. This was a much larger contribution than that offered by Brüll.

Both of them naturally wanted the journal to be Catholic, since they were intelligent enough to realize that only a Catholic journal stood any chance of being supported and promoted by the government of Dollfuss, and also that such a journal was a much more effective means for doing battle with National Socialism. But the Catholic aspect was for them of course only a means.

The audience with Schuschnigg took place first. He received me in one of the beautiful buildings at the magnificent square of the Minorite Church, where the Ministry of Education was then located. He was very friendly in receiving me. I told him that I wanted to become a lecturer at the University of Vienna, to which he answered that regrettably there was no vacancy at the time. I described my plan of establishing a journal, that is, I told him very generally about my hope of working as an intellectual officer against Nazism. He was interested, but of course what I was proposing was not within his jurisdiction to decide. He thought I should become a visiting professor within the humanities and theology division in Salzburg so that my academic activity would not come to a halt. On the whole, our discussion had been friendly and hopeful, and I went away satisfied.

True to my promise, I had also spoken to Schuschnigg about Wilhelm Wolf in an attempt to soften Fr. Alois' comments about Wolf. This was very stupid of me, as I later discovered—too late unfortunately. Schuschnigg had made a positive impression on me. He was still quite young at the time, about thirty-six, I think. There was something clean, elegant, and cultivated about him.

On this day, or perhaps earlier, I visited Funder,* the publisher and editor in chief of the *Reichspost*. I forgot to say that my article had appeared a few days earlier in the *Reichspost*, I think while I was in Hallein. A notice announcing my dismissal from the University of Munich had also appeared in the *Reichspost*. It was a short notice with the heading, "Dietrich von Hildebrand Dismissed!", yet with a certain hint of outrage over my dismissal, as if to say, "this goes too far." Klaus emphasized how important it was that I should seek out Funder on the grounds that a leading journalist had much more influence than I thought.

Funder received me with great warmth, and when I told him that I wanted to settle in Vienna, he clapped his hands enthusiastically. I no longer recall how much I told him about our plans. In any event, he encouraged me warmly and perhaps even offered suggestions for how I might go about getting a meeting with Dollfuss. He was very enthusiastic about my article in the *Reichspost*. I think it was already on this occasion that Funder asked me whether Klaus was Jewish—when I was alone with him. To take Klaus for Jewish revealed the complete lack of

---

* Friedrich Funder (1872–1959).

an eye for typically Jewish features. Yet Funder's question revealed that mistrust for the Jews—that old "Luegerian" anti-Semitism*—was also widespread among members of the Christian Social Party. Later on I still often encountered this anti-Semitism in Vienna.

The next day I went to see the adjutant in charge of scheduling audiences with Dollfuss. I waited for hours. Several people were there and I was the last in line. But when my turn finally came, I was told that Dollfuss had to ride immediately to Salzburg in order to speak with Rintelen† on the train. Rintelen, who was then governor in Graz and sympathetic toward Nazism, was on rather tense terms with Dollfuss. My chances of meeting with Dollfuss were thereby frustrated. It was uncertain how long Dollfuss would stay in Salzburg. I had the feeling that my chances of seeing him in Vienna were very slim, and it occurred to me that I might have greater success in Salzburg. I think I had already tried twice to get an audience with him. Now my third attempt was also turning out to be unsuccessful, thanks to Dollfuss' trip to Salzburg.

Waiting in attendance on people, especially when it requires self-promotion, is among the most uncomfortable things imaginable. The adjutant said to me sympathetically, "I can well understand your desire to see him; after all, it is your livelihood that is at stake." This only added to my dejection. I was not here to find a position but to offer something to Dollfuss in his interest, that is, in the interest of Austria. The adjutant saw in me a man whose only interest lay in finding a position—and, of course, one among many, even countless others, who came every day. This was all very depressing, so I decided to travel to Salzburg to attempt to speak with Dollfuss there. If this failed, I would try to secure a later meeting with Dollfuss with plenty of advance preparation, while returning to Florence for the time being. Klaus would remain in Vienna to prepare for the founding of the journal by raising more money for it.

So I left for Salzburg. In the meanwhile I had lost all my fear of being seen there, despite the fact that objectively nothing had changed

---

* Karl Lueger (1844–1910) had been mayor of Vienna until 1910.
† Anton Rintelen (1876–1946).

in the political situation. My attempt to speak with Dollfuss in Salzburg did not meet with success, as he had already left the next day.

Around the beginning of October, von Hildebrand decided to go to Vienna a second time, this time making preparations to meet Dollfuss. His friend Fr. Alois Mager suggested enlisting the help of his friend Gottfried Domanig (1895–1964), who was a close friend of Dollfuss. Von Hildebrand agreed and also went to stay with another person who might help him, Walter Breitenfeld (1878–1967), a prominent Catholic who lived in Saalfelden, a town near Salzburg.

Walter Breitenfeld picked me up at the train station in Saalfelden and drove me to his country house which sat on a large property. He was a man of about fifty-five years. He wore the traditional Austrian dress, and in general there was something outspokenly Austrian in his speech. But most importantly, he was an ardent Austrian patriot. We were very much in agreement about Nazism, which to my delight he rejected completely.

On the first day of my stay with the Breitenfelds (or was it the second?), news came that there had been an assassination attempt on Dollfuss. I was terribly upset and full of worry. So many of our hopes—for the continued struggle against Nazism and for Austria's awakening and recovery of its own identity—depended on the person of Dollfuss! The objective loss for Austria and for the world would have been enormous had the assassination attempt succeeded, while for me personally it would have meant the undoing of all my hopes. Thank God he was not injured. I breathed a sigh of relief and thanked God.

Breitenfeld was certainly for Dollfuss, but not to the degree I would have liked. He and Dollfuss had previously been colleagues, when Breitenfeld had held the same position in Burgenland as Dollfuss had had in Lower Austria. For this reason, he felt himself to be at least equal if not even superior to Dollfuss. He was an enthusiastic monarchist, and here we were again very much of one mind. He was also a very committed Catholic, which of course greatly won me over for him. He had previously served as president of "Logos," the Catholic intellectual association in Vienna with which I had already been familiar for many years. Breitenfeld struck me as a little too self-assured and at times he could be too sweeping in his judgments. He was also not entirely free of a certain anti-Semitism. These qualities certainly made me uneasy.

Yet he and his wife were very friendly to me, truly receiving me with the greatest warmth. They even offered to let me stay at their residence in Vienna located on Gumpendorfer-Strasse, with which I was quite familiar. They gave me the key and urged me to make myself completely at home. Breitenfeld was not close enough to Dollfuss to provide me with an introduction, nor was he able to contribute any important suggestions regarding my plans. But the days with him were stimulating and the relationship to him and his wife delightful and rewarding.

Von Hildebrand looked forward to having friends he could trust in Vienna when, as he hoped, he would be visiting the city frequently. The Breitenfelds told him of several friends, including leading legitimists who advocated for a restoration of the Habsburg monarchy. He stayed at the Breitenfelds' apartment in Vienna, near the house in which he had lived in 1911 and 1912, and in which his son Franzi had been born. "The unique world of Vienna," he writes, "spoke to me in a much more intimate and potent way than it had on my visit six weeks before."

Klaus' wife, Anneli, had also come to Vienna after visiting her parents. She had found an apartment very near the Danube Canal in the center city, not far from the beautiful church of Maria Stiegen. Klaus told me how he had already spoken once with Minister Ludwig,[*] the chief of the Austrian government press office. Klaus was full of hope, and Brüll and Marcuse continued to be interested. I still remember going with

---

[*] Eduard Ludwig (1883–1967), director of the Austrian federal press division that oversaw various official channels of communication.

Klaus to the Prater.* We sat there in a café drinking coffee while music played from records which transported me back to my life here in 1912. It was a popular tune. The sun was shining though it was somewhat pale—and I do not know why I so strongly perceived the contrast between the atmosphere evoked by the music and the world in which I was now living. And I don't mean the "world" embodied by the city of Vienna, so unique, grand, and beautiful, which stood out with particular clarity in light of the entire political situation and the awakening of Austria to its identity.

Soon after my arrival, I received a dinner invitation from the Domanigs who lived in Klosterneuburg. It was a very lovely evening with them, and I was very happy to see Mrs. Domanig again, whom I had not seen since 1924 when she had attended one of my afternoons in Munich following her return from Rome. She was engaged (though not yet officially) to Domanig at the time, whom she had gotten to know in Rome while she was working as secretary for Pastor.† Domanig delighted me: his seriousness and his deep piety were paired with a distinctively Austrian gracefulness which I found charming.

The rapport that soon developed between us was lively and warm. I told him about my plans, which he liked a great deal. He raised many intelligent questions, finally saying, "If you present all of this to Dollfuss as you have now, I am certain it will awaken his strong interest and that he will accept your proposal." I was overjoyed. Domanig said he would speak to Dollfuss and then let me know when and where Dollfuss would have time to receive me.

Domanig also told me many things about Dollfuss which interested me greatly and further intensified my enthusiasm and devotion for him. The Domanigs became great friends of ours, and I still have much to tell about both of them. I returned to the Breitenfelds' apartment in Vienna in a very happy state of mind.

---

* A large public park in Vienna.

† Ludwig von Pastor (1854–1928), German historian best known for his forty-volume *History of the Popes*.

I spent an interesting and satisfying evening with Fr. Frodl* at Klaus' apartment. I had already heard a great deal about him because of his famous debate over the Christian conception of ownership with Fr. Biederlack,† his fellow Jesuit in Innsbruck. He was intelligent and immensely likeable. There was also something incredibly warm and natural about him in the midst of great priestly dignity. In his debate with Fr. Biederlack, Fr. Frodl argued that the person is naturally ordered to community and, consequently, that property rights are essentially limited by the common good of the community. Fr. Biederlack, on the other hand, defended the inviolable dignity of personal property. The debate was eventually cut off by order of the superior.

Fr. Frodl's political outlook was wonderful. He saw with clarity the abysmal horror of Nazism in all its aspects, and he understood the absolutely unchristian spirit of anti-Semitism, an attitude which even opponents of Nazism in Austria did not always possess. It was a joy to speak with him. A friendship sprung up between us already on this first encounter, and it lasted throughout all the years I lived in Austria. I still have much to tell about Fr. Frodl.

Soon after, Domanig sent word that he would pick me up the next day to meet Dollfuss, who had invited me to his home after lunch. I was very happy. This was something quite different and far more personal than being granted an audience at the Chancellor's office in the Ballhaus. Dollfuss already knew the nature of my hopes and plans, and the fact that he was willing to let me come seemed to indicate that he was interested. I awaited our conversation with great anticipation and hope and with much prayer for a good outcome.

As Domanig and I entered, Dollfuss welcomed us with great warmth. From the first moment I was completely taken by his unique personality. He was quite short and of slight build, and he looked authentically Austrian. Everything about him radiated a great and specifically Austrian charm. His small stature was of the kind one often

---

* Ferdinand Frodl, SJ, Catholic moral theologian.
† Josef Biederlack, SJ (1845–1930), professor of moral and pastoral theology.

finds with great men of genius whose energy and abundance of life is so totally "concentrated" in their inner life that one has the feeling nothing much is left over for their body. Here I don't have in mind that spirituality which gives a person a certain ethereal appearance, such as one found, for example, in Nuncio Pacelli. This immaterial dimension also occurs in persons of large physical stature. No, it is a specific kind of concentration in which much spiritual energy and talent are compressed into a small body.

I began to lay out my plan for the journal and emphasized the great mission of Austria in the present moment as the bastion of the Church. Dollfuss said to me, "Indeed, politics today no longer deals with purely political matters but with fundamental questions of worldview. I see the battle against National Socialism as defending the Christian conception of the world. Hitler wants to draw on ancient Germanic paganism, but I want to draw on the Christian Middle Ages." I also spoke of the role of Austrian universities in the battle against National Socialism; they should provide intellectual guidance to young people vulnerable to Nazi ideology.

Dollfuss then said, "I have a plan. I want all professors of history and philosophy who sympathize with National Socialism to be replaced by professors from Germany who oppose it. Austrian professors with National Socialist sympathies should after all be glad to live and work in Nazi Germany. Of course, I want their replacements to be Catholics. As soon as this plan is executed and teaching positions in philosophy become vacant, I will appoint you as professor." This made me very happy, of course, yet I told him that meanwhile I wanted to pursue the journal so as to wage the intellectual battle against National Socialism on behalf of an independent and Catholic Austria. Dollfuss fully supported my plan and told me to discuss the details with his friend Weber,* the chief of the Austrian news service.

The entire interview, which was so decisive for me and my future and which found us in such deep agreement, lasted only about half

---

* Edmund Weber (1900–49).

an hour. I also met Dollfuss' wife on this occasion. In the midst of my visit, it was decided that Dollfuss and his family would travel to the countryside. My visit was in fact taking place on a Saturday. There was some uncertainty whether he could free himself for two days. When somehow it became possible, he asked his wife to make preparations for an immediate departure and also to ready the two children, a little boy and little girl, who were also to come along. As I heard this, and with everything unfolding so naturally and informally, the character of the interview became more special.

I was overjoyed as I left, not just because the path now lay open for me to accomplish what seemed to be the work God was asking of me, but also because my heart was overflowing with enthusiasm for Dollfuss: I already admired and revered him for his many deeds, yet his personality and his every word not only confirmed but far exceeded what I had seen from afar. A real love for Dollfuss had taken hold of me, and I was happy to be able to work with him—in the fight against the anti-personalism, the totalitarianism, and the racism of National Socialism, and on behalf of an independent and Catholic Austria.

I was beside myself with joy as I left and thanked Domanig from the bottom of my heart, for it was entirely due to him that I had been able to see Dollfuss. Domanig explained to me that, while Ludwig was the official minister in charge of press affairs, it was in fact Weber—a personal and likeminded friend and close confidant of Dollfuss—who really directed this division, even though officially he was only director of the news service. That same afternoon I was still supposed to meet with Weber, who had already been notified by Dollfuss.

Stupidly, I first went to see Wilhelm Wolf to ask his advice on how much money I should request for myself on a monthly basis. I did not want to be pretentious and ask for too much money, but at the same time I needed enough to devote myself completely to my work and to live in a place befitting my status and mission. I was thinking of 1,000 schillings, which was then about 600 marks. Naturally, it was ridiculous that I told Wolf anything about my success with Dollfuss, and that I should consult him in such a matter as what I should ask to be paid. I hardly knew him. Why did I not discuss this question with Domanig, whom I could trust completely?

Only later did I realize that in being so transparent with Wolf, I had let the fox into the henhouse. I had been so overanxious in Hallein, so silent in March, even toward my friends in Salzburg, yet now I was placing my confidence in a man about whom I really knew nothing. Of course, my confidence in Wolf stemmed from the fact that my friends in Salzburg had described him as their friend and that I had gotten to know him there. Still, it was madness on my part, especially when I think of the way things turned out with Wolf. He listened to me with astonishment; he was friendly, though showing no enthusiasm for my success with Dollfuss. I did not make anything of his passivity, thinking it was simply his manner. I was also too happy, too caught up in my good fortune to take notice. Wolf thought my proposal of 1,000 schillings appropriate.

Of course, I had sent word to Klaus about my success. I met him on the street, where he was waiting for me with Anneli and Brüll. When I told them the good news, Anneli jumped for joy and there was great rejoicing among us.

I went to meet with Weber. He greeted me in a very friendly way and our conversation was quite pleasant. I described my plan for the journal, which greatly interested him. I immediately told him that I had my eye on a highly talented young journalist to serve as editor and that without him I could not develop the journal as I intended. I also hastened to say that I would insist on bringing my own secretary. I did this from the outset to secure for Marguerite Solbrig the possibility of coming to Vienna and to facilitate a livelihood for her.

Yet our conversation focused primarily on the journal and the decision to proceed with its founding. When I mentioned that a number of men were ready to contribute money for the establishment of the journal, Weber responded that funds were available and that no further contributors were needed. Of course, that was just fine with me. He told me that at the Chancellor's wish I would be paid 1,000 schillings per month out of a discretionary fund over the coming six months. I told him I still had to return to Florence for a few days to get my family, but that I would permanently settle in Vienna before November 1. Then we could discuss all the many details and begin with the production of the journal.

There were of course still many questions to discuss. Who would be the official legal owner of the journal? (I thought it might be an association.) What would be the name of the journal? How much money had to be invested to launch the journal and to finance its operations until it could sustain itself through subscriptions? How much salary should be paid to the editors and to other employees? I do not think we discussed any of this at the time. Of the first and second questions, I am even quite certain they were only dealt with upon my return from Florence. Perhaps we did already discuss the amount of money that would have to be invested—I think it was 25,000 schillings. And perhaps I did also mention how much should be paid to Marguerite and Klaus. But on further reflection, I think these points were only discussed upon my return to Vienna.

Weber was very likeable and unaffected. He was then a man of perhaps forty-two. He came across as both adroit and intelligent, though with the impression that he came from a very simple family. He was not a lordly type. I think he had previously been an elementary school teacher. He was completely devoted to Dollfuss and totally given over to his role as adjutant. He could be quite charming when he wanted to be. On parting, he gave me my stipend for October, despite the fact that the month was almost over. But of course, the money was extremely welcome. One can imagine how I elated I felt as I left to tell Klaus about all of this.

I no longer quite recall whether I went again to inform Wolf of all the developments. It seems I did because I was in for a huge surprise the following morning—an unpleasant experience which in fact presupposes that I had met with Wolf again. The next morning I entered a café at the Ring near the University. Three men sat at a table.

One was Eugen Kogon,* whom I had met previously at the first

---

* Eugen Kogon (1903–87), journalist and political scientist, editor of the weekly newspaper *Schönere Zukunft* until 1932

Hochschulwoche in Salzburg. He was the editor of *Schönere Zukunft*,[*] the Catholic journal published by Eberle.[†] The journal was sympathetic to Nazism; at least it never adopted a clear stance against National Socialism. The reason was probably that the journal had 1,600 readers in Germany so that a ban on selling it in Germany would have been a heavy financial blow for Eberle. Yet it was precisely their stance toward Nazism which, among other reasons, necessitated the creation of the journal I envisioned. So Kogon was naturally an opponent of my plans at that moment.

The second man was a certain Flor.[‡] He had once come to visit me in Munich and the impression he had made was not confidence-inspiring. The third was a rather harmless man, whom I also knew but whose name I have forgotten. As soon as I entered, Flor came rushing over to me. The other two men also greeted me. "Allow me to congratulate you," said Flor, "on the realization of your plans. Now everything is taken care of for you." I was amazed, speechless, in fact. How could Flor know about my conversations with Dollfuss and with Weber? I replied evasively and asked, "And how would you know about this?" "Oh, I know everything—I always find out about everything." He then began to list all the details regarding the establishment of the journal which I had discussed with Weber.

This made me exceedingly uncomfortable, especially the fact that Flor and even Kogon knew everything. I could only conceive of one explanation, namely that Wolf had told them, which struck me as a serious indiscretion on his part. This marked the beginning of a certain reserve in me toward Wolf. But there was still much more that was soon to come. Brüll and Marcuse were naturally very disappointed that they were being turned down as financial contributors to the journal. Probably they had been hoping to secure a source of income. But above all it would have been somewhat flattering for them to be involved with a semi-official journal.

---

[*] An Austrian newspaper, tainted by anti-Semitism.

[†] Joseph Eberle (1884–1947), founder and publisher of *Schönere Zukunft*.

[‡] Fritz Flor (1905–39) belonged to a group of university students with strong nationalist leanings.

When I left from Salzburg that evening,* I boarded a train that was coming from Germany. It was very crowded and the compartment I entered was entirely filled with Jews—Jews who were emigrating, some to Palestine, others to America. They seemed very frightened. At first they looked at me with distrust. When I began speaking about Hitler and National Socialism in very harsh terms, they grew alarmed since even now it struck them as dangerous to speak openly about Nazism. But after a little while they began to warm up and to tell me about themselves.

I was deeply moved at how nobly they bore their suffering. They showed none of the embittered anger of Klemperer. On the contrary, they spoke about how beautiful it had once been in Germany; they spoke with love about the true Germany and about their great sorrow in now having to leave.

One of them told me in detail of all the disgraceful humiliations he had endured, such as the time a classmate, who had joined the SA, slapped him in the face for going into a café with an Aryan woman. He had to endure it; otherwise he would have been sent to the concentration camp. He said to me, "You can only imagine how humiliating it was for me in the presence of the girl who was a friend of mine." I spent almost all night, until our arrival in Villach, in conversation with these poor Jews, to whom I felt myself so drawn. They had undergone so much, and yet it was nothing compared to what was yet to come.

Having returned to Florence following his successful meeting with Doll-fuss, von Hildebrand gathered Gretchen and Franzi and moved to Vienna at the end of October.

The task awaiting me in Vienna filled me with hope and anticipation, for I was being given the chance to do battle with the Antichrist in

---

* The return journey to Florence from Vienna passed through Salzburg and Villach.

Nazism and Bolshevism and to fight for an independent and Catholic Austria. As far as my task was concerned, I felt I was approaching a new and deeply meaningful life.

The Breitenfelds had written us to say that we should stay with them at their apartment in Vienna until we had found a suitable apartment. This was extraordinarily friendly and a great relief for us. They picked us up at the train station and welcomed us with great warmth. In fact, they were meeting Gretchen and Franzi for the first time.

We now entered a period of incredible intensity, one of those which in hindsight cause one to marvel at everything that occurred in such a short time. I will now describe this time, which spanned from the end of October 1933 (perhaps the 27th) through Christmas, so not even two months. Klaus and Anneli naturally came to greet us the day after our arrival, and it was then that Breitenfeld first met Klaus. Breitenfeld immediately liked "Kläuschen," as he called him. He was enthusiastic and greatly impressed by Klaus' unusually sharp eye for politics. Breitenfeld soon had Klaus engaged in lively conversation.

My first visit of course was to Weber. He was very friendly as he greeted me, but I could sense that many obstacles still remained to be overcome before the journal could appear. Weber began by urging me to hire a young Austrian journalist to serve as the editor. I did not relent, of course, insisting that I absolutely needed to have Klaus Dohrn for the journal, that I could only work with him, that he was indispensable for me. Weber relented. Next we discussed the question of salaries. I told him Klaus Dohrn had to receive 600 schillings. He responded that this was far too much for such a young man who was just a beginner in journalism (Klaus was twenty-five years old at the time).

When he asked me how much salary I would require as the publisher, I responded with surprise, "What, am I still to be paid more? I am already receiving 1,000 schillings." Weber replied, "But that is something different. It is taken from a special fund for special circumstances and is meant to secure your livelihood. You must also receive something for your work with the journal." It was very naïve of me to have said this to him. I hadn't realized that these 1,000 schillings were an allowance, allocated for a period of six months to sustain me until I received the professorship. For the time being, this allowance was guaranteed for six months.

Obviously as publisher of the journal I needed to receive a stipend that was entirely separate from the allowance. Even if I had immediately been made professor, it would still have been necessary to be compensated separately for the journal. Weber thought that I should receive 600 schillings, while 400 would be enough for Klaus. I responded, "In that case, give me just 500 schillings and 600 to Klaus Dohrn." Shaking his head, he yielded. At my pressing request, 250 schillings were also allotted for my secretary.

Several questions remained open but Weber was not yet prepared to commit himself one way or another. Who would own the journal? When would we start the journal? Weber was of the opinion that the underlying owner of the journal should be an association. The reason was that the journal was not an official publication, even if the government was providing the startup money. But exactly whom we would involve he still wanted to leave open. I wanted to have people who would not interfere in my work, but naturally I could hardly object to having certain prominent people as members of this association. Among others I even thought of Wilhelm Wolf as a potential member, still considering him to be relatively reliable. It had been settled, as I already mentioned, that the government would invest 25,000 schillings for the creation of the journal. The journal would eventually have to become self-sustaining.

I sensed that Weber, and also Dollfuss, still hesitated to launch the journal since they hoped it could be done without driving *Schönere Zukunft* into a position of hostility. To this end, they wanted to draw certain people into collaboration to prevent them from complaining that they had not been given an official position. I did not grasp all of this at the time (and only later did I realize it), but I felt their hesitation, which of course made me anxious. There were still other questions. Who would print and distribute the journal? Above all, what would it be called?

Actually, for the distribution I already had my eye on someone, namely the publisher and bookseller Ferdinand Baumgartner. I think I had already met him on my second visit to Vienna at the beginning of

October. He and his wife had once been protégées of Stonner, at whose request I had given Baumgartner my essays on *Fundamental Moral Attitudes*[5] for publication. In any case, Baumgartner was, as I say, a publisher and bookseller. He sought me out together with his wife. I liked him very much thanks to his kindness and piety. He was very interested in my plan for the journal and was eager to take over the distribution. I had great confidence in him and I promised to hire him. Funder suggested we use the printer used by the *Reichspost*, called Prohaszka, and so we requested a cost estimate.

But all of this only began to develop in early November. The only thing that took place before the Breitenfelds left Vienna was the discussion with Weber, which I have already described, and perhaps also some conversations with Baumgartner.

These days in Vienna were primarily filled by the time we spent with the Breitenfelds and finding an apartment for ourselves. The Breitenfelds told us about friends of theirs who had their sights on a splendid apartment by St. Stephen's Cathedral, which was not terribly expensive. Their friends, however, were not able to move in for another two years and perhaps not at all. We could get this apartment if we promised to vacate in the event that they wanted to move in after two years. We went to see the apartment and it really was exceptional. The location was extraordinary. The house sat on the left side of the cathedral (when facing the façade of St. Stephen's). The auxiliary bishop Kamprath lived on the first floor.

From the third floor (where the apartment was) the view was of the left side of the cathedral and of the wonderful Baroque monument to St. John of Capistrano, which is built into the side of the cathedral. What an entire world of unbelievable beauty, greatness, and nobility! The house was a fine building, not a magnificent baroque palace, but about a hundred years old and defined by simple, elegant lines. Nothing in the construction was distasteful, and a great elegant stone staircase lent a stately quality to the whole.

We hoped to bring our beautiful furniture from Munich to furnish the new apartment. This was not easy, of course, because emigration from Germany was often penalized by a special tax known as the "Reichsfluchtsteuer," or "Reich Flight Tax." In the case of politically suspect persons their property, and if they tried to leave Germany, even their furniture could be confiscated.

We hired the excellent mover Perl in Vienna to pack up all of our furniture in the Maria-Theresia Strasse, which was then officially shipped to Budapest. We did this because Hungary was on relatively good terms with Nazi Germany and because shipments there were regarded with less suspicion than those to Austria. Since the furniture went to Budapest via boat on the Danube, it passed right through Vienna where it could easily be picked up by Perl and brought to our apartment. Perl's agent, with whom I dealt, was a Jew who could not have been friendlier or more thoughtful. He fully understood the situation and promised to arrange everything as cautiously as possible. We realized it would take several weeks for our furniture to arrive, and naturally we were very concerned whether our things would even make it out of Germany. We anticipated being able to move in around December 12.

Martha* later recounted the entire drama of the furniture to Gretchen. When objections were raised, Martha went directly to the official who did not want to permit the furniture to leave, i.e., she went to the director of the office in question. Greeting him with an emphatic "Heil Hitler," Martha began protesting energetically how unjust it was to make difficulties for the son of Adolf von Hildebrand, whom the Führer had so often praised, when for professional reasons he had to leave Germany. She came across so forcefully, not just as a National Socialist but also in her insistence that the furniture had to go, that she pulled it off. The furniture arrived in fine condition, and the apartment looked splendid. This marked the beginning of an entirely new life for us in Vienna.

One day Aurel Kolnai† came to visit me at the Breitenfelds' apartment. I had already heard about him on several occasions. A Jewish convert, he had previously worked, I think, at *Schönere Zukunft*. He was

---

* Martha Hummert, the von Hildebrands' housekeeper in Munich.

† Aurel Kolnai (1900–73), philosopher and political theorist who studied briefly with Edmund Husserl, under whose direction von Hildebrand had written his dissertation.

also the author of a book about sexual ethics. From afar he had always struck me as very talented. In greeting me he expressed his happiness at my coming and how he considered himself my student. I wanted to approach him in a spirit of friendship, but Breitenfeld stayed throughout almost as if he wanted to protect me from Kolnai. Breitenfeld kept asking him uncomfortable questions about his acquaintances, especially about Ernst Karl Winter,* which were really intended to force Kolnai to say things that would "expose" him before me.

The situation was terribly embarrassing for me, and I was irked by my friend's pronounced unfriendliness. He was too biased toward anyone with a leftward leaning, while for me the only thing that mattered at this moment was a resolute anti-totalitarian commitment, an opposition toward both Nazism and Communism. It is true that I had no sympathy for the Austrian socialists, but with a Catholic who was a very gifted philosopher and who approached me amicably and with respect, the fact that he had left-leaning sympathies was no reason to treat him in an unfriendly way. I had already heard about Ernst Karl Winter, primarily through his debate with Moenius†—which was actually an open letter exchange in Moenius' journal. Breitenfeld now told me that Winter had been a great opponent of Seipel,‡ and that Kolnai belonged to his circle. Poor, dear Kolnai, how unjust I was toward him, and after an unhappy conversation he left the apartment disappointed.

Von Hildebrand had hoped to be appointed visiting professor at the University of Salzburg until a position became available at the University of Vienna. Around this time, he was told that his envisioned anti-Nazi activities in Vienna would expose the theological faculty in Salzburg, which was financially dependent on the German bishops, to the wrath of the Nazis.

---

* Ernst Karl Winter (1885–1959), Catholic social philosopher, vice-mayor of Vienna (1934–36), known for his political maxim "stand right, think left."

† Georg Moenius (1890–1953), German priest, journalist, and opponent of the Nazis.

‡ Ignaz Seipel (1876–1932), Austrian priest, conservative politician, and—twice—chancellor of Austria.

Thanks to the intervention of von Hildebrand's friend and confessor, Fr. Alois Mager, OSB, the faculty in Salzburg finally agreed to appoint him, provided he did not seek to give any courses.

The coming period was totally taken up with preparations for the appearance of the journal. There were still various difficulties to be overcome, as I already mentioned. I recall a conversation with Weber in which he told me how he had been in Döbling in an attempt to convince Eberle that he should somehow unite *Schönere Zukunft* with the journal I was planning. Whether Weber thought I should conduct my battle against National Socialism as the editor of *Schönere Zukunft,* or whether he thought that Eberle should participate in the new journal, in any case, it was an attempt to draw Eberle in so that my journal would not be founded as a rival enterprise. I was very happy to hear that this attempt by Weber had totally failed. Eberle wanted to hear nothing of it and showed no inclination to altering the political orientation of his journal. In this, I had taken a significant step forward, for the attempt to avoid establishing a new journal or at least to combine it with something already existing would have cost me the freedom to structure everything as it seemed right and good to me!

On another occasion, Weber told me to visit Mataja[*] because Dollfuss very much hoped that he could also be drawn into the establishment of the new journal, perhaps even that he would serve as publisher along with me. The reason for Dollfuss' hope was quite transparent to me and Klaus. Having previously served as Minister and having played a major role in the Christian Social Party, Mataja was now on the sidelines. To prevent him from falling into the opposition, Dollfuss wanted to see Mataja drawn to a task that would tie him to the new government without actually giving him a position in the government itself.

This idea made me very uncomfortable, but naturally I could hardly refuse Weber's request. As I arrived one sunny morning to meet with

---

[*] Heinrich Mataja (1877–1937), politician and a previous Austrian foreign minister.

Mataja, I was pleasantly surprised both by his friendliness and also by the fact that he immediately stated, "I have no intention whatsoever to participate in the publication of your journal." I responded that I still hoped he would contribute articles, an invitation he neither declined nor accepted.

Mataja was an impressive personality. His stature was large and he had an intelligent and attractive face. He must have been about sixty at the time. Several years earlier he had suffered a bad case of meningitis, which left him in fragile health. His tremendous intellectual vitality, however, was undiminished. I would later get to know him well and would come to appreciate him. Our first encounter passed quickly and somewhat formally. The situation was really quite embarrassing for us both, and he spoke as if to emphasize very clearly, "Have no concern, I will not accept." Being quite clever, he had apparently recognized that the government was trying to compensate him for his non-involvement in the Dollfuss administration, that is, for being excluded from politics, and he did not want to take the bait.

One day as we were eating lunch at a good but simple restaurant on the Gumpendorfer Strasse, a piece of music came on the radio which I momentarily mistook for a piece by Braunfels but then immediately recognized as the dance of the sylphs from *The Damnation of Faust* of Berlioz. Walter had once composed a very similar piece. To my great joy, this music of Berlioz was followed by a piece of Walter's, namely the charming wedding of the doves from his opera, *The Birds*. I can scarcely describe how happy I felt and how moved. Just when Walter's music was prohibited in Germany as Jewish music, suddenly to hear the unique voice of his music on the radio in Vienna was deeply moving. But above all, I was able to perceive the entire beautiful world of his music, its great poetry, warmth, and inner joy—this music which was so deeply bound up with my own life, so interwoven with the great and significant times of my life.

I saw the Baumgartners often and of course we discussed the journal. Baumgartner was an utterly decent, good, loveable and pious man whom I came to cherish ever more. He was also highly capable and enterprising. Naturally, he was not a "cunning" businessman, nor did he possess the "efficiency" of the Prussians. He was authentically Viennese, being much more at home with the Viennese saying "Da kann ma halt nix machen" ("Not much you can do about it"), than with "Machen wir," the "Let's do it" attitude of the Berliners.

The name of the journal was the subject of much deliberation and many suggestions. Having turned down many of my proposals, Funder suggested that we should call the journal *Der christliche Ständestaat—The Christian Corporative State*. To my mind, the agenda of the journal lay in a different direction, namely the battle against antipersonalism and totalitarianism from the Catholic standpoint. I was therefore not terribly preoccupied by the idea of the "corporative state;" it was not my intention to offer a special defense of corporatism against democratic government. But, in the end, the corporative state was the goal of Dollfuss, among others, and so the name was not bad and we ultimately settled on it.*

Around this time, I was invited to give a lecture at the seminary in Vienna. I joyfully accepted the invitation, which came from the rector of the seminary, Fr. Handloss,† a deeply religious man whom I held in very high esteem. I naturally wanted to weave the battle against Nazism into my speech. I no longer recall the exact topic, but it was a religious lecture in which I touched on the current world situation.

At one point, I said something like this, "A sure indication that one is really thinking in supernatural terms is when one breaks with certain prejudices that represent a special danger in one's environment. And for you, my dear friends, this danger is anti-Semitism. There is a traditional anti-Semitism in Vienna and throughout Austria. Anti-Semitism, however, is incompatible with the spirit of Christ and his Church, and in the present moment, when a terrible antipersonalistic racism is raising its head in Nazi Germany, it is the special call of God to free oneself from this poison entirely!"

Having explained why anti-Semitism is incompatible with the

---

* For further explanation of the "corporative state," see p. 137.
† Karl Handloss (1871–1934), priest and seminary rector in Vienna.

Christian faith, I told the beautiful story of the Abbess of Wépion, namely how she spoke to the sisters on the evening before the entry of Pauline Reinach* into the convent at Wépion, "Tomorrow we have the great privilege of accepting someone into our convent who is a sister of our Lord not only in spirit but in blood." Having recounted this, a large number of my listeners left the hall, nearly half, according to what Karl Breitenfeld† later told me. What I said was too much for them. My words awakened anger and antagonism in this considerable group of seminarians. Others responded with great applause.

I also spoke of how one had to be grateful that God had given Austria many significant statesmen in times of great trial, such as Ignaz Seipel and now Dollfuss. This too aroused antagonism among many listeners. In any event, I was never again invited to speak in the seminary even though Fr. Handloss probably agreed with virtually everything I had said.

I experienced many disappointments, such as on the occasion when I sought out Verdross,‡ the professor of jurisprudence in Vienna. I had corresponded with him in the past and also written an article for his newspaper. I knew that he was a believing Catholic and had high expectations of him, including as a potential contributor to *Der christliche Ständestaat*. I found him to be very reserved and far from being unequivocal in his support for the Dollfuss government and in his opposition toward Nazism. Later I would experience even greater disappointments with him.

There was another professor by the name of Petritsch§ at the Vienna University of Technology whom I had met in the past at one of the Hochschulwochen in Salzburg. I had the happiest memories of him as a pious Catholic and as an authentic and loveable Austrian. When I visited him, I also noticed a great caution, even though he was much

---

* The sister of von Hildebrand's most important teacher in philosophy, Adolf Reinach (1883–1917).

† A seminarian and Walter Breitenfeld's son.

‡ Alfred Verdross (1890–1980).

§ Ernst Felix Petritsch (1878–1951).

friendlier and more open with me than Verdross had been. But when we spoke of the journal, he emphasized that it ought to bring together all the talented young voices in Austria, at which he proceeded to list various young people none of whom struck me as being sufficiently resolute in their stance against National Socialism.

One of these, however, was a certain Raimund Poukar.* He was then still writing articles that struck me as being somewhat too pro-German, yet he later became an enthusiastic collaborator with *Der christliche Ständestaat* and a member of my wider circle.

But I also noticed an attitude in Petritsch which disappointed me. He urged me to proceed in such a way that people of all perspectives would be represented in my journal. But in this I sensed in him a certain spirit of compromise rather than joy at my unequivocal stance. I no longer remember if it was on this visit to Petritsch or a later one that I was overjoyed by the unexpected arrival of Habbel.† It was encouraging to see my dear former student again, whose anti-Nazi stance was excellent. I had not seen him in a long time. Josef could come to Vienna on business since the 1,000 mark embargo did not apply to merchants. He had also brought money for me, royalties from my book *Zeitliches im Lichte des Ewigen [Earthly Concerns in Light of Eternity]*,[6] which he had published. Of course, the money was very welcome, and it was especially kind of him to find a way to give it to me, which he was actually prohibited from doing under Nazi law.

I remember one time when the Funders invited Gretchen and me for tea. Funder told me of the danger he had escaped in 1927 when the Justice Ministry was burned. The Socialist workers who were revolting forced their way into the editorial office of the *Reichspost* and wanted to take him along. He only escaped by climbing onto the roof of the building and then onto the roof of a neighboring building, from where he was able to slip into a street where no one recognized him.

The day finally came when the first issue of the journal appeared.

---

* Raimund Poukar (1885–1980), became editor of *Der christliche Ständestaat* in 1937.
† Josef Habbel (1903–74), one of von Hildebrand's publishers.

It must have been on December 1, 1933. I had written a long introductory essay about the mission and the aim of the journal. I had written another essay about a particular theme. Klaus Dohrn, of course, had also written an essay. Several distinguished persons had also contributed articles, though regrettably I no longer recall their names. The first issue looked impressive and we had made a good start. The reception was very favorable and, above all, Dollfuss was very satisfied, as Weber told me. This naturally was of greatest importance for me.

I had hired Dr. [Karl] Franke to manage the journal. He was not an editor but the business manager of the editorial office. Baumgartner was in charge of distribution and Franke was to attend to all the practical work of the editorial office. Klaus was only to be utilized for preparing articles or for securing personal contacts with people of political importance. His articles were excellent and as such an irreplaceable contribution. Franke's bureaucratic and excessively ordered style seemed to be a good counterbalance for Klaus. Franke also worked for me personally.

Shortly after the first issue of the journal appeared, Fr. Schmidt,* the famous priest of the Divine Word Missionaries, gave a talk in which he advanced disastrous ideas. He claimed that one had to distinguish between Jews who had been baptized lying down, that is, as infants, and those who had been baptized standing up, namely as adults. Only the former could be considered Christians in the full sense, since only they had undergone a Christian formation. Those who had converted as adults lacked this formation and hence could only be counted as half-Christians. This was of course an awful confusion in which the supernatural significance of baptism was completely ignored and Christian formation treated as the essential element. Aside from the lamentable theological nonsense, this was also an outrageous concession to Nazism.

I was overjoyed when Fr. Frodl brought me a brilliant and witty rebuttal, which of course we had to publish anonymously. The title of his piece was "Nazi Bacteria in the Baptismal Font?" We were all delighted, and so already in our second issue we were able to respond to this mis-

---

* Wilhelm Schmidt, SVD (1868–1954), leading Catholic anthropologist.

erable confusion. Weber told me that Dollfuss considered Schmidt's ideas unfortunate and that he did not agree with them in the least. I was immensely pleased to hear this.

At this same meeting, Weber and I also discussed the idea that I should begin hosting afternoon discussions at my apartment in Vienna as I had previously done in Munich. Of course, unlike in Munich, the theme here would be problems of *Weltanschauung* in politics, because bringing clarity to these questions was the great need of the hour. He was very enthusiastic about the idea and thought these afternoons should begin with a festive reception for the entire leadership of the Dollfuss government; I was to present on the fundamental philosophical questions of the state and the heresy of totalitarianism, etc., which could be followed by a discussion. I was of course enthusiastic about this plan. We decided that I could begin with these afternoons after Christmas, i.e., in January. This was to ensure sufficient time for preparation, which Weber thought was necessary if we were to launch the afternoons with an official event.

The Catholic University of Louvain invited von Hildebrand to give three lectures on epistemological questions in mid-December. He was also invited to give a political lecture in Paris on the same trip. "The news that I would give a political lecture in Paris was welcomed by the government in Vienna," he writes, "while the invitation from Louvain greatly increased my prestige in Vienna."

While in Belgium I very much wanted to visit the Empress Zita and Emperor Otto in Steenokkerzeel.* I asked Weber if there were any reservations about this given my quasi-official capacity, which naturally meant I could not undertake anything that might cast an undesirable light on the government. Since I would be making this visit entirely as a private citi-

---

* Zita von Bourbon-Parma (1892–1990), widow of Emperor Charles I of Austria (1887–1922), and her son, Otto (1912–2011), the claimant to the throne.

zen, Weber told me there were no obstacles. I was very happy as this visit meant a great deal to me. Being an ardent admirer of Emperor Charles, it would be a great gift for me to be able to speak with Empress Zita, and perhaps to get to know her. As well as I knew Archduchess Maria Josepha, the mother of Emperor Charles, I had never before met Zita.

The lectures in Louvain went very well. I was received by the philosophical faculty in the friendliest possible way. I remember various social events, particularly a large dinner hosted by Monsignor Noël,[*] which Monsignor Ladeuze,[†] the rector at Louvain, also attended. Monsignor Ladeuze was a very winning and noble man. I especially appreciated his resolute refusal to allow a plaque to be mounted on the newly rebuilt library in Louvain that was being suggested by the Americans and many others. This plaque was to state that the library had been destroyed by the barbarism of the Germans. Much as this may have been justified, and awful as the German occupation of Belgium had been, still it was sad that an inscription filled with such hate should be placed on the library of a Catholic university.

I was also invited to an evening with the experimental psychologist Michotte.[‡] Naturally, Monsignor Noël was also present. As I was speaking with someone in an adjoining room, I heard Monsignor Noël saying to Michotte, "He (by which he meant me) is not a German—there is nothing German about him, he is like a Latin." This remark made me happy, all the more so as it was a compliment coming from Monsignor Noël.

The overall atmosphere among the listeners was relaxed and I felt warm interest and a readiness to be engaged, even though I doubt many really understood what I had to say. I mean the completely new element in the conception of the *a priori*, which is the essence of phenomenology, and above all the tremendous implications of this insight. The one who understood most deeply was of course Edgar de Bruyne.[§]

---

[*] Léon Noël (1878–1953), Belgian priest and philosopher at the University of Louvain.

[†] Paulin Ladeuze (1870–1940), Belgian priest, theologian, and bishop.

[‡] Albert E. Michotte (1881–1965), Belgian priest and psychologist.

[§] Edgar de Bruyne (1898–1959), Belgian philosopher and professor in Ghent who discovered von Hildebrand for Belgium.

At the conclusion of my lectures, I mentioned how wonderful it was to speak at a university where truth was still being sought, at a moment when this was no longer the case in Germany. I no longer recall my exact words, but it was an unambiguous condemnation of Nazism that I connected with my expression of gratitude to Louvain. In his words of thanks Monsignor Noël responded with great warmth, also alluding to the tragic events in Nazi Germany and expressing his joy over my stance.

I mention this in part because of a completely negative review of my lectures which appeared in Germany. Sadly it was written by two young German Dominicans studying in Louvain. Particularly stupid was their claim that I had lectured in such poor French that I could hardly be understood. Apparently they did not know that my lectures had been translated by native French-speakers on the faculty, so that the text was flawless. Add to this that my French pronunciation is particularly good, and it is obvious that their reproach was motivated by their anger over my critique of Nazism. It made me terribly sad to see that there were still so many Catholics in Germany who were blind—indeed, even members of religious orders. I was reminded of my unhappy experience in Paris with the provincial of the Dominicans in April 1933.

But the great event of this trip to Belgium was at Steenokkerzeel. I went there from Brussels, probably only after having finished my lectures. The castle is an enchanting building from the Middle Ages, surrounded by water. The entrance leads over a small bridge. Two young Austrians received me—a Count Trauttmansdorff and a Count Czernin, I think. I was presented to the Empress. I had dressed elegantly and was wearing the frock coat still customary at the time.

The Empress made a very strong impression on me. There was something unbelievably elegant and aristocratic about her face, while her presence as a whole seemed to combine both strength and tenderness. She was immensely attractive. She represented the great Austrian tradition, its noble culture, yet at the same time she had a very strong individuality. Despite her tremendously courtly manner, her noble humanity kept breaking through in all that she said. I told her, of course, that I had long been an admirer of Emperor Charles, which she already knew from the commemorative card I had published in 1922.

Naturally I spoke with her about the present political situation, and especially about Austria. We found ourselves in complete agreement regarding Nazism. While she probably welcomed the politics of Dollfuss, she did not have my enthusiasm for him. She was naturally somewhat reserved toward a regime lacking a legitimate Habsburg.

Afterwards, I was able to meet Emperor Otto, who also made a very great impression on me. He was then still very young, about nineteen or twenty. He greeted me with warmth and expressed his satisfaction over the journal, which he read with pleasure yet "at arm's length." We had a stimulating and interesting conversation, and I was amazed how well informed he was about all the problems in Austria and how intelligently he spoke about them. He was then a strikingly attractive young man and there was something enchanting about his personality. I was very happy as I left Steenokkerzeel.

On my way to Brussels, I asked myself which of these two Austrian worlds attracted me more: Dollfuss and his program or the imperial family? Where did I feel more at home? Which of the two presented me with a more appealing world? The question was difficult to answer. Both attracted me, yet in one respect Steenokkerzeel more, while in another that of Dollfuss. In principle, the monarchy seemed to me the ideal solution for Austria. Also as far as the cultural milieu was concerned, I was drawn more to the imperial family. Yet the humble attitude of Dollfuss, his revival of the Austrian spirit, his battle against Nazism rooted in the spirit of the Church, was also a powerful draw for me.

In a certain respect, there was a great similarity between Dollfuss and Emperor Charles. Both wanted to orient themselves entirely according to the guidance of the Church. Indeed, Dollfuss wanted to base his constitution completely on *Quadragesimo anno.** Both stood in absolute docility toward the Church. Both were entirely free of ambition

---

* Social encyclical issued in 1931 by Pope Pius XI.

and both were deeply humble. Naturally Emperor Charles was far more pious in his daily life. But above all, I saw no contradiction in being an unconditional follower of Dollfuss while at the same time being a convinced monarchist.

While in Paris, I made a point of seeking out my old friend, Count Robert d'Harcourt. He received me with great warmth and proceeded to tell me that Cardinal Baudrillart had done nothing to publicize my lecture at the Institut Catholique. I do not know (or else I no longer remember) whether the Cardinal kept my presence somewhat hidden because he was embarrassed that a German was speaking at the Institut, or because he feared that my anti-Nazi lecture would somehow put me at risk. Probably it was the former, since in his eyes I continued to be a "German"—a misperception on his part, which even my stance against Nazi Germany could not dispel. To my great joy, I saw Foerster, who of course was also a great friend of d'Harcourt. I recall seeing a curious looking man sitting in the corner who from time to time would make horrid grimaces. When I inquired, d'Harcourt told me he was the famous philosopher Berdyaev,[*] who had this nervous tick. Afterwards, I was of course introduced to Berdyaev and we spoke together.

The next evening, I visited the Austrian ambassador. He was a priest, though he did not present himself in that capacity. The politician had entirely suppressed the priest. He had been a special protégé of Seipel in the past and had served as the Austrian representative in Berlin for a long time. I think he had once sympathized with the notion of a "Greater Germany," yet having been thrown out by the Nazis in the most brutal manner, he had become a radical opponent of theirs and thereby an Austrian patriot. He greeted me very warmly. Of course, he knew about my journal and appreciated it.

Just as we were speaking, a young man entered the room, a subordinate of his who worked at the Austrian press office. The ambassador introduced him to me as Dr. Fuchs.[†] He was a likeable, intelligent looking

---

[*] Nikolai Berdyaev (1874–1948), philosopher, Marxist during his student years, and convert to Christianity.

[†] Martin Fuchs (1903–69), Austrian journalist and diplomat.

younger man whom I would later still see frequently. The ambassador joined me for lunch at an excellent Parisian restaurant. He told me of his experiences in Berlin. We were in total agreement in regard to politics. But his liberal attitude and the way he had entirely "outgrown" the priesthood (he was dispensed from saying mass and had perhaps even been laicized) was painful and filled me with a heavy heart.

My lecture took place the next day before a very small audience. Even so, Cardinal Baudrillart offered some very friendly remarks at the opening, as he did also at the conclusion. I spoke about National Socialism, its absolute incompatibility with Christianity, and the political danger it represented. Above all, I spoke about Austria, its mission, and its entirely unique identity with respect to Germany. D'Hartcourt had naturally come to my talk.

Jacques Maritain had invited me to Meudon for the evening of December 22, which made me very happy. This was the same evening on which I wanted to take the night train back to Vienna, or perhaps to Salzburg, so that I could still reach Vienna on December 24 before Christmas Eve. Maritain brought me to Meudon himself. I had not seen him since 1928, and so I only knew him fleetingly. Now, however, our contact suddenly took on a new character in light of my fate, my flight from Germany, my battle against Nazism, and my work in Austria. He was incredibly charming toward me, and for the time I experienced the tremendous appeal of his religious personality. The great spirituality in his face, the reflection of a deep religious existence, impressed me deeply and won me over. I also met his wife, Raïssa, about whom I had already heard so much. She was very warm as she greeted me, but I did not come away that evening with a definite impression of her personality.

After dinner Maritain led me to his house chapel where we made a brief visit before the Blessed Sacrament. Then he accompanied me back to Paris, or at least far enough for me to find my way to the train station alone. He gave me his book, *Le Degrés du Savoir* [*The Degrees of Knowledge*], and asked me as we were returning to Paris what I would think if he were to send Dollfuss one of his books as a token of esteem. I was very happy that he seemed to have a real veneration for Dollfuss and urged him to do so.

I forgot to tell about an evening that took place in a house belonging to the German Order* behind St. Stephen's Cathedral. The occasion, I think, was a lecture by Mataja. Following the lecture, we sat together at a restaurant within the building, i.e., myself, Klaus Dohrn, along with Mataja and two of his friends, Oscar Bam† and Simon. The evening was important insofar as the acquaintance with Simon became an important factor. We became friends and he played quite a role in my life throughout the time I lived in Vienna.

Simon was an economist with a doctorate in the field. He had played a certain role under Seipel. He was a Jew, as one can already surmise from his name, but very liberal. He was the nephew of Johann Strauss. Strauss had married a Jewish woman, the sister of either Simon's father or mother. I detected nothing of this musical kinship in him; as educated as he was, and as many interests as he had, he was totally unmusical. I immediately liked Simon very much, while he showed great interest for me and our journal.

Oscar Bam was a senior member of the staff at the *Reichspost*. I think he always wrote the articles on foreign affairs; he may even have been an editor of this section. He was also a Jew, though probably baptized as a Catholic. Funder had already told me about him. Bam was a completely different type than Simon. He had a much more exclusive orientation to politics and he was not as intellectually independent as Simon. But he too was a very attractive person, approaching me in an extremely friendly way. He and I also struck up a lively contact, and Gretchen and I were often guests of the Bams. His wife was a Russian aristocrat.

This was also the evening our contact with Mataja—who was a strong personality and very interesting—finally became closer. The relationship to Mataja was a definite enrichment for me and turned out to be an important factor during our years in Vienna. Klaus also became quite attached to Mataja, whom he liked very much.

---

* The Teutonic Knights, which by then had a purely religious and charitable mission.
† Oscar Bam, author and journalist.

Simon showed a great interest in me, though, as I later noticed, the fact that he considered me a rising political star played a certain role in this. In reality, there was no basis for this. But he thought that I was the strongest intellectual influence on Dollfuss, in which respect I was supposedly his confidant. Simon said to me, "But after all, you have the greatest influence." This notion was immensely attractive for him, and so, for the moment, I was in his eyes surrounded by a glamorous halo, which had no basis in reality.

About this time, von Hildebrand was invited to a gathering of people in Ernst Karl Winter's circle who, he writes, "while being opponents of National Socialism, were also critical of the Dollfuss government." The philosopher Aurel Kolnai was one of them, as was Nikolaus Hovorka (1900–66), a publisher, and August Maria Knoll (1900–63), a sociologist.

Although some of their critique was not mistaken, I was not entirely comfortable in this company. It showed me how difficult the situation was—and how many difficulties Dollfuss had to contend with. Hovorka owned Reinhold Press, which I knew about because Moenius had published a book there. I also got to know Hovorka outside the context of this gathering. He had a handsome face and was very attractive as a person. He was a very pious Catholic, a daily communicant, who shared the political orientation of our journal. He was not a disciple of Winter, though he belonged to his circle, without sharing Winter's socialist sympathies.

A certain Karpfen* was his friend and collaborator. Karpfen was a Jewish convert. Hovorka recommended him to me as a contributor to the *Ständestaat*. Karpfen was very talented and thereafter he wrote frequently in our journal.

Back then I did something very unloving and ungrateful. Unfortu-

---

* Otto Maria Karpfen (1900–78), chemist, journalist, émigré to Brazil where he became a distinguished editor and literary critic (under the name Otto Maria Carpeaux).

nately it was one of those mistakes which one can no longer make good, that is, which one can only repent of but no longer undo. I had the impression that my friend from the year 1912, the old man Richard von Kralik,* was not entirely unambiguous in his rejection of Nazism. Was it because he had ties to the *Schönere Zukunft* or because, when I visited him in 1922, he had been so dismissive of Marc Sangnier and his pacifism? I was afraid of getting into discussion with him and for this reason did not immediately visit him upon arriving in Vienna. When Weber tried for the last time to connect the *Ständestaat* with the *Schönere Zukunft*—I have already described this—he told me that he had also visited Kralik, who was very offended that I had not sought him out.

Now the first months in Vienna were so incredibly filled with work, with practical things, and with meeting people in connection with the journal that I hardly could find the time to travel to Döbling to visit Kralik. But of course I should have made the time to do so. Kralik died in the course of the winter. How unjust it was of me to offend this noble man who in earlier times had been so kind to me, who had done so much for the old Austria and also for the Church, and who was such an original and charming personality. Now it was too late to visit him and to explain everything to him.

Why did I not immediately go to him after Weber told me this? Certainly, I feared that he would give me all sorts of suggestions for the journal, or even urge me to work together with Eberle. At the time, I thought I needed to avoid everything that might complicate the execution of my plans. But clearly this was a mistake. I should have recognized that a loving attitude toward the old man had greater priority, since objectively a visit on my part could not have hindered or even complicated my plans. After all, he did not have an influential position at that time.

I had asked Baumgartner whether he knew a priest by the name of

---

* Richard von Kralik (1852–1934), writer.

Oesterreicher.* I knew that the young Jewish medical student, who had written me in 1923 and who had later informed me of his ordination at St. Stephen's in 1927, lived in Vienna (or within the Diocese of Vienna in any case). Baumgartner told me that he knew Oesterreicher well, and so I asked him to tell Oesterreicher that I hoped to become acquainted.

It must have been just after Christmas that he came to see me one day. A blond priest entered the room. He was of middling height, a bit on the shorter side, and his face was attractive as far as his features were concerned. But he was incredibly awkward, one of those people who do not know what to do with their arms and legs. I could not quite understand why he was so awkward. He seemed always to have a slightly ironic smile. I received him very warmly, and we spoke about his letter to me, and mine to him. I told him how happy I was to see him again now that he was a priest. Not much came of this first encounter. But a contact had been established which soon began to develop and would lead to a friendship that would play a role over the course of many years.

Through Franke I had received an article for the *Ständestaat* by von Herrnritt,† who was a well-known jurist. Herrnritt had previously been chairman of an important government agency. I was very happy about the article, which was very good. It was of greatest importance that we also published articles by respected Austrian personalities. But they had to be articles which, at the very least, did not contain anything contrary to the spirit and to the political vision we represented, and that was not so easy. Herrnritt was a great acquisition for my work, and we would later develop a very friendly relationship. He also became a faithful attendee of the afternoon discussions which I later began to host. We also received an article from Count Dumba,‡ another distinguished man who had represented Austria in the League of Nations.

---

* Johannes (later, John) Oesterreicher (1904–93).

† Rudolf von Herrnritt (1865–1945).

‡ Count Konstantin Dumba (1856–1947), Austrian diplomat.

1934

In January, three related articles of mine appeared that in a fundamental way rebutted the Nazi ideology.[1] They formed a kind of triptych. The first article addressed the way Nazi ideology inverts the hierarchy of being by exalting the biological over the spiritual. I no longer recall the second article. The third, entitled "The Slave Revolt Against the Spirit," was the most important, and it was here that I also criticized racism. Soon thereafter another essay of mine appeared called "Ceterum censeo Carthaginem,"[2] in which I fought against all attempts to indulge in illusions about Nazism, and against all the wishful thinking that comes to expression in phrases such as "all revolutions initially undergo growing pains."

Klaus Dohrn had formed a very important and fruitful relationship with Morreale,[*] the Italian press secretary in Vienna. Despite being a Fascist and a special confidant of Mussolini, this man was a resolute and unambiguous opponent of Nazism. For this reason, he showed great interest in our journal. As the confidant of Mussolini, he was politically more important than the ambassador, who had a more social role. Morreale was a very intelligent and likeable person.

I initially had my qualms and reservations about him, since I saw my battle against Nazism as encompassing the battle against all forms of collectivism. Thus I also wanted our journal to criticize fascist tendencies of any sort. But Klaus exercised much better judgment here.

---

[*] Eugenio Morreale (1891–1976), Italian journalist, foreign correspondent, press attaché at the Italian embassy in Vienna, influential opponent of National Socialism.

His great political talent preserved him from being too doctrinaire. He recognized that Morreale was a man worth talking to and an important ally in our battle against Nazism.

I think it was also this month that Senator Pant,[*] the leader of the Germans in Polish Upper Silesia, came to visit me with Maier-Hultschin,[†] the editor of his journal. Pant was a defender of the cultural rights of the German minority in Upper Silesia; at the same time he was a loyal citizen of the new Poland. Above all, however, he was an ardent opponent of the Nazi regime and a pious Catholic. Of course, he could not be arrested in Poland and thrown into a concentration camp, but the Nazi regime, using money and covert activities, tried to mobilize the Polish Germans against Pant. We understood each other superbly, and he invited me to Katowice in April to give lectures, and I happily accepted. Pant's roots were in the "old Austria."

Years earlier, Pant had very much liked Hitler's sister,[‡] who was then living with Hitler. I mean he had courted her, though I no longer know how serious he was and whether he really wanted to marry her. In any case, he knew her very well and was therefore very knowledgeable about Hitler's youth and family. For this reason alone it was very interesting to speak with him, since I learned things that were not generally known. We also spoke about the very sinister incident of Hitler and his niece.[§] The niece was the daughter of Hitler's sister, Pant's former girlfriend. I had probably been vaguely aware that Hitler had had an affair with this niece and that she had suddenly taken her own life. Pant doubted that she had really committed suicide, suspecting that Hitler had killed her or had her killed.

Pant was often in Vienna during the years I lived there. Once, not

---

[*] Eduard Pant (1887–1938), teacher, politician, and publisher of the weekly journal *Der Deutsche in Polen* (*The German in Poland*).

[†] Johann Carl Maier-Hultschin (1901–58), editor of the largest German Catholic daily newspaper in Poland (*Der oberschlesische Kurier*) before taking over editorship of Pant's journal.

[‡] Angela Raubal (1883–1949), Hitler's half-sister, enjoyed Hitler's trust over the years and served as his housekeeper from 1928 to 1935.

[§] Angela (Geli) Raubal (1908–31), daughter of Angela and Leo Raubal, lived in Hitler's apartment in Munich beginning in 1928. Hitler's role in her death is a matter of historical dispute.

long after I had met him—perhaps half a year or even a year—Pant saw
Hitler's sister in Vienna, or somewhere in Austria anyway. He learned
a great deal about the death of the niece on that occasion. Pant accompanied Hitler's sister to the cemetery where her daughter's grave
was located. As they approached the grave, she was filled with deep
emotion. Pant said to her, "How terribly sad that this girl, who was so
young, would take her life. It's incomprehensible." Through her tears,
Hitler's sister answered, "But it isn't even true. She didn't take her own
life. She was murdered. . . ." She was cut short by her sobbing. Yet from
what she had stammered through her tears, Pant came away with the
definite impression that Hitler had arranged to have his niece killed, or
even done so himself.

Following the death of the niece (which must have been prior to
1930), there was a murder charge lodged against Hitler with the Bavarian Ministry of Justice—though I no longer recall whether Pant told
me this at the time. This charge was then dismissed by then-Bavarian
Justice Minister Gürtner.* For this Gürtner was rewarded after Hitler's seizure of power by being appointed Justice Minister in Hitler's
cabinet—meaning he became Justice Minister of the Reich.

Senator Pant occupied a most unusual position insofar as he was a
champion of German culture in Upper Silesia, while at the same time
being one of the most resolute, uncompromising, and courageous opponents of National Socialism. This was of course an inherently very
logical and consistent stance, for National Socialism was the greatest
antithesis to all that was truly great in German culture. Yet for a person
who had led an intense struggle against the Polish nationalists in Katowice, it was particularly commendable that he was able to see through
National Socialism, which presented itself as the defender of the German national interest, and to reject it at its very foundations.

For it is all too easy for people focused on a danger in one direction,
and who are fighting against this danger, to become blind to greater
dangers in the other direction. This was the tragedy of the initial stance

---

* Franz Gürtner (1881–1941).

of England and France toward Hitler—especially England before Hitler came to power. This tragic blindness was even more prevalent among many Hungarian nationalists, particularly in the case of figures like Monsignor Tiso.* Yet this is precisely why Pant's stance was so welcome and so commendable. He was simply a very pious Catholic and a very intelligent and courageous man. Pant introduced us to the leaders of the German minorities in Latvia and Livonia who were in Vienna at that time. Both had fled after Soviet Russia had occupied the entire Baltic region, and both were resolute opponents of National Socialism.

In mid-February, fighting broke out in Linz between members of the Heimwehr, the militia associated with the Christian Social Party, which by then had been merged into Chancellor Dollfuss' Patriotic Front, and members of the banned Republican Protection League, the militia of the Social Democratic Party. Dollfuss' government had received information that the Protection League had a large cache of weapons in Linz. The police sent to search the premises were fired upon and counterattacked.

The conflict quickly spread across Austria, with the worst fighting taking place in Vienna. Dollfuss eventually called upon the army, which suppressed the revolt in four days. The fighting was especially bitter, the culmination of years of hostility between different factions in Austrian society. By 1934, tensions were at a peak. The Austrian civil war left 196 dead among the Social Democrats, and 118 on the side of the government.

How is it that people who were opponents of National Socialism could allow themselves to play into Hitler's hands through such an uprising? In the face of such a dreadful and threatening enemy like Hitler, why could they not set aside all internal opposition to Dollfuss? How could they not understand that unity at this moment was indispensable for successfully resisting Nazi Germany? For all these reasons, it was

---

* Jozef Tiso (1887–1947), Slovak priest, politician, prime minister, and later president of Slovakia. His collaboration with the Nazis led to his execution for treason.

unforgivably shortsighted and politically obstinate of the Socialists not to stand with the government of Dollfuss in fending off a very great and imminent danger.

But to engage in an armed revolt was far worse. It was a crime. What more could Hitler have wished for than a revolution in Austria which would give him the excuse to march across the border on the grounds that he could not tolerate a revolution so close to Germany? Apparently the Austrian government had learned of Hitler's intent and so was prepared. The claim also spread at the time that in Linz the Heimwehr (which was very embittered toward the Social Democrats, and vice versa) had provoked the Social Democrats. It can hardly be denied that the Heimwehr, especially Major Fey[*] approached political questions in a fairly confrontational manner. The Heimwehr was also irresponsible.

But none of this can excuse the revolt by the Social Democrats. For no amount of internal tension, no degree of partisan antipathy, could justify radically jeopardizing the freedom and independence of Austria, which was also self-destructive for the Social Democratic Party.

Thank God the army remained dependable, which was to the credit of Vaugoin,[†] who had served as Minister of the Army under Seipel. Previously, Social Democrats had filled the army with party members, yet Vaugoin had seen to its complete depoliticization. This was the great service of Vaugoin, whom Austrians called "our good, beloved Vaugerl." An array of various volunteer fighter groups also emerged from among the university students: monarchists, followers of Dollfuss, the *Sturmscharen* of Schuschnigg, and the members of the Heimwehr. Of course, these young people were more like auxiliaries to preserve order in the city and they were not involved in the real battles.

I did not doubt for a moment that the government would succeed in suppressing the uprising. Yet I deeply regretted the disastrous fighting between Austrians at a moment when everyone needed to unite against

---

[*] Emil Fey (1886–1938), Austrian commander and conservative politician who was vice chancellor during the episode described by von Hildebrand.

[†] Carl Vaugoin (1873–1949).

the great enemy, Hitler. What a blow to the prestige of the Dollfuss government around the world that it became necessary to fire on the workers. There was great commotion on all sides.

Simon came to me the morning the uprising had erupted. He was quite agitated and asked me if I wanted to remain in Vienna under these circumstances. He considered the situation very serious and wanted to travel to Bratislava that afternoon. I told him the danger did not strike me as too great and that I wanted to stay. He did in fact end up leaving that afternoon.

There was no fighting within the Inner City of Vienna. But one could continually hear the shooting and in this way I experienced the situation fully. That evening, Franzi told me about patrolling with the volunteers groups, which he had joined. The Social Democrats had shot at them from the windows of nearby houses. A friend of his had been seriously injured in the groin. It was still dangerous, even in districts that did not witness the major fighting between the army and the militia of the workers, because Social Democrat workers were everywhere hidden in private homes and would suddenly shoot from the windows at anyone visibly affiliated with the government.

Repeatedly, Dollfuss and Prince Schönburg[*] turned to the militant workers, begging them to lay down their weapons; if they did so immediately, they would not be prosecuted in court. There was such nobility in their exhortations; nothing of hatred or demagoguery, only sorrow over the unnecessary and unfortunate fighting. I think the fighting lasted three days.

Klaus naturally came to see me frequently. Not only did we discuss the situation, we also had to plan the next issue of the journal with care. In this agitated and crucial moment, it was of great importance to find the right words: on the one hand, to condemn unambiguously the revolt of the Social Democrats, on the other hand, to remind everyone that the primary enemy of the government and of Austria were not the Social

---

[*] Prince Aloys Schönburg-Hartenstein (1858–1944), military officer and defense minister in the cabinet of Dollfuss.

Democrats but Nazi Germany. For members of the Christian Social Party, and above all for the Heimwehr, the real danger was that hatred for the Social Democrats, their traditional enemy within Austria, would completely consume them and so divert their gaze from the incomparably more dangerous, powerful, and radical enemy, National Socialism.

All of this made it very important to strike the right tone in the upcoming issue. Unfortunately, we received a completely unusable article from Schaukal,* whom we had met through Hegner,† which was filled with a deadly spirit of hatred for the Social Democrats and which succumbed to the most awful fantasizing about punishments for the Social Democrats. Naturally, we could not publish the article, yet the question remained how we could avoid irritating this incredibly conceited man and so turning him into a mortal enemy. I no longer remember exactly how we did it.

The uprising collapsed after the third day and the fighting came to an end. Those who had fought were granted amnesty, but the leaders among the Social Democrats who were responsible (and who had not fled) were punished. The Nazis exploited the revolt to present Dollfuss as murderer of the workers, as the man who shot at the Austrian working class to preserve his dictatorship. This abject defamation made an impression on many people, even outside of Germany.

Regrettably, it is so easy to influence even many well-meaning people with slogans, such as "enemy of the workers," "brutal dictator," etc. Even Jacques Maritain was swept into collecting signatures in Paris for a petition against Dollfuss who had ordered the army to shoot at the poor workers. This was the same Maritain who, as recently as our time together in Paris before Christmas, had wanted to send his books to Dollfuss as a token of esteem. Thank God, Gabriel Marcel refused to lend his name since he did not want to act on the basis of mere slogans without having precise facts.

There were many changes after the revolt. Richard Schmitz‡ be-

---

* Richard von Schaukal (1874–1942), Austrian Catholic poet.

† Jakob Hegner (1882–1962), publisher and translator.

‡ Richard Schmitz (1885–1954), journalist and Austrian politician.

came the mayor of Vienna, replacing the Social Democrat, Karl Seitz,[*] while also the deputy mayors were all replaced with new people.

In May, the Dollfuss government promulgated the constitution for a new Austrian state based on the principles of corporatism—the so-called Ständestaat. Inspired by Catholic social teaching—particularly Pope Pius XI's 1931 encyclical, Quadragesimo anno—Dollfuss sought an alternative to both laissez-faire capitalism and Marxist Socialism. His corporative model created professional groupings—the "corporations," such as manufacturing and financial services—that would bring together business owners and workers around shared interests. Dollfuss thought the Ständestaat, with its strong Catholic and Austrian identity, could also serve as a bulwark against aspirations by Nazi Germany to annex Austria.

The new Austrian state was authoritarian in the sense that the seat of legislative authority moved from the parliament to the chancellor. Dollfuss was criticized for adopting these measures, while he and his supporters maintained they were necessary, at least temporarily, to stabilize the country. Direct election to parliament was replaced by four councils whose members were appointed rather than elected. These councils in turn selected a federal diet, which had limited legislative power in the form of a "for" or "against" vote on laws proposed by the chancellor.

The primary theme for the government now lay in drafting the new constitution, which would replace parliamentary democracy with the corporative state—a corporative state, moreover, created entirely in light of the encyclical *Quadragesimo anno*. Alongside this were plans to work out a concordat with the Holy See through which Austria would gain the definitive character of a Catholic state.

The task of developing the new constitution had been conferred on

---

[*] Karl Seitz (1869–1950).

Dr. Ender,* the previous chancellor. Harkening from Vorarlberg, Ender was a man of highest integrity and respected by everyone. There was in him no trace, not even the slightest hint, of corruption or abuse of his position for personal gain, unlike so many other leading Christian Social politicians (notably Commerce Minister Stockinger). But Ender was himself a principled democrat, and so it was no easy task for him to draw up a constitution which was not entirely in accord with his convictions. But in his great loyalty to Austria, he undertook this task in a spirit of full commitment.

I visited Ender once during this period and asked him to write an article for our journal. It was an interesting and rewarding visit, for Ender was not only a very intelligent but also a very attractive personality. He treated me very warmly and also promised to contribute an article for the *Ständestaat*. Ender was one of those people in whose presence one has the feeling of breathing a pure air—of something completely unsullied and entirely righteous. As a real Vorarlberger, he had something more Swiss than specifically Austrian about him, or perhaps I should say that he embodied both elements, though, in comparison with someone like Seipel, who was authentically Viennese, Ender was Swiss.

I forgot to describe an important encounter that took place early in December or just after Christmas. This was my audience with the Austrian President, Miklas.† He greeted me very warmly and began to speak at length. He was a rather short and stocky man who came across less as a president and more like a high school principal—which had been his previous occupation, I think. But there was also something very attractive about him. He seemed to be a man of immense moral seriousness and piety, yet also of great simplicity and unpretentiousness.

He was quite distressed by breaking with the parliamentary constitution; everything that was not quite correct went against his grain. Presumably he saw the necessity of the step taken by Dollfuss, for whom he

---

* Otto Ender (1875–1960).

† Wilhelm Miklas (1872–1956), Austrian Christian Social politician.

had great esteem, yet he was unhappy that it had unavoidably become necessary to sacrifice democratic legitimacy. But Dollfuss, too, was a democrat by conviction. When Domanig told him he would have to close parliament, Dollfuss said, "What? Should I, who believe in democracy, play the dictator?"

But now Dollfuss was totally taken up with his great task of saving Austria from National Socialism. He wanted to prepare the ground for a democracy on a corporatist basis, as envisioned in *Quadragesimo anno*. And when I say "democracy," I mean an anti-totalitarian vision of individual freedom and the organic participation of all in public life. Miklas was a man of the old tradition of parliamentarian government, while Dollfuss was a man of the future. Miklas was in fact a monarchist, though he had voted for the Republic at a moment when many monarchists thought it prudent to do so for political reasons.

In the years between 1919 and 1921, many well-intentioned people thought it was impossible to overthrow the autocratic rule of the Socialists and form a Christian Social government while simultaneously supporting the monarchy. They considered the alternative between a Socialist regime and a Christian Social government on friendly terms with the Church to be of greater importance than the choice between a republic and a monarchy. They were objectively quite right to privilege the former alternative. Seipel thought and acted in exactly this way.

My time with Miklas was extraordinarily interesting. We had a discussion of real substance, free of all conventionalism. I primarily listened to Miklas who spoke without any diplomatic reserve but with great openness and in a human way. Bidding me farewell after about an hour, he said, "So, now go and tell the world what an Austrian president thinks." Of course I had briefly described my own point of view, in particular my view of National Socialism, which was already familiar to him through our journal. I had the heartening feeling that we were in complete accord. Establishing this contact with the President was obviously of great value for me. True, he had no direct political influence, but he did have certain important constitutional functions, such as appointing key members of the government.

During this time I was sought out by the painter Müller-Hoffmann,[*] a very dear person who had been a friend of Braunfels. He was a very winning and noble human being, and a very talented painter. His political views were very good. He was a total opponent of National Socialism and an enthusiastic supporter of Dollfuss. We were very much of one mind. During our Vienna years, Müller-Hoffmann was to play an important role in my life in many different regards. Already at our first encounter, a relationship of real friendship took root, and our contact from then on was always animated.

Another man I met at that time was a certain Dr. Missong.[†] His name was already familiar to me from various magazines. He had a great journalistic talent and became a primary collaborator with *Der christliche Ständestaat*. I think I got to know him through Klaus. His political views were excellent; he was a particularly radical opponent of National Socialism, not to mention a great Austrian patriot. He was among the most heartening figures within my Viennese circle because of his excellent political stance, in which over the years he never wavered even the slightest. We frequently saw him and his wife, who was very nice, and later they were among the most faithful attendees of my political evenings.

I also saw Oesterreicher with increasing regularity and our friendship grew. I was particularly impressed by his essays, which he gave me to read. They were of great beauty and depth. They were marked in a special way by a truly classical religious spirit, which set them apart from the majority of German religious writers at that time. Their lofty spiritual level and even more so their classical-religious style made a great impression on me and increased my esteem for him.

Also playing a great role in our lives in Vienna were Rudolf Allers[‡] and his wife. I already knew Allers from years before in Salzburg and

---

[*] Wilhelm Müller-Hoffmann (1885–1945), professor of painting at the School of Arts and Crafts in Vienna.

[†] Alfred Missong (1902–65).

[‡] Rudolf Allers (1883–1963), physician, philosopher, and psychologist. After emigrating to America he taught at both Catholic University of America and Georgetown University.

also from his lectures in Munich. I had heard a great deal about him and his conversion from Fr. Kronseder.[*] Allers was one of the most intelligent people I knew among Catholic thinkers of the day. The way he had overcome Freudianism from within, his phenomenological talent, and his deep piety—all this was a breath of fresh air for me. I felt very drawn to him, though it was not easy to become humanly close to him. Politically he was excellent, not only as a total opponent of National Socialism but also as an ardent Austrian and unconditional supporter of Dollfuss. Speaking with him was always stimulating and interesting. Klaus also appreciated him greatly; after all, Klaus was particularly attracted to intelligence.

Allers and his wife played a great role during our time in Vienna. Above all, they were regular attendees of my evening discussions, which only began later, because Weber's plan to inaugurate these with a festive event came to nothing.

I waited a long time before starting to host these gatherings because I kept thinking that Weber would return to the idea himself. But the Socialist uprising had pushed everything into the background, while Dollfuss was so taken up with developing the new constitution that he had time for nothing else. The moment for the sort of official event Weber had envisioned was over.

But a far more serious concern for me was that Dollfuss had become completely inaccessible due to the approaching conclusion of the concordat and adoption of the new constitution. Even Weber—at least so he claimed to me—was unable to discuss anything else with Dollfuss.

At this time, Oesterreicher invited me to a meeting which I think he held in the house where Dr. Rudolf[†] lived. The purpose of the meeting was to lay the groundwork for a new association that sought the conversion of the Jews. This association would later be founded under the name Pauluswerk. Oesterreicher spoke very beautifully about the

---

[*] Friedrich Kronseder, SJ (1879–1957), theologian, university chaplain, and retreat master.

[†] Karl Rudolf (1886–1964), Austrian priest, leader of the Austrian Catholic youth movement.

purpose of this association, though still with a certain timidity. For my part, I said it was paramount at this particular moment that Catholics everywhere should take up the fight against anti-Semitism so as to reveal the true face of the Church to the Jews. Oesterreicher answered that this was not possible for him, being of Jewish descent, to which I responded that I wanted to do so myself.

A lady who had been invited to the meeting by Oesterreicher later commented to him how unbelievable it was that I should act as if I were not myself a Jew, even though I had a Jewish grandmother. While the lady was in fact correct about my grandmother, this had never led me to feel Jewish, nor did it ever play even the slightest role in my stance toward anti-Semitism. I had never known my Jewish grandmother, nor did I ever feel in any way rooted in the cultural world of the Jews. The fact that I was drawn to many Jews, the fact that I had a great love for various people of Jewish descent, such as Marguerite Solbrig, Hamburger, or Adolf Reinach, all this was a pure value-response to their personalities and in no way an expression of special affinity for Jews. Thus I felt completely justified in saying that I as a non-Jew could take up arms against anti-Semitism.

In March, a friend of von Hildebrand received two tickets from Richard Coudenhove-Kalergi (1894–1972) to a performance of Antony and Cleopatra *and gave one to von Hildebrand. Coudenhove-Kalergi had begun the Pan-Europa movement in the mid-1920s.*

After the performance, the two of us, Hegner and I, were invited to a supper with Coudenhove. This was the occasion I personally became acquainted with Coudenhove, who was fighting for European unity and was called "Europapa," and also with his wife. He was a strikingly handsome man, with a noble and aristocratic countenance marked by a mysterious Asiatic note. Of course, he was half Japanese. They lived in a magnificent place, a charming old house located in a beautiful courtyard and decorated with very beautiful furniture.

• • •

Around this same time, von Hildebrand met several supporters of his journal, including the Benedictine Fr. Augustin von Galen, OSB (1870– 1949), brother of the bishop of Munster, Clemens August von Galen (1878–1946), one of the Nazis' strongest opponents among the German bishops.

At the beginning of April, von Hildebrand traveled to Katowice, passing through Bohemia into Upper Silesia.

Several of the cars on the train I was riding were going to Germany, while others were going to Poland. The train was divided at the border. I cannot say how many times I had to reassure myself that the car in which I was sitting was going to Poland. Just the thought that by mistake I could suddenly find myself in Germany sent shivers down my spine. It was the nightmare of nightmares.

Arriving in Katowice, I was received with great warmth, residing as Pant's guest in his spacious home. I think I gave three lectures. I no longer recall the subject, but surely I spoke on questions regarding the individual and the state, questions which I had dealt with in my book, *The Metaphysics of Community*, though naturally with application to the current problems in the struggle against Nazism. The lectures took place in a room where Pant usually addressed his own circle, not a very large room. The audience consisted of about thirty to forty people. The lectures, which were not public but addressed to the associations led by Pant, were meant to deepen understanding for the battle against Nazism and to help in the formation of an elite leadership. I cannot say I got the impression that my lectures had a strong effect. While I know what I presented was certainly not bad, I felt the audience did not understand it very well. They did not seem to be engaged to the same degree that my audiences in Vienna often were.

In April, Dollfuss appointed Ernst Karl Winter as the fourth mayor of Vienna, with the special task of reestablishing friendly relations with the working class after the unfortunate socialist revolution. Winter was very close to the Social Democrats without really being one himself, primarily because of his monarchism. Though he was not a legitimist, he was a staunch monarchist.

I still recall an event in Vienna that left a very deep impression on me. I was with Marguerite Solbrig at the Michaelerplatz when Dollfuss came out of St. Michael's Church where a mass had just taken place for those who had died in the socialist revolution in February. Marguerite and I were close enough that I could clearly hear the speech which Dollfuss addressed to all who had attended the mass and to the crowd standing outside the church. He spoke about all who had died in February with deep seriousness and in a spirit of noble recollection. He emphasized that the mass had been celebrated as much for the poor, misguided workers who had fought against the government as for the soldiers who had died for the government. In his words one sensed the full extent of his kindness, his nobility, and his deep piety. Both Marguerite and I were deeply moved.

Around this time there was another public gathering at which Dollfuss spoke. Was the occasion a birthday celebration or the ratification of the constitution? I no longer remember. But I was there and heard the delightful speech given by Dollfuss. Among other things, he said, "Not only am I the youngest chancellor in Europe, I am also the shortest." His endearing humor, his lack of any complexes due to his unusually small stature, his inner freedom, and his unassuming manner—all this came to expression in his words.

As I was leaving, I tried to get into his proximity. I succeeded, and he shook my hand, a little absently, but for a moment he held my hand firmly and looked me in the eye earnestly. I will never forget that moment, for it was the last time I saw up close this man whom I so loved and revered. It was also the second time I had been able to shake his hand.

One day I received a visit from Professor Kastil,[*] the well-known stu-

---

[*] Alfred Kastil (1874–1950).

dent and scholar of Franz Brentano,* who was professor of philosophy in Innsbruck. He told me that he had left Innsbruck "because the conduct of my colleagues was such that I could only see brown."† He visited me primarily because of our shared political stance. Being a strict follower of Brentano, he was philosophically very critical of phenomenology, seeing both Meinong‡ and Husserl as traitors. He was very humorous and attractive, and we got along very well. We saw each other frequently, and he became one of the more significant figures in my Viennese circle of acquaintances.

We were immensely pleased to receive the articles Mataja sent for our journal. It was truly a joy because his articles were excellent and because he was a significant political mind. I also saw him frequently, and it was always very enriching to speak with him. He was indisputably a "lordly type," unlike most Christian Social politicians. Not even my beloved Dollfuss, who came from a very modest background, was a "lord," though in him it did not seem a deficiency because of the way he transcended this entire sphere through his genius, his piety, and his humility. Neither Funder, nor Schmitz, nor Stepan were "lords" in this sense. Even Schuschnigg, though an aristocrat, was not lordly like Mataja.

In the past, Mataja had not been very Catholic, neither in his lifestyle nor in his political positions. He had also been something of a rival and opponent of Seipel. He then became seriously ill and, following his illness, he converted. By the time I met him, he had become markedly pious and was living happily married to his very friendly and deeply Catholic wife. In contrast to many of the "bigwigs" in the Christian Social Party, he was very cultivated, a man of great knowledge, and a brilliant orator.

He was also free of that foolish anti-Semitism displayed by Funder and all the more by the previous chairman of the party. When someone

---

* Franz Brentano (1838–1917), priest, philosopher, and psychologist, left the Catholic Church in opposition to the declaration on papal infallibility.

† A reference to the "Brownshirts," the Nazis' original paramilitary wing.

‡ Alexius von Meinong (1853–1920), Austrian philosopher and psychologist.

pointed out to this chairman that a Catholic could not be anti-Semitic because Christ was a Jew, he replied, "I beg you, only a half-Jew!" Mataja was far above this kind of theological ignorance and philistine spirit. The fact that he was on good terms with Simon and with Captain Bam, as well as with Kunwald, already showed that he was free of any anti-Semitic prejudice. He was just too intelligent for that.

His attitude toward the government of Dollfuss was one of reserve. He had always been an opponent of the Heimwehr, which was also part of the government. He was also, as a longstanding democrat, critical of the new constitution. Finally—and this was perhaps the primary reason—he was offended that he had been passed over and not appointed to a position in the new government. But his main interests lay in foreign affairs where he found himself in full accord with the government, for his anti-Nazism was absolute and principled. His articles were therefore well suited to our journal, even if he had a different stance toward Dollfuss.

"Lordly" in a still more pronounced way—because he was both "courtly" and aristocratic—was von Wiesner,* the leader of the legitimists. Under the emperor he had been active in a government ministry (foreign affairs, I think) and he had lost nothing of the regal etiquette, the elegance, the bearing, and the courteousness. I think he was half-Jewish. But above all he was an important man and a superior political mind. I got to know him through Klaus, and it was always a special pleasure to speak with him, indeed, it was always interesting and stimulating. It was mostly in my later Vienna years that I saw him with regularity, but I already met him in my first year there.

In the meantime, I had naturally met Eduard Ludwig, the minister in charge of public relations. Klaus had in fact already met with him even before my decisive conversation with Dollfuss. Ludwig was the type of official who is superficial, perfectly mannered, and lacking any real personal convictions. He had already outlasted several regime

---

* Baron Friedrich von Wiesner (d. 1940).

changes in his post. In contrast to Weber, he was much more polished, agile, and proper. But he was extremely shallow and insipid.

Weber at the time at least seemed to be much less of a Polonius and to have real political convictions of his own. He was a very strong Catholic, while Ludwig was liberal through and through. Weber was also wholeheartedly devoted to Dollfuss in a way that Ludwig was incapable of being to anyone. Yet Ludwig was far more clever and cunning than Weber.

Around this time, Stepan,* who was director of Styria Press, became the leader of the Patriotic Front, the party of Dollfuss. To my mind this was a fortunate choice because Stepan was surely among the leading figures within the Christian Social Party. I also welcomed this development personally because I knew Stepan, thanks to the fact that my book *Liturgy and Personality* had been published by Anton Pustet, which was an imprint of Styria. The recommendation of our journal by the Patriotic Front played a very significant role in our expansion.

I quickly sought out Stepan who received me warmly. The building which housed the leadership of the Patriotic Front was located near the square "Am Hof" where the Jesuits had both their principal church and their main residence. I think that Stepan had already become governor of Styria before being made leader of the Patriotic Front. Rintelen, the previous governor of Styria, had become the Austrian ambassador in Rome, where it was thought that this very unpleasant and dangerous man would be less of a threat.

During the summer semester, I was invited to give a lecture in Graz. I think my theme was again "state and individual." I had been invited there two years before by a church historian with whom I had gotten along very well (he was not a narrow Thomist). Regrettably, he was now strongly sympathetic to National Socialism, which prompted a fierce debate between us. As on my previous visit, I stayed with the Vincentians. My lecture was organized, I think, by the delightful student

---

* Karl Maria Stepan (1894–1972).

chaplain, Fr. Zemanek, a Vincentian with whom I already had a good rapport from my time in 1932. His political orientation was excellent, which was especially important and welcome considering his influence with the students.

The day after my lecture I met Professor Dobretsberger,* an economist, who had been present at my talk. How rare it was to meet a person who opposed Nazism entirely on principle and who understood with great clarity why there could be no possibility of compromise. Dobretsberger told me how Rintelen, while still governor of Styria, repeatedly attempted to win him over or to catch him in his net. Yet Dobretsberger was not someone to be tricked. Despite many invitations, he never paid Rintelen a visit. Finally, when Rintelen left him no peace, Dobretsberger wrote to him, addressing him, "Götz von Berlichingen."† I could not help laughing at Dobretsberger's crude, impertinent manner.

Many important things happened during the months of May and June, 1934. On one occasion we learned of the approach of a German plane carrying a high-ranking Nazi who was coming for negotiations with the Dollfuss regime. Klaus and I were very dismayed, fearing that it could pave the way for an unfortunate peace, which, aside from being totally intolerable on intellectual and moral grounds, would just have been a tactical deception by Hitler, offering no guarantee for the security of Austria.

As I expressed my concern, indeed, my horror, to Weber, he replied, "Come now, what do you want? Eventually we will have to arrive at some *modus vivendi* with Nazi Germany. In the long run, this 'state of war' will become unbearable." I was very upset by Weber's response. I was certain that Dollfuss would never compromise at the level of first principles. But the danger remained that he might believe in the possibility of a "peaceful coexistence," as it was called twenty years later

---

* Josef Dobretsberger (1903–70), served as Austrian minister for social affairs.

† An allusion to that sixteenth-century knight whom Goethe immortalized in his eponymous play, whose name conjures up his saucy line, "Lick my ass."

in regard to Soviet Russia. I feared that perhaps he did not sufficiently realize that a promise from Hitler was worthless and that an agreement with him was not even worth the paper on which it was written.

On the other hand, I was committed not only to the defense of a Catholic and independent Austria—which, in terms of *Weltanschauung* represented the absolute antithesis to Nazi Germany—but also to the glorious battle against Nazi Germany, to the active struggle against National Socialism for the sake of Germany, to its liberation from this criminal regime, and to the banner which Dollfuss alone had raised, as the rest of the world was frightened and adopted a wait-and-see attitude while making one concession after another. The great mission that Austria in this moment had taken on for the entire world could not be abandoned—to say nothing of the fact that not to progress is to regress, just as in the spiritual life.

I mean simply that only by going on the intellectual offensive and only by resisting all forms of peaceful coexistence could the "true Austria"—as seen by Dollfuss—be realized and its independence saved. Writing out of these convictions I published many articles in the *Ständestaat*, including one entitled "Ceterum censeo, Carthaginem esse delendam."

Thank God, this attempt by Hitler was frustrated by Starhemberg.[*] Upon hearing this, my perception of Starhemberg changed, for until then I had seen him as a loyal Heimwehr member, a follower of Mussolini, and as someone whose outlook was quite muddleheaded. But now I saw a refreshing simplicity: the clear-cut categories of the soldier and that loyalty which is inimical to all considerations of diplomacy—a great gift at that moment.

Starhemberg's loyalty and honest dependability were probably the reason Dollfuss favored him over Major Fey, who was capable yet incredibly ambitious and enigmatic, and appointed Starhemberg to the Vice-Chancellorship. Fey and Starhemberg were old rivals in the Heimwehr. The relationship between Dollfuss and Fey became increasingly

---

[*] Ernst Rüdiger Starhemberg (1899–1956), then Austrian vice-chancellor.

tense and by July Dollfuss had firmly resolved to dismiss Fey, who until then still held an important post in the government, I believe as Minister of Security.

Another unfortunate incident was tied to the introduction of the death penalty. As such I was quite happy that the death penalty was reintroduced, for the assassinations and other political crimes committed by the Nazi underground urgently called for the death penalty. Yet I was very unhappy when Weber said to me, "Hopefully the first criminal to receive the death penalty will be a Communist and not a Nazi. Otherwise it will be politically unbearable, given the effect on Nazi Germany." This did not please me at all. Why should the effect on Nazi Germany even be a consideration? After all, the Nazis would interpret any actions by the Dollfuss government in the most dishonest and defamatory manner.

But looking back, perhaps my reaction was too black and white. The situation was so difficult, yet somehow one had to discern a way forward. The first person to receive the death sentence was neither a Communist nor a Nazi but an ordinary arsonist. This was deeply unfortunate because the sentence was totally disproportionate. In what—I believe—was an act of revenge, the arsonist had set fire to a barn, for which he would normally have received a ten-year sentence. There was now general relief that one had found a first victim who was not a Nazi. The verdict was too harsh, and Dollfuss was terribly distressed that this draconian sentence should be carried out for political reasons.

He went into his room and prayed an Our Father for the poor arsonist as the sentence was being carried out. He believed that he had to make this concession, that it was his duty, even though it was very difficult for him personally. Yet I think that it was a great mistake on his part.

I recall that Gretchen and I along with the Matajas were invited to dinner that evening by Captain Bam and his wife. Mataja was beside himself over the sentence, and he was right. His indignation was genuine and a sign of his deep sense of justice. He rightly felt that an unjust sentence—let alone a death sentence, the sacrifice of a human life—was not a legitimate concession to the national interest. I will never forget this evening. We were all deeply downcast. Mataja's indignation over this terrible situation was fully shared by Captain Bam.

Dollfuss was on good terms with Mussolini. Now, to be sure Dollfuss was a principled opponent of Fascism, which is why he said to me, "Mussolini wants to build on pagan Rome, I by contrast want only to build on the Christian Middle Ages." But Mussolini had taken a decisive stance for the independence of Austria and was the primary bulwark for Austria against Nazi Germany.

Beyond this, Mussolini also had tremendous respect for Dollfuss, whom he liked a great deal. So it was that a real, personal relationship had formed between the two men. Mussolini invited Dollfuss and his family for a vacation on the Adriatic and listened with interest to what Dollfuss had to say about his basic outlook and convictions. In fact, he respected Dollfuss' faith and almost envied him for it. I think Dollfuss knew how to appeal to what was noblest in Mussolini, for despite all his flaws, Mussolini also had potential for good. Klaus also learned a great deal about this from a most reliable source, namely Morreale, with whom he had become quite friendly.

Despite their collaboration on foreign policy and despite the warmth of their personal relationship, as a true statesman Dollfuss remained ever attuned to political possibilities of any sort, preserving his complete independence from Mussolini even in areas where they worked together, like foreign policy.

Around that time, Mussolini met Hitler for the first time in Stra.[*] Although, as I later found out, this meeting made a very negative impression on Mussolini, still it was a brilliant "chess move" by Dollfuss to meet the French foreign minister and Prime Minister, Barthou,[†] at the train station in Vienna. Barthou was returning from Bucharest to Paris, and they were able to have a lengthy discussion about foreign policy. This was immediately following Mussolini and Hitler's meeting in Stra.

I was very pleased by this swift countermove, since relations be-

---

[*] The meeting took place June 14–15, 1934.

[†] Jean Louis Barthou (1862–1934), his discussion with Dollfuss took place July 19, 1934.

tween Mussolini and France at the time were rather tense. As I later found out, when Mussolini saw Hitler for the first time ever in Stra, he said to his adjutant, "Questa faccia é un ontà per l'umanità" ("this face is a disgrace to humanity"), a very striking remark which proves that Mussolini did have a sense for quality and that he saw through Hitler's pathetic and tawdry appearance.

I think I paid my second visit to President Miklas at the beginning of June. Once again, it was a substantive discussion, throughout which I was impressed by the moral earnestness, the great conscientiousness, and the modesty of the man. I think we also discussed the execution of the arsonist, which Miklas was very unhappy about. Beyond this, I do not recall many particulars, but I mention the visit because I had already formed a certain relationship to him by the time I visited him for the third time at the end of July in a highly dramatic moment. But I will only describe this later.

During this spring Klemperer came to see me, or perhaps he telephoned. He had moved from Florence to Vienna and lived at Schönbrunn Palace in one of the most beautiful apartments I have ever seen—the most magnificent parquet floors imaginable, enchanting baroque furniture, wonderful ornamented blankets, and above all a view into the little garden filled with roses. It was an absolute Figaro-world: a highpoint of culture and beauty. The Emperor Charles had previously lived here. The Klemperers invited us on many occasions. I got to know his wife and his daughter, Lotte, who was still very young at the time, perhaps ten or twelve. His wife was originally from the Rhineland. She was quite likeable and made a very sound impression.

I can hardly find the words to express how beautiful it was to be invited there for dinner. I remember one occasion especially. It was still bright, because the sun in June sets quite late. We ate outside in the garden in front of the house, and it was the most blissful experience to be surrounded by this unique world—the world of Austria, of the Rococo, the world of Figaro. Schönbrunn as a whole is uniquely beautiful, but this section with the little rose garden in the golden light of the summer evening was particularly wonderful.

To experience such a distinctive and refined world, filled with the special air of Mozart, and embodied in such a concrete and individual manner, is something very rare. How unusual it is to find the beauty and nobility of this world realized in such perfection, concreteness, and fullness. And what a great and unusual gift it is to find oneself unexpectedly in this world, not for the sake of enjoyment but transported there by life circumstances, not as a spectator but as someone inhabiting it in an entirely natural way.

At the Klemperers I saw Paul von Klenau,* the Danish musician, whom I had not seen in many years. He was married to a Jewish woman, whose maiden name was Simon, which was probably the reason he had left Germany. He spoke as if he were an opponent of National Socialism, but soon after he returned to Germany without his wife. In fact, he divorced her and chose to conform himself to Nazism. I had never had an especially positive impression of his character.

Through Klemperer, I also came to know Klenau's Jewish son-in-law, Soma Morgenstern, a talented writer to whom I owe my knowledge of many wonderful Jewish anecdotes. Being with the Klemperers was always very stimulating, for he was intelligent, cultivated, and a strong personality. From time to time he would conduct and give us tickets to his concerts.

In the meantime, my relationship with Oesterreicher had greatly developed. I saw him often, and once he invited me for a long walk in the Vienna woods, a walk which took up nearly the entire day. He invited me to become the godfather of Georg Wassermann, the son of Jakob Wassermann,† who had recently converted under his direction. I accepted with great joy, and Georg Wassermann, then about twenty-two years old, was baptized in the church of Notre Dame de Sion.

---

* Paul August von Klenau (1883–1946), conductor and composer.

† Jakob Wassermann (1873–1934), one of the most widely read German authors during the 1920s and 1930s.

Of great importance were my visits to Bishop Gföllner* of Linz. Early on, I stopped off for two hours to be received by him while on a trip to Salzburg. Among the Austrian bishops there was no more resolute opponent of the Nazis than Bishop Gföllner. From the very beginning, he had ordered the churches in his diocese to offer the prayers against evil doers (*contra malum agentes*), with special application to the Nazis. I was delighted by the way he had stepped forward to attack the Nazis forcefully in various ways.

This is why I felt a strong need to see him. He received me in the most gracious way and we understood each other extremely well. He was very enthusiastic about our journal, which he received and read. A very authoritarian bishop, Gföllner had something of a cramped personality. He was also a strict Thomist. Yet none of this then struck me as decisive.

The discernment of spirits, which alone mattered in that moment, simply required one to ask whether a person clearly grasped the nature of National Socialism and whether they rejected it completely on the basis of the right philosophical and moral reasons. Where this was the case, differences of opinion could be postponed for a later time. This was why Bishop Gföllner was my favorite among the Austrian bishops. During my Vienna years, I went variously to see him in Linz on my way to Salzburg. I also befriended his secretary, Prelate Ohnmacht,† who often visited me in Vienna and whose political orientation was excellent.

A closer look at Bishop Gföllner reveals the complexity of the situation in which von Hildebrand had to navigate. Even courageous Catholics who condemned Nazism were not immune to a form of religious anti-Semitism that viewed Judaism and Jews as morally and culturally "harmful."

Von Hildebrand must have known that on January 23, 1933—a week

---

* Johannes Maria Gföllner (1867–1941), Austrian theologian and bishop.
† Karl Ohnmacht (1893–1954), Austrian priest and politician.

before Hitler was named chancellor of Germany—Gföllner had issued a pastoral letter denouncing Nazism. While Gföllner condemns hatred of the Jews, he writes at length of the harm secularized Jews allegedly have on Christian culture. His letter provoked widespread criticism and moved the entire Austrian episcopacy to respond. In December 1933, the Austrian bishops issued a collective pastoral in which they more clearly condemned anti-Semitism.

One evening Klaus brought me to a small restaurant called the Griechenbeisl to meet former German Chancellor Joseph Wirth, who always went there when he came to Vienna. Klaus had already become acquainted with him before, while I had already heard so much about him in my life. He struck me more as a sergeant than a statesman.

He was of large stature, with an enormous blond moustache. His face was rather flushed, and he had a jovial, light-hearted, and friendly expression. He spoke in a very pronounced Baden accent and with the gusto often found in people from Baden, and especially from Württemberg, who greatly enjoy speaking their dialect. This also occurs in people from Berlin and the Rhineland, while in Swabians and Allemanians there is an additional note of optimism and even a certain self-importance. Wirth also had this quality. He said to me, "Professor, you will find the very best beer in all of Vienna at the Griechenbeisl!" He avoided serious topics, including politics, told jokes, and praised the beer.

My relationship to Domanig grew increasingly warm, and sometimes he would drop by unannounced. I think my introduction of Domanig to Prince Hans Schönburg already dates to this time. In any event, I was happy to bring together these two noble personalities who, as far as social position went, came from vastly different worlds. They got along very well.

In those days, Domanig told me of a remark by Dollfuss which was incredibly characteristic of him. Dollfuss was speaking about his progressive hardness of hearing. He said, "I hope my hearing lasts another two years, since I want to retire as soon as we are able to secure an independent future for Austria—as soon as the threat of National Socialism is averted." This statement was very typical of Dollfuss for it showed how free he was of any ambition. He remained Chancellor, not out of ambition, but because he considered it to be his God-given mission. This is a trait rarely found among talented statesmen.

Domanig also told me about a time he and Dollfuss were riding on a train together. As they pulled into the station, they could see into the train parallel to theirs. A man sitting in the compartment of the other train looked at Dollfuss with an expression of such hatred that Dollfuss and Domanig were deeply shaken. How could one hate Dollfuss, who was so noble, so kind, so well-wishing toward everyone, who fought against the Antichrist of National Socialism! But Domanig told me that seeing the man's expression was like looking into an inferno of hatred.

I have not yet written anything about the two young men, Bosch[*] and Canaval,[†] who played a leading role in Schuschnigg's Catholic *Sturmscharen*.[‡] I met them through Klaus and Franzi. They were also publishers of a newspaper called *The Storm Over Austria*.[§] Both were deeply committed Austrian patriots and fellow soldiers in the great battle against National Socialism.

On June 30, news began to reach us about unrest in Germany, and on July 1 the reports were already more detailed. With the first rumors on June 30, Klaus and I began to hope it might be internal unrest in Germany that could signal the beginning of the end. But already on July 1 we heard about the murder of Röhm[¶] and it soon became clear that the unrest was in fact a gruesome "purge" by Hitler. I can still see Klaus as he came to me with the initial reports, saying with satisfaction, "It

---

[*] Franz Xaver Bosch.

[†] Gustav A. Canaval (1898–1959), also chief editor of *Telegraf* and founder of the *Salzburger Nachrichten*.

[‡] A political and paramilitary organization drawn from Catholic youth.

[§] *Sturm über Österreich*, the newspaper of the Heimwehr, the militia associated with the Christian Social Party.

[¶] Ernst Röhm (1887–1934), leader of the SA, or "Brownshirts."

appears that there has been shooting in Germany and now great confusion, which makes me very hopeful."

That evening we went to the Griechenbeisl to see Chancellor Wirth and to find out more from him thanks to the good sources he had. We did find him there. He was very agitated and anxious to know in greater detail whether it was an uprising against the National Socialist regime, an internal power struggle, or even something else. I still see him putting down his beer every fifteen minutes to rush to the telephone to find out if further news had come in. But that evening it was impossible to confirm anything. But it was not long before we began to get increasing detail about the terrible murders that had been committed: Röhm and Gregor Strasser[*] from the National Socialists, Klausener[†] from the Catholics, and Schleicher[‡]—to mention only the best known—had been murdered.

All together, more than a thousand were massacred on June 30 and the following night. Unfortunately it was not an uprising but a purge—the so-called "Night of the Long Knives"—in which Hitler had anyone murdered who made him the slightest bit uneasy, while also giving his followers *carte blanche* to exact revenge on their personal enemies and opponents.

On July 2, Fr. Thomas Michels[§] came to visit me in a state of intense agitation. He told that Willi Schmidt[¶] had also been taken from his home on June 30 and immediately beheaded. This was completely mysterious. Willi Schmidt was certainly a decisive opponent of National Socialism, yet he was not politically prominent in any way, nor did he have any personal enemies. Fr. Thomas was very close to him and his wife (a charming Jewish convert), and so he was completely beside himself over the murder. It soon turned out that the murder had happened "by mistake." The people from the SS who had arrested him came to Mrs.

---

[*] Gregor Strasser (1892–1934), a leading member of the Nazi Party until 1932.

[†] Erich Klausener (1885–1934), German politician and head of Catholic Action in Berlin.

[‡] Kurt von Schleicher (1882–1934), the last chancellor of Germany before Hitler was appointed.

[§] A Benedictine monk of the Abbey of Maria Laach and acquaintance of von Hildebrand.

[¶] Wilhelm (Willi) Schmidt (1893–1934), writer and music critic in Munich.

Schmidt to apologize, saying that they had taken the wrong person. They had been searching for a completely different Wilhelm Schmidt. They were sorry and asked if they might be allowed to attend the burial. Mrs. Schmidt thanked them but asked them to stay away.

I also soon found out that my friend, Fritz Beck, had been murdered on June 30. This shook me deeply. I thought of our farewell and how I tried at the time to convince him to leave Germany. He had said he could not, just as a captain could not abandon his ship. I later heard the details from a reliable source.

It was an act of revenge by a doctor who as a student had plotted against Beck and had hated him from that time. The doctor hired several people to kill Beck. They came to Beck's home and declared they were to arrest him and bring him to Dachau. Beck believed it to be an official arrest and so went with them. On the way to Dachau, they shot him in the car, threw out his corpse, and drove away. A homeless man who lay hidden behind a bush heard the shot and saw that a dead body was being thrown out of the car. Thinking it was a robbery and a murder, he informed the nearest police. They found the corpse and identified Beck by his papers. His nephew Huber was notified and called to confirm the identity.

It was particularly tragic that Beck had been home that day. Had he not been found by these people on the "Night of the Long Knives," the next day no one would have bothered him anymore. After all, there was no serious, political basis for his arrest. Poor, noble Beck! Thus ended his life, in which he had done so much good for others, and in which in the most inspired way he had enriched the communal life of the university students. Here was a man deserving of every honor, yet he was thrust aside in this disgraceful way. He was not even brought before a court, but simply killed like a dog and thrown onto the street.

And yet, Beck's death was also emblematic. For even though his murder was a pure act of personal revenge, his entire life's work was so antithetical to National Socialism that in the long run he could not have lived in its midst. Sooner or later, Beck had to become a victim of National Socialism.

His death was a great loss for me personally. I had great respect for him and we were bound together in friendship. He had played a great role in my life in Munich between 1920 and 1933. Above all, his death was objectively a great loss, since Beck could still have done so much good after 1945 in the work of rebuilding after the end of the Third Reich.

Thus June 30 was not, as we initially hoped, a weakening of National Socialism, the onset of its disintegration, but only a gruesome event, a massacre which also wiped out noble and valuable men—this was the occasion of Fritz Gerlich's murder in Dachau—and a slaughter within the party from which Hitler emerged strengthened. Naturally, we did not miss the opportunity to respond appropriately about June 30 in the *Ständestaat*. I wrote several articles on this subject, one of which was called, "Eritis sicut Deus," in which I argued that National Socialism had now completely dropped its mask and that Hitler had clearly shown himself to be a mass murderer.

Fr. Alois Mager came occasionally to Vienna and I saw him from time to time, sometimes in Salzburg, sometimes in Vienna. He told me of a conversation he had with Dollfuss about the Catholic university to be established in Salzburg, for up until that time all that existed was an extended theological faculty. He told me that the way Dollfuss had spoken about the university for half an hour made a great impression on him. Dollfuss was no specialist about universities and schools, yet Fr. Alois thought he had arrived at more important and essential conclusions in his remarks than any of the experts he had heard on the topic.

With an amazing intuitive grasp of all the issues, Dollfuss had sketched an extraordinary vision of the university to be established, even touching on teacher-student relations, the common life of students, and so forth. All of this confirmed my impression of Dollfuss' genius and his intuitive ability to find a clear and pertinent solution, without the benefit of preparatory study, to a problem presented to him in the moment.

On July 25, I went to see Weber about various things I wanted to discuss with him. He received me in an especially friendly way and told me that I had been the subject of conversation between Dollfuss and

Stepan, who were on a trip together and that Dollfuss had expressed great satisfaction with my activity. He had emphasized that Schuschnigg ought to take care of the professorship soon, and that he would discuss it with him.

Then he said to Weber, "We really should give him some additional money, so that he can get some good rest in August." I was overjoyed, above all because Dollfuss, whom I cherished, was satisfied with me. This was a great and deep source of joy. The contribution for a vacation was also a great help for me and thus very welcome, though it primarily made me happy as an expression of Dollfuss' satisfaction and his understanding for me. The prospect of being able to resume my teaching capacity in the near future was also very satisfying for me. I left Weber in the sort of happy state one rarely experiences. My heart overflowed with love for Dollfuss, with gratitude to God for the existence of such a noble opponent of National Socialism, that it was granted me to work with him, and that he was satisfied with my work.

Elated, I rushed home to tell Gretchen the wonderful news. The telephone rang. It was Oesterreicher, who said to me, "An announcement was just made on the radio that Dollfuss has resigned and Rintelen become the chancellor." Did I know anything? What could this mean? I was dumbfounded and said to him, "This cannot be true. I just spoke with Weber fifteen minutes ago, and he would have been the first to know something about this." Still, I was disturbed that it was even possible for the radio to make such an announcement. Soon after Oesterreicher called again to say that the radio station had been temporarily taken over by Nazis who had spread this news. Now it was again in the hands of the government. What we had heard about Dollfuss and Rintelen was thus a false report.

Yet there was unrest in the city, something was not in order—though at the moment nothing was yet certain. I was seized by a terrible anxiety. Not much later we found out that the chancellery was occupied by Nazis, that Dollfuss was in their hands, and that it was impossible to break in forcibly because they threatened to kill Dollfuss otherwise.

I knelt down at my desk and begged God to save Dollfuss. I broke out into sobs at the thought that this noble warrior against the Antichrist, this person who was so good, so deeply devout, was in the hands of criminals, that he might be forced to some compromise, if he were even allowed to live. It was terrible to be in a position where one could not free him, could not get into the chancellery to wrest him from the hands of his criminal enemies. Having our hands tied like this, the fact that we were forced to remain passive while wanting to save him, made these hours a time of unspeakable torment. I had naturally telephoned Klaus immediately and he had informed me of the awful course of events. But we were unable to get any clear reports on the exact course of events.

After terrible hours of anxious waiting, dreading, hoping, praying, the awful news came at seven o'clock: Dollfuss was dead. The Nazis in the chancellery capitulated. They had been unable to realize their demand to have Rintelen appointed chancellor and so they surrendered. Words cannot express how deeply I was struck by the death of my beloved Dollfuss, how my hopes for Austria and the battle against National Socialism collapsed.

As later came out, Dollfuss lay on the floor and slowly bled to death. A guard, who was permitted to remain close to him, reported this later. Dollfuss asked for a priest and a doctor, yet the Nazi thugs refused both. He was forced to endure a slow death by bleeding in the knowledge that he would be unable to receive the sacraments. Two guards among the captured were called over and they applied a bandage. He said to them, "Children, you are so kind to me. Why not the others? I never wanted anything other than peace. We were never the aggressors. We were always forced to defend ourselves. May the Lord God forgive them." Major Fey was permitted to speak with him for a moment.

I no longer recall whom Dollfuss entrusted with asking Mussolini to take care of his wife and children. It seems he believed it was an uprising of the army, that all was lost, that the Nazis would take over the Austrian government, and that no one in Austria would be able to care for his wife and children.

Thank God, however, it was a putsch organized in Berlin and carried out by certain underground elements. While the putsch was successful in eliminating the soul of the new Austria as embodied by Dollfuss, it was actually unsuccessful, considering that the goal had been the chancellorship of Rintelen and thereby the transition to a National Socialist regime. President Miklas is primarily to thank for categorically rejecting Rintelen and for placing the government under the control of the ministers who had gathered at the Army Ministry, and among whom Schuschnigg was the most prominent. There was not yet an announcement of a successor—it was not yet known that Dollfuss had been murdered—but Miklas had issued this interim authorization to prevent confusion from arising.

Funder later told me an interesting episode. During these hours of anxious waiting, he suddenly ran into Rintelen. That Rintelen should now appear in Vienna was very conspicuous and worrisome, as if he needed to be on hand in order to take over the chancellorship. Funder then did what may well be his lasting claim to fame.

He said to Rintelen, "Oh, you are urgently being awaited by the ministers who are at the Army Ministry. Please, come with me and let us go there immediately." Thinking Funder was referring to his appointment and that he should be present to discuss the situation, Rintelen voluntarily got into a car with Funder and rode off to meet the ministers. Arriving at the Army Ministry, Funder accompanied him all the way to the room where the ministers were meeting. There Rintelen was of course immediately arrested on suspicion of having played a role in the conspiracy, or at least of having been aware of it.

I cannot portray in words what I felt that evening. The terrible irreplaceable loss for Austria, for the future of Austria, which alone had taken up the heroic struggle against National Socialism. I realized clearly that whoever the successor of Dollfuss might be, the struggle would no longer be carried on in the same way. But apart from the irreplaceable loss in regard to the international political situation, the death of Dollfuss—the tragic death—broke my heart. It was a pain rooted in a very personal love and veneration. Dollfuss for me was not only the David who had taken up the heroic battle against the Goliath Hitler, he was also an embodiment of the so precious Austrian spirit—he enchanted me with his humility, his deep faith, his genius, and with the great charm of his being.

Although I had only spoken with him at length one time, I loved him in a very personal way and his death affected me as only the death of a beloved person can do. Beyond this there were the tragic circumstances of his death, the terrible agony he endured as he slowly bled to death. The moving way he bore everything and the way he died were certainly a source of great consolation, still our hearts were seared by these events. Marguerite was so shattered that she could not stop crying for days.

Oesterreicher came to me the day after the murder of Dollfuss, demanding that I immediately request an audience with President Miklas to implore him to appoint Schuschnigg and not Starhemberg as successor to Dollfuss. Under the circumstances I did agree with Oesterreicher that Schuschnigg, a pious and outspoken Catholic, offered the greatest guarantee for a continuation of the political course that Dollfuss had taken.

This supposition later proved false. Yet even today I cannot say with certainty that Starhemberg would have been a better choice, despite the fact that he was probably less encumbered than Schuschnigg by "Greater German" sympathies. I do believe Starhemberg would have made a greater effort to carry on the work of Dollfuss fully in his spirit and that he would have adopted a more unbending stance toward Nazi Germany. Yet he lacked the genius of Dollfuss, was naïve in many ways, and would not have been up to the situation.

But I was not aware of any of this at the time, nor was Oesterreicher. Our fear was simply that we would get a Heimwehr government if Starhemberg were appointed.

I had no desire whatsoever to go to Miklas, and it seemed completely inappropriate to push myself forward at such a moment. The President would have no time, and why should my opinion matter to him? Besides, I had many inhibitions. It went against my nature. Only when I have the clear consciousness that it is God's will that I do something do I have the strength to overcome my inhibitions. I did not have this consciousness, and so I did not want to go to Miklas.

This occasion marked the first time I experienced in Oesterreicher, who until then had often struck me as timid, a will of steel and an ability to exert such pressure on others that it was almost impossible to resist. He kept repeating that it was my duty and dragged me to the door of the President's office. I actually succeeded in speaking to Miklas. In greeting me, his adjutant said that he was ashamed to speak German after what had happened. The depth of his outrage over the murder of Dollfuss was a consolation for me. What he said came from his heart. I regret that I have forgotten his name.

The President was very gracious as he received me and I could see how deeply shaken he was. He told me that nothing was yet certain regarding Dollfuss' successor. I laid out my thoughts—that Schuschnigg was surely the right choice and that he should be chosen over Starhemberg. Miklas responded, "Yes, this by far would be my personal preference as well." Like me Miklas had no particular fondness for the Heimwehr, while as a pious Catholic he felt a greater solidarity with Schuschnigg. The rest of our conversation focused on the tragic death of Dollfuss and on the terrible crime of the Nazis. It had unquestionably been orchestrated from Berlin. Naturally I only stayed with Miklas for a short while. As I emerged, Oesterreicher expressed great satisfaction that I had gone and also about the outcome of the conversation.

On the same day as the occupation of the chancellery (July 25), there was also an uprising of the National Socialist underground in various parts of Austria, though everywhere it was suppressed by the army and the police with relatively little effort. In a very important development typical [of Mussolini's policy toward Austria at the time], large numbers of Italian troops were amassed at the Brenner border with the charge of marching into Austria the moment the Germans attempted an invasion, and so to prevent this interference. From the start I was an opponent of Fascism and of Mussolini, yet at this moment I could only feel deep gratitude to Mussolini that he came to the defense of Austria's independence and also of Dollfuss' legacy.

I was very upset when Funder enthusiastically told me that von Papen had been appointed the German ambassador in Vienna. Funder believed this signified a complete transformation in Austria's relations with

Germany and pointed to a hopeful future. I countered that I viewed von Papen's appointment as very dangerous and that after the murder of Dollfuss it was less than ever possible to speak of a *modus vivendi* with Germany. He replied that I failed to take into account the armed conflicts with National Socialist rebels taking place throughout Austria and that the appointment of Papen was therefore really a sort of conciliatory gesture. There was no point in further discussing the matter, since he was very stubborn and considered himself much more politically astute than me. But I saw clearly that Papen was a Trojan horse and that he was being sent to throw sand into the eyes of Catholics in Vienna.

According to Winston Churchill, Papen told the U.S. ambassador in Vienna that he planned to play on his reputation as a devout Catholic to win the confidence of Catholics like Cardinal Innitzer of Vienna.

The solemn funeral took place on July 28. We were able to attend the ceremony, at least the first part, and to get close enough to witness much of it. It was incredibly moving to see Mrs. Dollfuss, deep in sorrow and on the arm of Starhemberg, as she approached behind the coffin in which Dollfuss lay. Of course, the entire government was present. Yet I was struck that it was Starhemberg, and not Schuschnigg, who accompanied Mrs. Dollfuss. On a purely personal level, Starhemberg was apparently closer to Dollfuss than Schuschnigg was. The military band played "I had a comrade, a better one you'll not find." It is difficult to describe what went on within me at the time, how my heart bled at the thought that Dollfuss was being buried and that this beloved and noble man, on whom Austria's hope rested, this heroic and selfless opponent of the Antichrist embodied in Hitler was no longer in our midst!

During this time, we received a visit from a French businessman from Lyon, a pacifist and a man greatly interested in politics. But we really got to know him at a party hosted by Gabriel Puaux, the French ambassador. Puaux was a very likeable and cultivated man. He was also a Protestant, which is relatively rare in France—there can hardly be more than 100,000 Protestants in all of France. The party was a luncheon and there were about twenty-five guests. The gathering took on a special note thanks to Puaux's remarks about the terrible event of July 25. He spoke simply but with great warmth. He said he had hoped to work for a long time with Dollfuss, whom he deeply revered. Tears ran down his face as he spoke. Puaux's heartfelt empathy and his genuine veneration for Dollfuss were very consoling for me. Naturally I also met the embassy counselor, Vicomte de Montbas, as well as various other staff members of the embassy.

During these days of mourning, as I waited full of anxiety over my personal plans and also over the future of my work in Vienna, I met with Klemperer on various occasions. He too had been affected deeply by the death of Dollfuss. He invited us to a sort of operetta, "The Princess on the Ladder," in which his friend Karlweis sang the principal role. It was around this time that Klemperer and Oesterreicher got to know one another. Klemperer, after all, was always seeking contact with Catholics and above all with priests. Even though he was not a very consistent Catholic, nor very fervent, still he possessed a yearning for the Church. He liked Oesterreicher a great deal. He had need of an intellectual priest—like Münch, through whom he had found his way to the Church, or like Pinsk, who had been his great friend in Berlin.

After several days, President Miklas appointed Schuschnigg as chancellor. I was happy, since I saw this as the lesser evil for the reasons I gave above. During a visit with Weber, he told me that Schuschnigg soon intended to secure my appointment as professor at the university. This was a part of Dollfuss' legacy which he absolutely wanted to fulfill.

I looked toward the future with great anxiety. The task of the journal now seemed to me more important and urgent than ever; indeed, the death of Dollfuss had made it even greater. The journal *Storm Over Austria* was simply not on a sufficiently high level to conduct the incredibly necessary philosophical and political battle against Nazi Germany. But on a purely personal level too, ending the journal would have been a great blow for me.

Klaus, whose wife was soon to give birth to a child, would have had nothing to depend on, while Marguerite would also have come into great distress. At least I could hope to make ends meet through my salary as professor. But more important than any human consideration was the significance of the journal in the battle against National Socialism and for the independence of Austria, of a Catholic Austria.

During this time, I received an invitation from Fribourg that greatly honored me. A circle of theologians was meeting there at the beginning of October to discuss various sociological questions, new problems that had arisen in the wake of the changed conditions of life since the Middle Ages: themes such as just war, the relationship between the state and the individual, and so forth. All of the participants in this discussion were French theologians. I was the only layman invited. Naturally I accepted the invitation with joy, for I was very interested in these discussions. The symposium was scheduled for late September or early October.

Unfortunately I can no longer say with certainty whether my afternoon discussions already began in May 1934 or whether it was not until October.[*] In any case, the first of these gatherings was a grand affair. I must have invited nearly eighty people, and while I cannot exactly remember everyone by name, among them were surely Allers and his wife, Kastil, von Herrnritt, Oesterreicher, Fr. Frodl, various other priests including Dr. John.[†] Then there were Count Thun,[‡] Count Kinsky,[§] Mataja, Missong, Simon, Bam, Klaus and the entire staff of the journal, Weber (who did not come), and Dr. Rudolf. The discussion went well, though only over time did the regular and truly interested attendees begin to emerge. At that first gathering, it was the social aspect that predominated. Hovorka and Karpfen also came to the afternoon discussions.

During the course of the 1934/35 winter semester, the gatherings developed more and more into what they were meant to be, namely a political discussion which gave me the repeated opportunity to shed

---

[*] Witnesses from the time say the gatherings began in early fall.

[†] Robert John (1899–1981), priest, professor of German literature, and Dante scholar.

[‡] Count Paul Thun (1884–1963), poet.

[§] Count Rudolf Kinsky (1898–1965).

new light on the absolute impossibility of any kind of compromise with National Socialism. For it is unbelievable how vulnerable our human nature is to falling into illusions and to growing numb in our indignation over injustice which we come to accept. Here, as in so many others in life, we must be like the conductor of an orchestra, in continually renewing the call to alertness. The moment one lets up, people fall asleep, or at least become indifferent.

Allers was one of the main participants in the discussions and was always excellent. Naturally, Klaus was also one of the best—with respect to politics usually the very best. Mataja, when he came (his health prevented him from coming often), also had many excellent things to say. In short, the intellectual level was very high. I will still have quite a bit to say about these afternoon discussions, which later would sometimes draw as many as a hundred twenty participants.

Von Hildebrand then traveled to Fribourg in Switzerland for the symposium on social questions with a group of leading French theologians. But even here he stepped forward in his role as "intellectual officer" addressing the burning questions of the day. In addition to Monsignor Bruno de Solages (1895–1983), the rector of the Catholic University of Toulouse with whom von Hildebrand formed a lasting friendship, he also met various other priests who deeply impressed him by their learning and spiritual life.

Our conversations were chaired by the elderly Fr. Albert Valensin, SJ, a very intelligent specialist on political and social questions. He was extremely likeable and we got along superbly. His family was originally Italian-Jewish. Their name was Valensini. He had a niece, Georgia Valensini, who was half-Jewish. There were two Valensin brothers who were Jesuits. Fr. Albert's brother was professor of philosophy at the Institut Catholique in Lyon. I rather think I already knew Fr. Albert Valensin from Munich, that he had once visited me there.

Also present was a young philosopher, Fr. Fessard, SJ,[*] a complete non-Thomist in the sense of holding that it is impossible to separate faith and philosophy. He made a very intelligent impression, but I did not sufficiently understand his position, thinking it was tinged by a slight fideism like that of Rosenmöller.[†] I failed to recognize the many avenues for mutual understanding that were opened by his critical stance toward Thomism. Having raised an objection to him on this point, he said to me after the meeting, "Don't you see that everything you write is much closer to my perspective than to the Thomistic one?"

I was the only layman in the group. The discussion focused mostly on questions I had either addressed in my book *The Metaphysics of Community* or were the subject of many articles in *Der christliche Ständestaat*. I was in fact much better prepared to speak about these questions than any of the others, and so I had much more to say than they did. The group received my contributions with great interest and comprehension. These discussions were as stimulating for me as they were fruitful. Everything about the Catholic milieu delighted me, and I was given the chance to awaken in this group of professors and priests, who had great influence in their own country, a deeper understanding for the nature and danger of National Socialism, to show them the radical incompatibility of National Socialism and Catholicism. This was necessary because the Concordat with the Vatican as well as the stance of the German bishops and also of some German theologians contributed to concealing the abyss that separates National Socialism and Christendom.

What gave me the greatest joy, though, was a comment by Fr. Desbuquois, SJ,[‡] after I had served at a morning mass he had celebrated. He said to me, "Do you know that God has granted you a rare *sensus supernaturalis* (sense for the supernatural)? And do you realize clearly the responsibility that such a gift entails?" He had formed this impression

---

[*] Gaston Fessard, SJ (1897–1978).
[†] Bernhard Rosenmöller (1883–1974).
[‡] Gustave Desbuquois, SJ (1869–1959).

during the discussions. I have to admit that this remark made me much happier than a great deal of the praise I had received for my books and lectures. It was the most beautiful thing anyone could say to me, since I considered the primary theme of all of my religious writings to be the articulation of the essence of the supernatural in its qualitative character, beginning with my essay "The New World of Christendom"[3] and continuing through to my book *Liturgy and Personality*.[4] The book in which this theme is most central, *Transformation in Christ*, did not yet exist at the time, nor had it even been planned. These words were particularly precious coming from Fr. Desbuquois, who deeply impressed me by his saintly being. From then on, these discussions were held every fall, and I participated in 1934, 1935, and 1936.

Upon returning to Vienna, I soon noticed a great change in Weber's attitude toward me. He was, as I had already come to notice, really more of a subordinate by nature, and so the fact that I was not nearly as much *persona grata* with Schuschnigg as I had been with Dollfuss did in fact influence him a great deal. Of course, Weber's position became much weaker with Dollfuss no longer there to support him. But this should not have been a reason why our own personal relationship, which had developed over the course of a year of collaboration, should wane as it increasingly did. This was particularly unfortunate for the continuation of the journal.

But much worse, as I soon noticed, was the fact that Austria's struggle against National Socialism no longer possessed the same character as it had under Dollfuss. There had been something totally unconventional and inspired about Dollfuss. This had won him affection from outside of Austria, particularly the friendship of Mussolini. He embodied Austria and everything about him had an Austrian charm.

By comparison, Schuschnigg was much more conventional, stiff, and Germanic than Dollfuss. And he was completely lacking in genius. Schuschnigg was a decent, pious, and dutiful man. He was also cultivated, in many respects more so than Dollfuss, yet he lacked Dollfuss' brilliant intuitive perception. Schuschnigg was surrounded by many German nationalist elements, and even by traitors, like Wilhelm Wolf, yet he could not see through them. Above all, Schuschnigg himself, being burdened by a certain German nationalism, was not entirely free of sympathies for a "Greater Germany." This showed itself on many occasions.

I noticed more and more how the notion of the "brotherhood" of Austria and Germany began to poison the entire politics of Schuschnigg. The fact that every step against Hitler was of course a step toward the liberation of Germany sheds light on the error at the root of this notion of "brotherhood," namely that it makes an unfortunate and naïve identification of a nation, or people, with the political regime presently in power. One simply had to see that Germany had fallen into the hands of criminals, just as had also happened to poor Russia. Second, Austria and a Prussian Germany free of National Socialism were politically two different worlds, regardless of their many cultural links. Austria is a nation of its own. In the past, it had been a synthesis of East and West, North and South, a sort of European microcosm, which continues to animate the smaller Austria of today. Austria is therefore something totally distinct from Prussian Germany, which in reality has always been the traditional enemy of Austria.

Stepan approached me to ask whether I would like to write a book about Dollfuss, both his personality and his work. Otto Müller of Anton Pustet Press was to publish it. (Pustet was also the publisher of *Liturgy and Personality*.) I accepted this offer with great joy, for I desired to commemorate this singularly beloved and revered man. I also had the feeling that I understood his character and his greatness better and more clearly than anyone else who might have been considered for such a book. But it had to be completed in a very short period of time, because Müller wanted it to appear while the shock over Dollfuss' murder was still in the air—a very understandable request for a publisher who was also very business savvy.

I pressed myself into an unbelievably intense state of work, much like the time in Munich when I was writing *Liturgy and Personality*. I worked from morning until night without interruption, received no visitors, and did not even write any articles for the journal. Balduin came from Salzburg to Vienna for a few days to help me, for I felt the need to show him what I had already written as well as to discuss with him the overall structure and the parts that were still to be written. I wrote the book, *Engelbert Dollfuss*,[5] in twelve days, which allowed it to appear before Christmas. I think it was in October that I wrote it—just after my return from Lyons—and the book appeared in the beginning of December.

The book even found its way to Germany, where several copies were sold before the Gestapo, upon becoming aware of it, confiscated and banned it. The book had great success in Austria. I received many appreciative letters. Even Professor Kastil called to say that from the moment he had gotten a copy one evening he had been unable to stop reading and that he had continued until five in the morning, so much had it captivated and moved him.

But Mrs. Dollfuss was not as pleased. I had mentioned in the book that Dollfuss was an illegitimate child, which was well known, to avoid any appearance of wanting to conceal anything. It fit very well in the passage where I was contrasting his simplicity, modesty, and above all his humility, with his genius and his courage. But Mrs. Dollfuss thought that my mention was superfluous, somehow indiscreet. I felt incredibly sorry about offending her, but I was also sorry about her tepid response to everything in the book which ought to have made her happy.

Domanig's response to my Dollfuss book was very great, which made me very happy. Domanig had been one of Dollfuss' closest friends, and it is from him that I had received most of my material for the book, above all the utterances of Dollfuss.

An official at the Ministry of Commerce by the name of Raimund Poukar, who had written various articles in many journals, increasingly became a collaborator of the *Ständestaat*. His articles were extremely useful, well written, and increasingly expressive of our basic orientation. It was very important for our journal that we also had many Austrian collaborators drawn from various circles and groups. This was so because Klaus and I often felt resistance toward us as "emigrants."

In the case of Austria, this was a particularly foolish objection considering that many of the greatest Austrian patriots were foreigners, and that it was precisely these foreigners who understood the phenomenon of Austria in a special way and in certain respects even embodied it—from Prince Eugene to Metternich, Schlegel, Gentz, and Pastor. Regardless of the stupidity of this prejudice, still we had to be concerned with the reputation and dissemination of our journal, and thus we sought to dispel this prejudice by presenting many Austrian voices in our pages. To this end, Poukar was very helpful. Other Austrian collaborators included Missong, Mataja, Count Dumba (the Austrian representative at the League of Nations), and Ender. Later on, there was a very intelligent Protestant from Hermannstadt,* along with various others whose names I have forgotten. A regular collaborator was Karpfen, the colleague of Hovorka.

I had been invited by Fr. Gemelli,† the rector of the Catholic University of the Sacred Heart in Milan, to give a lecture at the university. The subject was a critique of the foundations of National Socialism. The lecture went well and I succeeded in carrying out my critique of the totalitarian ideal of the state without offending various attendees who were Fascists. Of course, my critique was primarily directed toward elements that were entirely lacking in Fascism, such as racism.

Some years later, in 1938, Italy passed the first of its race laws, which severely restricted the rights of Jews. Even so, von Hildebrand means that racism was not intrinsic to Fascism as it was to Nazism, and in 1934 it was still possible to criticize racism to an audience of Fascists.

Regrettably, I spoke too freely in an interview that I gave, without considering what could be harmful to my effectiveness in Austria and to my battle there against National Socialism. I mentioned that my paternal grandmother was Jewish—a completely needless revelation, as I was soon to find out, because it was able to do great harm to my position in Austria and because it had no real importance. After all, this fact did

---

* The city of Sibiu in present-day Romania.

† Agostino Gemelli, OFM (1878–1959), Italian theologian, philosopher, and psychologist, founder of the Sacred Heart University in Milan.

not have the slightest influence on my stance and had never, even in the past, played any role in my life.

While focusing primarily on my love for Italy, the interview had mentioned my Jewish grandmother, which various "neutral" Austrian newspapers eagerly seized upon. In truth, I spoke about my Jewish grandmother because I was proud of her. It was certainly important not to conceal this fact artificially, and to allow myself to fall into the attitude of denying any trace of Jewish ancestry, which even many anti-Nazis did in Austria.

Yet in this case it was also a mistake not to recognize that, having not been asked, there was no reason to make this revelation. Doing so would decisively weaken my struggle, not just against National Socialism, but also against the moderate anti-Semitism in Austria, if people could say of me, "But of course, he is speaking on behalf of his own people." Soon after I heard that Funder—the same Funder who had received me with such incredible warmth in August 1933—had said of me, "Well, that was only said by the Jew Hildebrand." Through this interview I had become fully Jewish even in the eyes of someone who was relatively well disposed to me.

Let me briefly describe a visit from Ludi Pastor.* He came to see me and asked if I would consider accompanying him to Rome on a particular mission. Wilhelm Berliner, the leader of the Austrian branch of Phönix, a brilliant businessman and a major entrepreneur, wanted a report on the general climate of opinion toward Nazism in Vatican circles. Naturally, he would finance the journey. He was not just looking for a report from me, though this was the primary purpose; I was also supposed to brief these circles where possible. Ludi would accompany me on the trip. I could choose the time.

Ludi also intimated that I might be able to secure some support for my journal by talking with Berliner prior to the journey.† Apparently Berliner valued the journal and considered it very important. This of

---

* The son of historian Ludwig von Pastor.

† Berliner died suddenly in 1936 just as the scandal broke that "Phönix Wien" was in bankruptcy, having lost $150,000,000. Some historians suggest Berliner committed suicide.

course was very appealing for me, for it could lead to a source of support just when Schuschnigg was leaving me in the lurch as far as the journal was concerned. The trip to Rome was also very enticing, and I had especially high hopes for what might come out of an audience with the Secretary of State, Cardinal Pacelli, whom I knew so well from Munich.

At the end of 1934, von Hildebrand would finally be appointed as associate professor of philosophy at the University of Vienna.

Schuschnigg wanted to impose me on the faculty, not because he had any particular appreciation for me, but because Dollfuss had wanted it this way, and he wanted to be loyal to Dollfuss. This is the way things were around the middle of December 1934.

It was around this time that I made my first visit to Cardinal Innitzer.* In retrospect it now seems unlikely to me that I would only have visited him after being in Vienna for a full year; that would have been very impolite. I had probably visited him *pro forma* at the beginning, and this was the first time I had a serious conversation with him.

He received me with very great warmth. He said, "I am so happy that we finally have a practicing Catholic teaching in the philosophical faculty." It was a good conversation, and I was particularly pleased to hear him say that he had not received Papen and did not want to receive him. Before leaving I ventured to ask him for an article for the *Ständestaat*, and he agreed.

He embraced me as I left and I went home feeling quite satisfied at our meeting. I knew, of course, that he was a weak man. Though he was certainly a very warm and kind person, one said of him that he always agreed with the last person he spoke to. He was too weak to say "no"— except in matters of sin. And so I did not overrate his friendliness.

But I certainly did not expect from this meeting something I soon

---

* Theodore Cardinal Innitzer (1875–1955), archbishop of Vienna.

found out. Wilhelm Wolf came to Cardinal Innitzer asking him to sign a petition drawn up by Wolf and others and addressed to Schuschnigg: it was a petition requesting that I not be appointed professor. Wolf said to the Cardinal: for the sake of peace we have to prevent von Hildebrand from becoming professor, he will just stir up trouble. With this argument, or rather by means of this pressure brought to bear on the Cardinal, Wolf was able to get him to sign the petition. This happened soon after my meeting with the Cardinal and about two weeks before my appointment. Schuschnigg ignored the petition and appointed me in spite of it. He certainly realized that the Cardinal's signature on this petition was of little value.

1935

My appointment as associate professor of philosophy at the University of Vienna took place during this time, probably beginning January 1, 1935. Although my classes in the spring semester would only begin on February 1, my inaugural lecture, the official ceremonial event for an academic appointment, was scheduled for early January (sometime around January 10–12). I had sent numerous invitations to many friends, including quite probably all the participants of my evening discussions. The theme of my lecture was completely nonpolitical, a purely philosophical analysis of the difference between "value" and the "subjectively satisfying."

The lecture was set for the afternoon, at five o'clock. I arrived at the university fairly late. This was a bad habit I had formed in Munich, always rushing to my lecture at the last moment. In Munich I would ride my bike, arriving breathlessly, with just moments to spare, in fact often somewhat late. I did the same this day as well. Upon arriving at the university and seeing that it was already quarter after five, I paused for a moment to consider whether I should just go directly to the auditorium and hang my coat there rather than first going to the dean's office to deposit my things.

As I ascended the stairs, I passed a female student on her way down. Seeing that I was going up in haste, she said, "I assume you, too, want to attend Professor von Hildebrand's lecture. You won't be able to enter. The hall is packed." This news made me happy: I thought it bode well that my lecture could elicit such great interest. But upon entering the dean's office, I immediately realized that the reason for the crowded hall was in fact quite unfortunate. Looking pale as a ghost, Kralik[*] approached me and said, "My dear colleague, you cannot hold the lecture. A great demonstration has been launched against you."

"On the contrary," I replied, "there can be no question about my presenting my lecture. If I relent today, they will repeat the demonstration, and I will never be able to give the lecture." Standing next to Kralik was someone from the Ministry of Education, who was also very frightened. He too said, "It is impossible to hold the lecture." I renewed my insistence and explained what a defeat it would be for the government if students had only to hold a demonstration to prevent the lecture of a government-appointed professor. "We have to ask the Minister," replied the official. He telephoned Pernter,[†] the Minister of Education at the time, who of course agreed completely with my position and declared that the lecture had to take place at any cost.

A few minutes later, we were joined by the chief of security of the university, a former officer by the name of Baron Stein.[‡] As an attendee of my evening discussions, I already knew him. His political views were excellent. The position of chief of security of the university was a relatively new one. It involved working with the police to maintain order at the university, which was very necessary during these stormy political times. Baron Stein approached me and said, "You'll only have to wait a brief while. I'll soon have order restored, and then you can give your lecture. I have sent for forty-eight armed policemen who will remove the protestors. Your lecture will take place in another hall where only those with an invitation from you and those who are students in the division of humanities will be admitted."

After some waiting, Baron Stein came to get me. Passing many heavily armed police, we went through a special hallway into an auditorium where I could give my lecture. Thunderous applause greeted

---

[*] Dietrich von Kralik (1884–1959), son of von Hildebrand's friend Richard von Kralik and dean of the humanities faculty.

[†] Hans Pertner (1887–1951), official at the Austrian ministry of education who rose to become minister of education.

[‡] Karl von Stein, chief of security for the Austrian Student's Union.

me as I approached the podium. I can still see the tall, noble figure of Prince Schönburg as he stood clapping vigorously. Of course, this was the response to the demonstration of the Nazi students. Dispensing with any political remarks, I turned directly to delivering my properly philosophical text. After about ten minutes, a few students exited the auditorium, angrily slamming the door behind them.

Following my lecture I learned the following details. Professors in the faculties of medicine and law had used the classroom to incite their students to prevent my inaugural lecture through demonstrations and, where possible, through violence. The initiative thus came from the professors.

About six hundred students were present, of which very few belonged to the humanities division. They wanted to beat me up. Instead, they were greeted by the police who forced them out of the hall with batons. The students began singing "Deutschland, Deutschland über alles" and the *Horst-Wessel Lied,* but they were driven out of the university, where they then dispersed. Baron Stein then announced the new location for my lecture and that entry would be limited to those invited by me and those in the division of humanities.

None of the protestors were allowed to enter, though a few Nazis, who were in this division, did manage to enter. These were the same students who, disappointed and enraged, had then stormed out of the lecture. They had expected me to deliver a highly political lecture, which would have given them the chance to protest. My purely philosophical remarks bored them, of course, all the more so because they surely did not understand a word of what I said.

My debut at the University of Vienna was thus very tumultuous. But I was happy I had insisted that the lecture take place. I decided to ask several young men, who were members of a legitimist student organization and friends of Franzi, to attend the actual opening session of my class, which took place three weeks later. This was to protect me against any further harassment, unlikely as this seemed following the failure of the first demonstration.

. . .

It was just after this inaugural lecture that I traveled with Ludi to Rome. The evening before our departure, I had a lengthy discussion with Berliner, whom I met with Ludi in a café. Berliner began by reiterating what he expected from my information-gathering mission to Rome. Apparently he had great respect for the Church—as a moral and spiritual force, though for him the Church was, of course, a merely human institution. But because he considered the Church to be a great power, it was very important for him to know from reliable sources what the climate of opinion was in Rome toward National Socialism, including what people there saw as the likely future of Nazism. At the same time, he hoped that I would inform key people in the Vatican about Austria's situation.

Having discussed the trip, I broached the subject of the *Ständestaat* and its financial difficulties. I hoped to be able to convince him to contribute 600 schillings per month. This was too much, he countered: the most he could put at our disposal was 480 schillings per month. He understood how vital the continued existence of the journal was for the struggle against National Socialism, and so was ready to do something for it. But 480 schillings per month, around 5,700 annually, was the maximum. Even so, I was very relieved to secure his pledge.[*] The next day, Ludi and I made the journey to Rome.

Just before or after his trip to Rome, the referendum in the Saarland was held. The Saarland was a small area to the southwest of Germany, administered from 1920 to 1935 by France. Many opponents of the Nazis had fled there. Ninety-one percent of the population voted to join Germany.

Schuschnigg had decided to defend Germany's right to the Saarland. This disastrous decision was in part motivated by his "national" sentiments toward Germany. The Saarland was inhabited by Germans,

---

[*] Berliner continued to support the *Ständestaat* until his death in 1936.

by people who spoke German; thus Germany was well within its rights to demand that these Germans belong to Germany, at least, so Schuschnigg thought. Instead of seeing that the National Socialist regime was Germany's greatest enemy, and that it was fortunate for Germany if Germans there were living outside of the Third Reich, Schuschnigg allowed himself to be blinded by the notion of a national German state—for an Austrian, a particularly unfortunate error.

Schuschnigg also mistakenly believed that by making a friendly gesture toward Nazi Germany, i.e., by improving relations between Austria and Germany, he could bring Germany to recognize Austria's independence. This was a catastrophic error and a compete misjudgment of Hitler's mindset. Any concession in dealing with such a person only serves to whet their appetite, without in any way changing their stance toward the one making the concession. It is in fact typical of the mindset of totalitarian states, such as Nazi Germany and Soviet Russia, that they make their plans completely independent of the conduct of their opponents. It does not matter whether a country approaches a totalitarian state under friendly or hostile colors; it has absolutely no influence on how the totalitarian state will treat the other.

Suddenly we noticed that all the newspapers in Austria began expressing hope that the Saarland would vote to be incorporated into the Third Reich. I had no intention of joining this chorus, and we made very clear in our journal our conviction that the people of the Saarland, assuming they were even able to vote freely, would vote for their independence from the Third Reich. Even if they do not vote for incorporation into France, at the very least they would oppose incorporation into the Third Reich. Such a vote would have been of greatest significance, for it would have shown the world that the Nazi regime is not a true representative of the German nation.

Just at this time, we received a submission for the *Ständestaat* on a neutral theme from Minister Ludwig, who was clever and smooth-talking. I had to accept it, of course, as I could hardly reject an article from the Minister of the Press, from the man who at any moment could censor us. Being far cleverer and more adept than I at detecting things going on beneath the surface, Klaus immediately grasped Ludwig's

plan: he wanted to publish an article promoting the Schuschnigg position on the Saarland just before the referendum. To prevent this and
to protect our journal from being forced into "capitulation," we did the
typesetting on Wednesday instead of Thursday, as usual.

That Wednesday, Schuschnigg delivered a political speech in the
presence of an invited audience. I too had been invited. Upon arriving,
I ran into Ludwig, who greeted me very warmly. He thanked me for
accepting his article in our previous issue. Then he said, "Here, I have
another article for you. I'd ask you to include it in the upcoming issue."
I had no doubt that this was the article which would cause our journal
to "capitulate" on the Saarland question. I replied, "I would have been
delighted to publish your article, but the typesetting has already been
finished. I really have no way of getting it into the upcoming issue." He
was very disappointed.

Of course, as the referendum was already next Sunday, he did not
give me the article for the issue being typeset next week. Once the referendum was over, the article no longer had any significance, as it would
cease to be timely. I do not know if Ludwig ever noticed that we had
called his bluff and outwitted him, or if he believed that the typesetting
had been completed sooner than usual.

Schuschnigg's speech was in many ways depressing. While it made
clear that he was a noble person, with the best of intentions, it also revealed that he was politically clueless and burdened by German nationalist sympathies and ambiguous ideas about the brotherhood of blood.

At the end of his lecture, he read a letter that had been sent to him by
a German. Written with great warmth, the letter praised Schuschnigg
and sent him best wishes for the New Year. The author of the letter
was clearly an opponent of National Socialism, who therefore looked to
Austria and its struggle against National Socialism with great hope and
yearning. But Schuschnigg, who was apparently very happy about the
letter, said, "I don't know whether the sender is a National Socialist or
not. Regardless, the letter shows that it is possible to get along with a
German." I could hardly believe my ears!

When he should have recognized that the letter came from someone
who, filled with hope, saw him as the diametrical opposite of National

Socialism, that clearly this was someone unhappy about the Nazi regime; when he should also have felt compelled to carry on the uncompromising struggle against National Socialism for the sake of many unfortunate Germans; and when through this letter he should have been strengthened in this struggle, all Schuschnigg could take from the letter was that it was possible to get along with a German (by which he really meant with a National Socialist). The effect was to encourage a certain optimism, as if to say, "Really it isn't so bad, we can find a *modus vivendi*." I began to be increasingly concerned with the politics of Schuschnigg following this lecture.

Von Hildebrand now returns to recollections of his trip to Rome, which took place in early 1935.

My strongest recollections from this visit are of the audience I had with Secretary of State, Cardinal Pacelli. I had not seen him in a very long time, perhaps even since 1925—so not in ten years. After his previous guest had left, Pacelli came to the door where he greeted me with his charming, kind smile, saying, "E come va, e come va?" ("How is it going, how is it going?")—this repetition being especially typical of him. As in the past, I was again completely enchanted and delighted by his unique personality. He first asked me how I was doing, and I answered his questions.

Then I began to speak. "Do you know, Your Eminence, that there was a moment in Germany of the kind that only comes around every three or four centuries, a moment in which millions of Protestants and Socialists would have converted had the bishops in Germany spoken a completely uncompromising *"non possumus"* toward National Socialism, had they built up a wall against National Socialism and called its crimes by name, had they uttered a total anathema?" He replied, "Indeed, but martyrdom cannot be commanded from Rome. It must come about spontaneously."

And then he said to me, "What do you want, when even a good

friend of yours is enthusiastic about Hitler?" I knew to whom he was alluding, namely Baron Cramer-Klett.

So I said, "Yes, and what is worse is that even a friend of Your Eminence, Baron Cramer-Klett, has become enthusiastic for Hitler." He replied, "Yes, he is the one I had in mind."

When I told him about all the terrible deeds done in the name of National Socialism, he said, "You'd be amazed at what I said in my letters to Nuncio Orsenigo* I laid it out in black and white. If it comes to a break in relations with Germany, I will publish these letters." To which I exclaimed, "When will this blessed day come?" Naturally, we spoke to each other in Italian. As I described the situation in Austria, he said, "Indeed, Chancellor Schuschnigg is a courageous person."

Before leaving, I said to him, "Eminence, what does the future hold? How will things develop with National Socialism?" He replied, "It looks very serious; it will get bad if the moderate forces within National Socialism don't gain the upper hand." "Oh, don't say this, Eminence!" I cried out. "The moderate elements are the most dangerous. Far better that we have people like Rosenberg,† who drop their masks and openly reveal the absolute incompatibility of Nazism with Christian faith, than those who confuse and mislead Catholics by concealing their attack on Christ. It is not a question of moderate or radical. National Socialism in its very substance is filled with the spirit of the Antichrist." To this he replied, "Yes, you are right. Racism and Christianity are utterly incompatible, like fire and water. There is no room here for peace, there can be no bridge."

I was very pleased to hear him speak this way. Upon receiving his blessing, I departed. I was with him for perhaps an hour. Naturally we spoke of many things, but unfortunately this is all I can still remember in any detail. I was satisfied because I could see that he recognized the absolute incompatibility between National Socialism and the Church. But I also could see the incredibly complex and difficult situation of

---

* Cesare Orsenigo (1873–1946), the apostolic nuncio in Berlin.

† Alfred Rosenberg (1893–1946), the Nazis' major theoretician, notably through his 1930 book, *The Myth of the Twentieth Century*.

1. One of innumerable pages of outlines Dietrich produced in writing his memoirs. This page summarizes his several attempts to meet Austrian chancellor Engelbert Dollfuss to win his support in founding an anti-Nazi newspaper.

2. Dietrich's first major public clash with the Nazis took place in April 1921 when he denounced German nationalism at a peace conference organized by the French Catholic philosopher Marc Sangnier (second from right), depicted here in later years with a group of students.

3. Nazi Brownshirts look onto the crowd gathered on the Marienplatz in Munich during Hitler's attempted coup on November 9, 1923. The so-called Beer Hall Putsch forced Dietrich, who was on the Nazi blacklist, to flee Bavaria.

4. Hitler's appointment as German chancellor on January 30, 1933, played a crucial role in Dietrich's decision to leave Germany. Hitler is depicted here with his first cabinet. He is speaking with Franz von Papen, a Catholic who paved the way for Hitler's rise and who was later to propose a plan to assassinate Dietrich.

5. The decision to leave Munich when Hitler came to power in 1933 was "inexpressibly painful." It meant giving up their beautiful home at Maria-Theresia Strasse 23, above where Dietrich and Gretchen had lived since his parents' death in 1921 and where so much of Catholic life in Munich had been centered.

6. Dietrich's wife, Gretchen, as a young woman. Despite embarking on a path of total uncertainty, she committed herself unreservedly to her husband's fight against Nazism.

7. Chancellor Engelbert Dollfuss, pictured in 1933, welcomed Dietrich's proposal to found an anti-Nazi journal and committed the support of the Austrian government.

WAS WIR WOLLEN

Europa, das christliche Abendland, das wahre Deutschtum richten ihre Augen voll Erwartung auf Oesterreich, das den christlichen, deutschen Ständestaat zum Programm erwählt hat. Dieses Programm reicht weit über die Grenzen der Politik im engeren Sinn hinaus. Es erfordert eine tiefgehende, geistige Klärung weltanschaulicher Art. Falschen und verwirrten Vorstellungen, dem wirtschaftlichen Materialismus und dem Materialismus des Blutes, dem liberalen Individualismus und der heidnischen Staatsomnipotenz, müssen die großen klassischen Formulierungen abendländischen Denkens entgegengestellt werden. In einer Zeit der Abkehr von Irrtümern, die sich selbst ad absurdum geführt haben, aber auch einer Zeit neuer Gärung und Verwirrung müssen die ewigen, allgemein gültigen Ideen von Staat, Nation, Volksgemeinschaft, Recht, Autorität, Freiheit und Persönlichkeit klar herausgearbeitet werden. Es müssen verkehrten Gefühlen und Idealen die großen Traditionen wahren und echten Deutschtums, wie es in Oesterreich seine besonders schöne, allen zugängliche Ausprägung gefunden hat, entgegengestellt werden. Dieser Aufbau erfordert eine geistige Erneuerung, eine innere Umkehr in den führenden Schichten der Intelligenz, die zum Unterschied von weiten übrigen Teilen des Volkes noch zögernd und abwartend beiseite stehen.

Die Arbeit an dieser Aufgabe Oesterreichs hat aber weit über die Grenzen Oesterreichs hinaus entscheidende Bedeutung. Für die deutschen Minderheiten in erster Linie — aber auch für alle großen und kleinen Staaten Europas, in denen die Zeitwende sich geltend macht.

Der ideologischen Eroberung Oesterreichs für seine Aufgabe will diese Zeitschrift dienen. Abseits von aller Parteipolitik will sie helfen, die ganze Fülle klar herauszuarbeiten und zu vollem blühenden Leben zu entfalten, die in dem Wort des Mannes enthalten sind, dem die Führung Oesterreichs in eine große, wahrhaft deutsche, christliche Zukunft anvertraut ist: „Austriam instaurare in Christo."

---

8. This mission statement appeared in the inaugural issue of Dietrich's Vienna journal in December 1933. It includes these key lines:

Our Purpose

The eyes of Europe, of the Christian West, of the true German world, look with high hopes to Austria, which has chosen the path of a Christian, German corporative state. The significance of this path extends far beyond the boundary of politics (taken in the narrow sense). It is a path that calls for deep philosophical clarification of first principles. The great teachings of classical Western thought have to be opposed to various false and confused conceptions, to economic materialism and to racial materialism, to liberal individualism, and to pagan conceptions of unlimited state sovereignty. At a time of great ferment and confusion, when certain errors are being abandoned because they have proved to be unlivable, we have to present clearly the eternal, universally valid ideas of state, nation, people, right and wrong, authority, freedom, and personality. Against disordered feelings and ideals we have to set the great traditions of true and genuine German culture as it is expressed in Austria in a particularly beautiful and universally accessible way. This cultural structure must be renewed from within; an inner conversion is needed in the cultural elites, which in contrast to large sectors of the population stand irresolutely on the sidelines waiting to see what will happen.

(2) Abf. 1 gilt nicht für Beamte, die bereits seit dem 1. August 1914 Beamte gewesen sind oder die im Weltkrieg an der Front für das Deutsche Reich oder für seine Verbündeten gekämpft haben oder deren Väter oder Söhne im Weltkrieg gefallen sind."

Die oben genannte Verordnung bestimmt zu § 3 in Nr. 2:

„(1) Die erste Ausnahme des § 3 Abf. 2 ist gegeben, wenn der Beamte bereits am 1. August 1914 planmäßiger Beamter gewesen und seitdem ununterbrochen Beamter geblieben ist. Einem planmäßigen Beamten in diesem Sinne kann gleichgestellt werden, wer am 1. August 1914 sämtliche Voraussetzungen für die Erlangung seiner ersten planmäßigen Anstellung erfüllt, insbesondere die hierfür erforderliche letzte Prüfung mit Erfolg abgelegt und sich während seiner Tätigkeit als Beamter in hervorragendem Maße bewährt hat.

(2) Eine Tätigkeit als Angestellter oder Arbeiter im öffentlichen Dienst am 1. August 1914 genügt nicht."

4. Haben Sie im Weltkrieg an der Front für das Deutsche Reich oder für seine Verbündeten gekämpft? *Nein. Erst freiwilliger Krankenpfleger im Lazarett – Lazarettzug – dann Aussortierlazarett z. Januar*

Der Begriff „Frontkämpfer" ist im Sinne des Gesetzes zur Wiederherstellung des Berufsbeamtentums vom 7. April 1933 zu verstehen. Hierüber bestimmt die Dritte Verordnung zur Durchführung des Gesetzes zur Wiederherstellung des Berufsbeamtentums vom 6. Mai 1933 (RGBl. I S. 245) zu § 3 in Nr. 3:

„(1) Frontkämpfer im Sinne des Gesetzes ist, wer im Weltkrieg (in der Zeit vom 1. August 1914 bis 31. Dezember 1918) bei der fechtenden Truppe an einer Schlacht, einem Gefecht, einem Stellungskampf oder an einer Belagerung teilgenommen hat. Auskunft darüber geben die Eintragungen in der Kriegsstammrolle oder in der Kriegsrangliste. Es genügt nicht, wenn sich jemand, ohne vor den Feind gekommen zu sein, während des Krieges aus dienstlichem Anlaß im Kriegsgebiet aufgehalten hat.

(2) Frontkämpfer ist insbesondere, wem das Abzeichen für Verwundete verliehen worden ist.

(3) Die Teilnahme an den Kämpfen im Baltikum, in Oberschlesien, gegen Spartakisten und Separatisten sowie gegen die Feinde der nationalen Erhebung sind der Teilnahme an den Kämpfen des Weltkrieges gleichzustellen."

5. Sind Sie Sohn (Tochter) oder Vater eines im Weltkrieg Gefallenen? . . . . *Nein*

Der Begriff „gefallen" ist im Sinne des Gesetzes zur Wiederherstellung des Berufsbeamtentums vom 7. April 1933 zu verstehen. Hierüber bestimmt die Dritte Verordnung zur Durchführung des Gesetzes zur Wiederherstellung des Berufsbeamtentums vom 6. Mai 1933 (RGBl. I S. 245) zu § 3 in Nr. 4:

„ „Gefallen" ist auch, wer einer Verwundung erlegen ist, die er als Frontkämpfer erlitten hat."

Das in Ziffer 4 Gesagte gilt entsprechend.

6. a) Sind Sie arischer Abstammung im Sinne der Ersten Verordnung zur Durchführung des Gesetzes zur Wiederherstellung des Berufsbeamtentums vom 11. April 1933 (RGBl. I S. 195) zu § 3, Nr. 2 Abf. 1? *Nein*

Diese Vorschrift lautet:

„Als nicht arisch gilt, wer von nicht arischen, insbesondere jüdischen Eltern oder Großeltern abstammt. Es genügt, wenn ein Elternteil oder ein Großelternteil nicht arisch ist. Dies ist insbesondere dann anzunehmen, wenn ein Elternteil oder ein Großelternteil der jüdischen Religion angehört hat."

Entscheidend ist aber nicht die Religion, sondern die Rassezugehörigkeit der vier Großeltern.

b) — wenn 6a zu verneinen ist —:
Welcher Großelternteil oder welche Großelternteile sind nichtarischer, insbesondere jüdischer Abkunft? . . . . *Grossmutter väterlicherseits jüdischer Rasse, protestantischer Konfession*

9. In his memoirs, Dietrich describes the questionnaire on racial purity sent by the University of Munich to all faculty in 1933. His response was an act of open defiance. He notes that his paternal grandmother was Jewish but was baptized Protestant as a child. Under the German race laws, he could therefore have considered himself non-Jewish. But he was fundamentally opposed to the question itself—thus his firm "Nein"—"no" in response to question 6a, "Are you of Aryan descent?"

10. Klaus Dohrn, a relative of Dietrich's sister Eva by marriage, was his key initial partner in developing a "Catholic, antiracist, and anti-totalitarian journal." Here Dohrn is pictured in 1942.

11. Dietrich was deeply concerned that the Concordat between the Holy See and Germany could easily mislead ordinary Catholics into thinking that the Church had endorsed Nazism. This photo was taken at the signing of the Concordat on July 20, 1933. To the far left is Monsignor Ludwig Kaas, whose birthday telegram to Hitler outraged Dietrich. German vice chancellor Franz von Papen sits next to Kaas, and at the center is Vatican secretary of state, Cardinal Eugenio Pacelli.

12. Kurt von Schuschnigg, the Austrian chancellor after Dollfuss' murder, hoped to defend Austrian independence by pursuing a policy of peaceful coexistence with Nazi Germany. When they met in the United States many years later, Schuschnigg acknowledged to Dietrich that he had been right about the true nature of the Third Reich.

13. Franz von Papen became German ambassador to Austria in 1934. In 1937, Papen complained to Dietrich's brother-in-law, "That damned Hildebrand is the greatest obstacle to National Socialism in Austria. No one does more harm!"

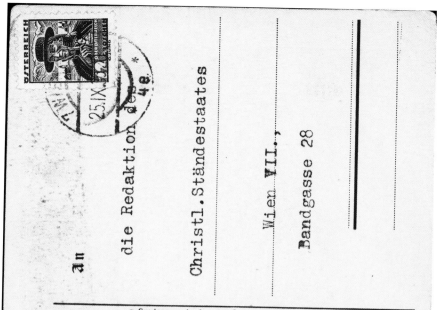

An

die Redaktion des

Christl.Ständestaates

Wien VII.,

Bandgasse 28

Nichts kennzeichnet Euere Einstellung
zur"christl.Moral"besser,als dass der
alte Gauner Mataja,die Mizzi Schmidt,
der sein ergaunertes Geld unter fremden
Namen verheimlichte,Euer Mitarbeiter ist
Und er wagt es vom Evangelium zu schrei-
ben!Seine Zeilen triefen von Religiösi-
tät.Ja,so seid Ihr`alle,Ihr Lumpen!!!
Ihr wisst genau warum Ihr alle zusammen
"kämpft"--!Die Vaugoins,Matajas,Seifert
Schmitz,Kimmels,Poukars usw.sie alle
sind Haderlumpen und tief religiöse
Mitarbeiter des Juden---Hildebrandt-!
Eine feine Richtung !!!!

14. A caustic message sent to the Vienna editorial offices of Dietrich's journal in September 1936. The author expresses the anti-Semitism Dietrich had to combat even among fellow Christians. It concludes, "All of you know the real reason for your struggle. Each of you good-for-nothings—Vaugoin, Mataja, Seifert, Schmitz, Kimmel, Poukar, etc.—are in fact extremely religious collaborators of that Jew Hildebrand! What a contemptible point of view!"

15. One of the most outspoken Catholic apologists for Nazism was German bishop Alois Hudal. Dietrich countered one of Hudal's books with a scathing review in his journal.

16. At the University of Vienna, Dietrich found virtually no support for his anti-Nazi work among his fellow Catholic colleagues. But an outspoken fellow warrior was the philosopher Moritz Schlick, whose logical positivism could hardly have been more at odds with Dietrich's philosophical outlook. Yet the two found common cause in the battle against Nazism.

17. Selections from a secret dispatch to Hitler from the then-Nazi ambassador in Austria, Franz von Papen. Though Papen does not explicitly use the term "assassination," Dietrich had learned that a decision had been made to kill him. So it is reasonable to assume that Papen was not only referring to assassination but was perhaps even the instigator of the plan.

Streng geheim!

Inhalt:
"Der Reichsbund für deutsche Freiheit."
(Drei Durchschl. an A.A.)

Vor kurzem wurde hier, wie auch die "Essener Nationalzeitung " schon berichtet hat, ein "Reichsbund für deutsche Freiheit" gegründet. Diese Organisation, deren

As the *Essen National Times* has already reported, a *National Union for German Liberation* was recently established here. This organization...

Dostali sind, erstrebt den Sturz des nationalsozialistischen Regimes und versucht, die Gegner des nationalsozialistischen Deutschlands unter einheitlicher Leitung zu sammeln. Als Inspirator steht hinter diesen Machenschaften der sattsam bekannte ausgebürgerte Emigrant Professor Dietrich von Hildebrandt, der Herausgeber des " Christlichen Ständestaates ". Der " Reichsbund für deutsche

seeks to overthrow the Nazi regime and is trying to unite the enemies of Nazi Germany under a single leadership. The mastermind behind these intrigues is the well-known expatriate emigrant Professor Dietrich von Hildebrand, editor of the weekly journal, Christliche Standestaat...

Der Wichtigkeit halber und im Hinblick auf die Möglichkeit, durch eine Warnung Spuren verwischen zu können, habe ich das angegebene Material sofort an den Reichsführer der SS Himmler gesandt.

Because of the importance of this matter and fearful that the suspects might be warned and their tracks covered, I have immediately sent copies of the enclosed documents to the Director of the SS, Himmler...

bostel.
Ich sehe die Möglichkeit, einen ganz grossen Schlag gegen diese schlimmsten und gefährlichsten Feinde des Reiches in Österreich führen zu können. Zu diesem Zwecke bitte ich, das

We may be able to strike a severe blow against these extremely evil and dangerous enemies of the Reich in Austria....

An den   Legitimisten der Richtung Dr.v.Wiesners.
Führer und Reichskanzler,   ./.
        B e r l i n .
        durch Kurier.

E272603

● Gogo   Mimoires.

11 Maerz 1938: ich erwarte Shuster um ihnen meinen Möbel zu
                verkaufen. In meiner Wohnung befanden sich: Gilbert
Gretchen. Amata. der jüdische Rechtsanwalt. Kustan (Lindie) Muihi-
Um 6 Uhr meldete das Radio dass die Abstimmung abgesagt sei.
Um 6 Uhr 15 erschien Frau Shuster. und ich vollzog die Erklärung
des Verkaufes der Möbel. als Zeugen: der Rechtsanwalt und
Lindie Kustan. Um 7 Uhr. die Meldung dass Schuschnigg abgedankt
hat. Als Schluss spielte das Radio den Quartett Satz von Schubert.
und das Kaiser Quartett von Haydn.
Um 8 Uhr telefoniert mir Klaus: ultimissimo Momento.
Wir packten rasch das Wichtigste zusammen. und ich ging
um 8:45 ohne Gepäck mit Gilbert und Muihi um ein Taxi
zu finden. Ich fand 2 Taxis: in dem einen fuhr Muihi an
meiner Wohnung um Gretchen. Amata. Koffer zu holen.
Ich fuhr an den ... West Bahnhof. nach ¼ Stunde Bangen Warten
trafen (Muihi) Gretchen. Amata ein.
Der Zug ging um 9:10. Voll besetzt mit zitternden Juden und
ein Grauenvoller Nazi. er schaute volle Stunde auf seinen
Opfer in allen Coupés. An der Grenze, mussten allen aussteigen
(Marchegg) hiess die Grenze. Allen Österreicher wurden die
Ausreise verboten. Ich stieg mit Gr. und Amata in einen
anderen Zug der zur Fahrt nach Pressburg bestimmt war.
Zu dem Coupé, ... ein Deutscher Herr mit einem Ausland
Pass. Der Pass Beamter stieg ein zu Untersuchung, Gr. und
ich zeigten unser Schweizer Passe. In meinem Pass
stand: Univ. Professor. aber nicht wo. Darunter stand
der Heimatsort. Zürich. Der Beamter fragte mich ob ich
Professor in Zürich sei. Ich sagte: Ja. Als Univ. Professor
in Wien, wäre ich beschränkter Staatsbürger.

18. Just three days before his death on January 26, 1977, Dietrich
added gripping details about his final escape from Vienna on March
11, 1938, in a dictation to his wife, Alice von Hildebrand. He
noted, "At seven o'clock, we learned that Schuschnigg had stepped
down [as Austrian chancellor]. In closing the radio played the
Quartettsatz of Schubert and the *Emperor Quartet* of Haydn."

19. On March 1, 1938, Hellmut Laun (pictured) drove Dietrich and Gretchen to the Czech border in what they perceived as a desperate escape. Though it turned out to be a false alarm, the real escape took place just ten days later.

20. Hitler arrived in Vienna on March 14, 1938. Here he is greeted by jubilant crowds.

21. After their flight from Vienna on March 11, 1938, Dietrich and Gretchen spent several weeks at the home of his student, Balduin Schwarz, near Fribourg, Switzerland. Pictured at the Schwarzes, he briefly sported a beard for disguise.

22. Edmond Michelet (left) saved the lives of Dietrich and his family by providing false French identity papers. This meant the Hildebrands did not have to register with the French authorities, who would have been required to turn them over to the Nazis. Michelet and Dietrich are pictured here together in 1946.

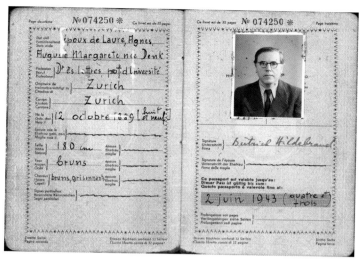

23. Dietrich would not have been able to leave Vienna after Hitler's invasion had he possessed only an Austrian or German passport. But thanks to his grandfather, he was also a Swiss citizen. His concern was shared by other leading figures, including his friend Eugenio Cardinal Pacelli, Vatican secretary of state. The original Swiss passport used in fleeing Vienna is probably lost, but this passport, issued in 1940, tells the story—in its many visas—of his desperate escape from France and from Europe in 1940. The French exit visa (bottom right) was provided by a French Catholic embassy official who was fired for issuing false papers to refugees. Dietrich had to entrust his family's passports to this man over the weekend, hoping against hope that they would be returned with the necessary visas.

24. A photo from the final leg of the escape from Europe, the voyage by ship from Rio de Janeiro to New York in December 1940. Gretchen looks out smiling while Dietrich sits third from right. Also pictured is the eminent German philosopher of education, Friedrich Wilhelm Foerster (second from left) [and his wife], who enriched Dietrich's grasp of the poison of nationalism.

25. Dietrich and Gretchen with their granddaughter, Catherine von Hildebrand, on the ship en route to New York.

the Church, which had to consider the twenty-five million Catholics in Germany.

Von Hildebrand had a very high regard for Eugenio Pacelli, papal nuncio to Germany (1917–1929), cardinal secretary of state (1930–1939), and Pope Pius XII (1939–1958). He always believed that Pacelli's anti-Nazi stand merited praise.

The second interesting visit I made was to Monsignor Kaas. We had on various occasions criticized him in the *Ständestaat*. One time, in response to a rumor that he had been transferred to South America, we even expressed our delight that his dangerous influence would come to an end. Paying him a visit was not a pleasure. But I think it was actually Monsignor Kaas who had expressed the desire that I come.

He began speaking to me as I was still at the door, and before I could even say a word of greeting. He burst out, "You are doing me a grave injustice. I'm in no way guilty for the position of the German Center Party." And then he began a desperate apologia in which he heaped all the blame on Brüning while presenting himself as a clear opponent of National Socialism. I no longer remember all that I said to Monsignor Kaas, or whether I brought up the telegram he had sent congratulating Hitler on his birthday in April 1933. At any rate, it was an unpleasant conversation. He did not convince me, but then I was in no position to judge whether his accusation of Brüning had any merit. In general, however, his conduct smacked a little of *"qui s'excuse, s'accuse"* ("He who excuses himself accuses himself").

Upon returning to Vienna, one of my first orders of business was to meet with the chief of the secret police, Mr. Weiser.* He had expressed

---

* Ludwig Weiser (1887–1944).

the desire that I pay him a visit. I was very curious to find out what he wanted from me, and since, because of my trip to Rome some time had passed since he had initially asked me to come, I hurried to see him as soon as possible.

As I entered the room and introduced myself, he said to me, "How do you feel?" He was a very intelligent-looking Sherlock Holmes type, with strong, clear features and a calm and expressionless face. I did not understand what he was getting at, but answered, "I feel very well." He proceeded, "You know, as chief of the secret police, a political murder would be very unpleasant for me." Of course, I immediately understood his allusion. "Indeed," I said, "that would be extremely awkward for me as well." He replied, "We have our spies, of course, who find out what is going on in the Nazi underground, things about which you could hardly be aware. We know that it has been decided to get rid of you. You must therefore take special measures to protect yourself. Is your name listed on the door of your home?"

"Of course," I answered. "This is a great mistake," he continued. "Not only must your name disappear from your door, it should not even be listed in the telephone book or address directory. Do you receive people at home who you do not know?" "Yes," I said, "refugees from Germany often come to me. Naturally, I always receive them."

He replied, "This is a great mistake. Any Nazi can present himself as a refugee. You cannot allow anyone into your home if you do not know exactly who they are. You cannot receive anyone alone unless they are very close friends. Someone must always be present as a witness. A favorite trick of these people is to force a chloroform mask over someone's head and then to suffocate them. By the time your wife happens to come into the room and find you, the murderer will long be gone. You also cannot ever get into a car if you do not know exactly who is driving, nor can you ever go alone to an appointment arranged by telephone, unless you can determine with certainty that the voice on the phone is that of a friend you know well. Be on guard for anyone who might be following you, or when someone appears at your home behaving suspiciously. As soon as you notice anything of the sort, please notify me immediately." Finally, he said, "It could be that they will be content to put out your eyes instead of killing you."

I thanked him profusely for his warning. Naturally, it made a certain impression on me, but I cannot say it even crossed my mind to withdraw, that is, to give up my political activities to avoid danger.

Though I am fearful of physical dangers, I was not afraid; I was not intimidated by what Weiser had said. I had the consciousness that I was conducting a struggle willed by God, and this gave me an incredible inner freedom. On the other hand, Weiser's words had a very unsettling effect on poor Gretchen, when I later recounted them to her. From then on she lived in great anxiety over my life, even accompanying me to my classes, despite the fact that there was no particular danger along the way, nor would she have been any protection in an assassination attempt.

As I already described, a group of legitimist students attended my first class to protect me in the event of any demonstrations by Nazi students. But there were no further demonstrations and the course proceeded in a calm and matter-of-fact way. The actual number of attendees was satisfactory (my bodyguards came only the first time and not as participants in the class). There were perhaps twenty-five students.

I had gotten to know various musicians while I was in Vienna, perhaps through Klemperer. One of them was Krenek,* whose opera *Jonny spielt auf* I had heard in Munich. Now Krenek had composed an opera called *Charles V*, regrettably on an atonal basis. He had completely immersed himself into the world of the Church through the libretto, which he had written himself. He was a Catholic, though he had lost his faith and now was coming back to the Church. Naturally this drew me to him greatly, while his interest in me was probably motivated by the fact that he was seeking contact with Catholics.

I often visited him, and he would play for me passages from his *Charles V* and try to win me for atonality. In this he did not succeed. On the contrary, I regretted the fact that he, whose talents one could not

---

* Ernst Krenek (1900–91).

deny, had committed himself to atonality. The text of the piece was very good. Krenek's political orientation was excellent. He was a stimulating and interesting human being, and my interaction with him was enriching. Sometimes he would write something for our journal.

The other musician I got to know was Wellesz,[*] a Jew who had become Catholic. He was assistant professor of music history at the University of Vienna as well as a composer. He was hardly of Krenek's stature, yet he was far more conceited and convinced of his talents. Through good connections, he had managed to get an honorary doctorate from Oxford, which no German musician since Haydn had received. He told me this with great pride, while mentioning a letter in which someone had said to him, "You write history and you make history."

Krenek and Wellesz became attendees of my evening discussions. Krenek also introduced us to a friend of his, Dr. Willi Reich. He was a music critic, and I liked him very much as well. He had a great love for the Church and was very drawn to Catholicism. Later, he asked me to bring him to a priest since he wanted to convert. But this was much later.

On one occasion, we were invited for tea at the home of Alma Mahler-Werfel.[†] There we also met Alban Berg, the atonal composer, who had written, among other things, the opera *Wozzeck*. He struck me as very unostentatious and modest, but also earnest and dignified. There was a nobility in the expression of his face. I still remember how in the conversation about Nazism, Franz Werfel spoke critically about Wagner, whereupon his wife exclaimed, "Hands off my gods—Alban, come to my aid in the defense of Wagner!" Naturally, my contributions to this discussion went exactly in the same direction. I was happy about Mrs. Mahler's love and reverence for Wagner, and especially about Alban Berg's stance toward Wagner.

I met several other people at this tea. I particularly remember a

---

[*] Egon Wellesz (1885–1974).

[†] Alma Mahler-Werfel (1879–1964), wife of composer Gustav Mahler (1860–1911). Following his death she married, first, the architect Walter Gropius, and later the writer and poet Franz Werfel (1890–1969).

completely unique and angelic figure, the daughter of Alma Mahler from her marriage to the architect Gropius. She was about twenty-two. There was something unbelievably pure and kind about her. This purity was especially conspicuous considering the milieu in which she had grown up, both in regard to Alma and also to Mahler's daughter Anna (whose married name was Zsolnay). This girl possessed something extraordinarily pure, otherworldly, gentle, and kind.* One could not but love her. I am sure this visit did not take place any later than the winter of 1934/35.

It must also have been around this time that a Hungarian by the name of Thewrewk-Pallaghy visited me.† He was an ardent legitimist and knew several archduchesses. He was an assistant professor of history and also held a post in the Hungarian Ministry of War in Budapest. His political orientation could not have been better, and he was also a pious Catholic.

He invited me with great urgency to give a lecture in Budapest which he wanted to arrange under the auspices of an institute for foreign affairs. My trip to Hungary was also to include a visit to the Benedictine monastery in Pannonhalma, where the abbot, who knew my books, had warmly invited me to spend several days. All this was very appealing, and I told Thewrewk-Pallaghy that in principle I would like to come to Budapest to speak there, which pleased him greatly.

I had been invited to give a lecture in Salzburg about Emperor Charles on the occasion of his death anniversary (April 1). The invitation came in the name of various legitimist groups in Salzburg. Since the death of Dollfuss, I had become increasingly active in legitimist circles. The more I became disappointed by the political orientation of Schuschnigg, the more I saw only one real solution for Austria's

---

* The girl's name was Manon and she died soon after. Alban Berg dedicated his 1935 violin concerto to her ("to the memory of an angel").

† Attila von Thewrewk-Pallaghy (1901–89), historian, contributed several articles to the *Ständestaat* in the first half of 1935.

independence in the long term, namely the return of the Habsburgs, i.e., of a constitutional monarchy.

The new Austrian constitution, now that Dollfuss was no longer alive, did not seem to have a future. It had been robbed of its soul, and there was no longer any hope that it would take the form that Dollfuss would surely have given it. In the hands of Schuschnigg, it became something formal and empty. A constitutional monarchy, on the other hand, which would gather all true Austrian patriots, which would definitively banish all talk of a greater Germany and all Anschluss-ideals, a monarchy in the spirit of Emperor Charles, this I thought would be the true antithesis of National Socialism and of all German nationalism.

For this reason, I focused more and more on these circles and spoke increasingly at legitimist gatherings. There were also many Jews among the legitimists, so that I was often invited to speak before an exclusively Jewish audience of legitimists. My relentless struggle against all forms of anti-Semitism made me extremely popular in these Jewish circles. Often I would begin my lectures with an absolute condemnation of anti-Semitism, adding, "I condemn anti-Semitism with all my heart because I am a Catholic. Anti-Semitism and Catholicism are absolutely irreconcilable." My words would be greeted with thunderous applause.

My lecture, which took place in the evening, proceeded splendidly. It was well attended and I was very much "in form." The theme was very near and dear to my heart and allowed me to connect the true mission and nature of Austria with a treatment of the saintly figure of Emperor Charles. The lecture was a great success and a source of great joy for me.

Upon returning to Vienna, I learned from Hefel* that they wanted to move into the apartment where we were living at the Stephansplatz in the fall of 1935. We had foreseen this possibility, and it was the condition under which they had made the apartment available to us. This meant that we had to move before the summer holiday, and so we began searching for a beautiful and suitable apartment. Naturally, if at all pos-

---

* Ernst Hefel (1888–1974).

sible we wanted to stay within the Inner City, i.e., in the First District of the city of Vienna, which architecturally is by far the most beautiful.

It was not until late June, or even early July, that we found a suitable and very beautiful apartment in the Palais Cabriani located on Habsburgergasse, and we moved at the end of July. The Palais was a very beautiful Baroque building—probably from the beginning of the 18th century—far more beautiful than the house where we lived by St. Stephen's Cathedral. Of course, we lost the magnificent view of St. Stephen's, but on the whole our new surroundings were architecturally much more beautiful.

In the course of May 1935, I received the official invitation to lecture in Budapest from the institute devoted to issues of foreign affairs. This made me happy because I was very interested in getting to know all the people whom Thewrewk-Pallaghy had told me about, and because I was attracted to the Hungarian milieu as a whole. I was also happy for the opportunity to fight the Nazis in Hungary and to lend support to the cause of legitimism.

On the other hand, in light of what Weiser had told me about the intention to eliminate me, a trip to Hungary, where, unlike Austria, the Nazis could move about freely and without restraints, did pose a certain risk. The Nazis would often wait until a politically undesirable person was traveling and then do away with them. So I resolved to take Franzi along with me as a bodyguard.

But Franzi's protection did not suffice for Gretchen. Without even the slightest mention, she wrote a letter to Schuschnigg describing the danger I faced. "Surely, Herr Kanzler," she wrote, "you are in far greater danger, but you are surrounded by detectives who can protect you, while my husband is completely vulnerable. Now that he is going to Budapest, he is especially in need of protection." That, anyway, was the gist of her letter. It was somehow typical of Gretchen's character. She was by nature reserved and reluctant to step into the foreground or to make any special demands. Yet if it was a matter that affected someone else, especially me, and if she became outraged or felt impelled to intervene, she could suddenly become very courageous and even quite sharp in her manner. It is true that she had to act in the moment, for once she reentered her normal rhythm, she no longer had the strength to assert herself in this way. I departed for Budapest with Franzi without knowing anything about Gretchen's intervention.

As we arrived, Baron Thewrewk-Pallaghy was at the train station to greet me. He was accompanied by a man I did not know. He introduced himself as a detective by the name of Del Medico. I was quite surprised that a detective should come to pick me up. But then I concluded this was perhaps a standard precaution when a politically controversial figure like myself came to speak publicly in Budapest. Del Medico was a very nice and friendly man. He told me that he had been assigned to accompany me everywhere and that I was not permitted to go anywhere without him. We went straight to the hotel.

Del Medico brought us to our room but first carefully inspected everything, the closet, under the bed, etc., to make sure that a bomb had not been hidden somewhere. Having found nothing suspicious, he allowed us to enter. I believe this took place the evening before I was scheduled to give my talk. I no longer recall how long we stayed in Budapest, but so many events took place that it must have been two or three days. I do remember that after dinner Del Medico brought us back to our room. Having once again checked carefully, he told us that we could not leave the room until he came to fetch us the next day. Indeed, our room was to be locked from outside. This greatly displeased me, as I wanted to go to mass the next morning and Del Medico told me that he would only come to get us at 9:00 a.m. By then it would be too late to attend mass. I suddenly felt that I was a prisoner. I could not conceive of a satisfactory explanation for my predicament. Only when I returned to Vienna, where Gretchen told me about her letter to Schuschnigg and showed me a copy, did I finally understand why I had been so carefully guarded in Budapest.

The next morning, as Thewrewk-Pallaghy drove us to see the cathedral and the royal palace, Del Medico noticed a car that seemed to be following us. He became concerned and had our car stopped. As he strode toward the other car, he signaled for it to stop as well. It turned out to be harmless tourists and not at all the assassins Del Medico feared.

My lecture took place in the afternoon. It was held in the parliamentary building, where I was warmly greeted and escorted in by Bersewicki, the old president (then about eighty years old) of the institute on foreign affairs that had invited me. Quite a crowd had come, above all many legitimists, retired generals, and aristocrats. My lecture was warmly received. Speaking in this setting, which still embodied so much of the old Habsburg monarchy, I felt transported into a beautiful cultural atmosphere. This trip to Budapest granted me a much richer contact with Hungary, which has its great charm, than I had experienced in the summer of 1934 when I had visited with Marguerite.

I still remember going to a Hungarian restaurant that evening. Again, Del Medico entered first to search for anything that might be suspicious. Only after he had completed his inspection was I allowed to enter.

I also paid a visit to Fr. Anton Schütz, who had come to see me in Munich and who was so enthusiastic about the afternoon gatherings I had hosted. He had been the confessor of the famous Archbishop Prohászka.[*] But I was deeply disappointed when I saw that Fr. Schütz, from whom I expected so much, sympathized with the Nazis. He urged me to write purely philosophical books and to give up the journal. I was appalled, but none of my arguments succeeded in convincing him otherwise.

Thewrewk-Pallaghy took me to meet a very talented journalist who edited a journal. I met him on the last morning of my stay in Budapest on Margaret Island. His name was Eugen Katona. The actual publisher of the journal was Count Széchenyi.[†] I think it was only later that I got to know Széchenyi when he came to see me in Vienna; on this trip to Budapest I was not yet acquainted with him.

Katona struck me as a very likeable person, and we had a very animated conversation. He was of course an opponent of Nazism, yet he

---

[*] Bishop Ottokár Prohászka (1858–1927), theologian and Catholic bishop of the Hungarian diocese of Székesfehérvár.

[†] Katona and Count Georg Széchenyi, editor and publisher, respectively, of the journal *Korunk Szava*. Both wrote several essays for *Der christliche Ständestaat*.

made a point of saying that he was attracted to the revolutionary and dynamic aspects of National Socialism. I objected vigorously by showing him that there was nothing natural or organic about National Socialism as a movement, which in no way deserved to be called "alive," but that the pressure of brutal terror had given rise to a purely artificial conformity.

I did not have to convince him of the Antichrist in National Socialism, nor of its diabolical immorality. Being a pious Catholic, he already saw this clearly. Yet at the time he was clearly still somewhat under the influence of trends in the youth culture, which greatly overrated dynamic movement as such. Katona would later be completely freed of these ideas.

Back in Vienna, von Hildebrand and his wife were invited to dinner at the Kraliks with others from the humanities division at the university.

This was the evening I made the acquaintance of Moritz Schlick.[*] He greeted me very warmly, in no way disguising his delight that I was now a member of the faculty—his words, I think, were "that a man of your political orientation is joining our faculty." Philosophically, Schlick and I could not have been further apart. Every one of the bland and insignificant philosophers in the department was closer to me in philosophical regard than Schlick. And yet it was only Schlick who greeted me in a cordial and friendly way.

This was how much a person's political stance took precedence at that moment, when the real line of separation was one's bearing toward National Socialism. It was this question which determined whether someone was seen as friend or foe. This flowed from the fact, first, that a person's stance toward National Socialism was not just a question of politics but of first principles. But then it was also a matter of extraordinary immediacy.

---

[*] Moritz Schlick (1882–1936), leader of the Vienna Circle of logical positivists.

These two factors gave the question a priority over all the other points of difference and commonality that otherwise played a role. I felt closer to a believing Protestant who was an unambiguous opponent of National Socialism than I did to a Catholic who was a Nazi. I even felt a greater solidarity with Schlick than I did with a philosopher who had been "infected" by Nazism, despite the fact that Schlick was an atheist who belonged to the most awful philosophical school, and that I considered everything he taught to be totally false and extremely harmful.

As the general conversation touched variously on occurrences in Nazi Germany, the other professors limited themselves to neutral observations. Only Schlick expressed his full agreement with my clear condemnation of what had happened.

It must already have been this year that Kestranek[*] came to visit me. An attendee of my classes in Munich, he had impressed me by his warmth, his faith, and his intellectual openness. I was very happy to see him again. Of course, he was a strong opponent of Nazism and an ardent admirer of Dollfuss. He had read my book on Dollfuss with great enthusiasm. Kestranek held my father in esteem and was himself a sculptor, I think. He was part of a circle in Munich to which Theodor Haecker[†] also belonged, along with various other young people. I never learned exactly why, but he was always saying that he needed to go back to Munich. Clearly he had some spiritual mission there that he cared about deeply.

Kestranek was in many ways very close to me. Our mutual understanding was especially good. Among those I knew at the time, very few had his degree of interest in intellectual questions. It was always a special joy when he came to visit.

I have not yet said enough about the Scottish Abbey[‡] which played a great role in my life. There was above all Abbot Peichl,[§] a fine man,

---

[*] Hans Kestranek, sculptor and close friend of writer Theodor Haecker.

[†] Theodor Haecker (1879–1945), German Catholic writer, translator of Kierkegaard and Newman, and friend of von Hildebrand.

[‡] A Benedictine abbey in Vienna.

[§] Herman Peichl, OSB (1887–1966).

whom I knew from the very start of my Vienna years and with whom I was on particularly good terms. He was a noble and spiritually refined man and a very edifying monk. He had carried out a Benedictine liturgical reform in the Scottish Abbey that had not at all been easy to achieve. One really had him alone to thank for the beautiful liturgies and the deeply monastic spirit of the abbey. His political views were very good and he was completely untainted by any form of anti-Semitism.

I have already mentioned Father Richard Beron* from the Abbey of Beuron. He had led rehearsals for the laity to participate in the choir which sang, that is, made the responses, at the solemn mass. Over time, however, his political stance became very unfortunate. I think it was only in the fall of 1935 that he suddenly declared—in contrast to his previous position—that National Socialism was inexorable, that it represented God's will, regardless of whether one welcomed it or not, that Nazism must now come to Austria, and that it was senseless to resist as I was doing. For various reasons I wanted to avoid reaching a breaking point with him.

In complete contrast, the political orientation of the Franciscans in Vienna was excellent. The head of the community was a German priest who was a particularly radical opponent of National Socialism and an enthusiastic reader of my journal. But the other Franciscans too, some of them from Germany, were also completely clear in their total rejection of National Socialism.

I must say that the stance of the Franciscans and the spirit which imbued their political views was immensely consoling and encouraging for me. There were a host of people who viewed my rejection of National Socialism as exaggerated and who perceived my sharp tone as un-Austrian. Even many Austrians whose political views were relatively good found my stance too abrupt and not in keeping with Austrian sensibilities.

Even my old friend Count Paul Thun raised objections to me along

---

* Richard Beron, OSB (1903–89), leading member of the Catholic Academic Association.

these lines. My unrelenting principled stance was perceived as typically German. The Austrian, by contrast, was supposedly much gentler and not so rigidly insistent on principle. This was very painful for me because I liked Count Thun very much, and because I suffered a great deal under this tendency, which represents a particular danger for my beloved Austrians. But it was also painful to see that even noble Austrian patriots like Thun did not grasp the full magnitude of the Nazi horror, that they did not completely comprehend the danger which threatened Austria, indeed, which threatened it more every day.

But my afternoon discussions and the journal had drawn a large circle of aristocrats who completely shared my stance against National Socialism. One of these was a very fine man, Count Heinrich Waldstein, along with his wife.

Around this time, Gilson came to Vienna where he was to give a lecture on Dante. I no longer recall the setting in which he spoke, whether under the auspices of the *Kulturbund*, or perhaps organized by the French embassy. In any case, he visited us for tea. He spoke rather pessimistically about the political situation, saying, "I don't know whether I will speak again next year at the Hochschulwochen in Salzburg. After all, who can say what will have become of Austria by then." This distressed me greatly. But I was immensely happy to see him again and to build on the contact we had begun in Paris in 1933.

His lecture was very interesting, even if his thesis struck me as rather strange. He argued that Dante was the first to shatter the unity of the Middle Ages: that Christian unity to which everyone felt connected, even when they belonged to various countries; that Christian unity which everyone assumed and which found its political expression in the realm of Charlemagne. Dante's *De Monarchia*, according to him, set the disintegration in motion with his theory of the two swords. The experience of unity among Christians everywhere was no longer taken for granted as before. Knowing Dante too little, I could not form an opinion on the matter. But as a great historian of philosophy, I assumed that Gilson surely had good reasons for presenting such a thesis.

· · ·

A strong hostility had arisen against the journal and against me, even in circles that were not ill-disposed to me. I do not mean any of those who completely shared my views, such as Mataja, Bam, Simon, Allers, or close friends, like Prince Schönburg, or any of the aristocrats who came to my evening gatherings. Thank God, none of these people had changed their position in the slightest.

Still, there were others who, while having no sympathy for the Nazis and while initially being well-disposed to the journal, now called me an alien presence in Austria—an "emigrant"—and accused me of adopting a tone that was too harsh and thus unbearable. Even Count Thun, whom I had known already in Munich and whose mother had been the great friend of Rilke,* now opposed me. When I once visited him, he declared that my way of polemicizing against the Third Reich was no longer bearable, that it had no place in Austria, and so on and so forth.

On top of this, the financial situation of the *Ständestaat* was becoming increasingly grave. The journal had not achieved the distribution we had expected during the first year. The endorsements from the Patriotic Front and from official government channels had ended, while the sum of money initially promised had only been paid in half by the government because Schuschnigg lacked any interest in the journal.

Weber had completely withdrawn from me. I was forced to the sad realization that he after all had a bureaucratic soul. The warm relationship that had developed between us while Dollfuss was alive vanished shortly after his death. Once it became clear that Schuschnigg harbored less than friendly feelings toward me, Weber's attitude toward me became one of definite reserve, indeed, of fear that any connection to me could be compromising. The lack of money meant that we were irregular in paying the stipends of our writers and sometimes even the salaries of our employees or the bill from the printer.

---

* Rainer Maria Rilke (1875–1926), poet.

In mid-October von Hildebrand went to Fribourg for the symposium he had attended the year before. A friend, Fr. Konstantin Noppel, SJ (1883–1945), took part for the first time.

My joy in Fr. Noppel's presence was soon destroyed when, to my horror, I noticed that he had become heavily infected by Nazism. We clashed during the discussions and our earlier friendly relationship went completely to pieces. During the discussions, he sought to present a completely false image of National Socialism to the others and unfortunately made a certain impression on them. This was in part because he spoke as a Jesuit, a Jesuit who had previously been known as a pacifist and who for a time had been the rector of the Germanicum in Rome. Second, thanks to a touching kindness, they were very open to being taught and to learning about aspects they had perhaps overlooked.

Another factor was that Fr. Delos lived in Germany, where from conversations with many people he had formed the impression that race after all might be more important than assumed in Catholic circles until then, i.e., that perhaps there was something in the notion of race that had been overlooked. Naturally I very strongly objected to the hypothesis proposed by Fr. Delos—he had only mentioned it as a possibility—but also, and much more pointedly, to the rosy picture painted by Fr. Konstantin Noppel. I think I succeeded in convincing all the participants, including Fr. Delos. He was simply too intelligent to reject the validity of the arguments I offered against racism, and not to see the biological materialism buried in the notion of racism.

I even succeeded in showing Fr. Delos that anti-Semitism on top of everything is a particularly stupid form of racism, given that in many cases one does not even know whether a person is Jewish. There are Italians who look very much like Jews, and Jews whose Jewish ancestry is invisible. Anti-Semitism was clearly not just anti-Christian and immoral but also quite foolish. Fr. Noppel, however, was furious about my remarks and clung fast to his position.

· · ·

When I returned to Vienna, I found out to my great joy that Kern* had decided to settle there permanently. He had a deep sense for all that is great and beautiful in art as well as in the realm of truth. He was profoundly reverent and possessed a deeply value-responding attitude. At the same time, he was full of humor and had all the charm of an Austrian. I soon came to feel not just close to him but also free to be myself in his company. His presence would be an important factor in the significant period now beginning in my Vienna years.

I was now thrust into a time of extraordinary intensity in various different respects. I began waging a battle on two fronts. The one targeted the circles I just mentioned, namely those who attacked me for being an "emigrant" and an "alien presence in Austria." These political attacks led me to take the bull by the horns and to write an article titled "The Emigrant."[1]

I pointed out how contradictory it was for Austrians to denounce as "emigrants" people who came from other countries and became Austrian patriots. For as I already mentioned, many of the great Austrians of the past were "emigrants" precisely in this sense, from Prince Eugene, Metternich, Schlegel all the way to Pastor. Thus, I publicly challenged those who found my position offensive and refuted their arguments. I also wrote various articles along similar lines, including one called "The True Germany,"[2] through which I openly confronted these attacks (which in fact tended to take the form of grumbling).

It must have been sometime in the fall that I made the acquaintance of Dr. Kunwald,† to whom I frequently went to seek counsel about the financial woes of the *Ständestaat*. I had already heard a great deal about Dr. Kunwald, who of course was a famous man and a great authority on questions of economics. He had for years been the advisor to Seipel. One of Kunwald's students was Kienböck,‡ who had brilliantly stabilized the Austrian currency and who in 1935 was still the Austrian Min-

---

* Theodor Kern (1900–69), an Austrian painter.

† Gottfried Kunwald (1869–1938), lawyer, banker, one of the most influential figures in Austria until his death in 1938.

‡ Viktor Kienböck (1873–1956), Austrian politician who served as finance minister.

ister of Finance. Kunwald had counseled him about the stabilization of the currency, though now he no longer agreed with Kienböck's policies. Kunwald was also on very good terms with Mataja.

Kunwald could not walk: his legs were either crippled or too weak to carry his fairly substantial girth. He had to be carried to the car when he wanted to go out. Upon entering the room, one would find him sitting at his desk on a chair with wheels. He had long white hair and a long white beard. He looked like a rabbi. He had a shapely head with intelligent blue eyes. The expression on his face was kindly and patriarchal, yet more than anything else he made the impression of being a person of importance. One felt that he not only possessed great intelligence but also that he was a very powerful personality.

It was always a joy for me to visit him, and a very warm relationship soon arose between us. He treated me in a fatherly way that was moving. He would not accept any payment for advising me, for which, since he was a famous expert, others paid a great deal. He said to me, "You are a child of the light. One must help you." Naturally, Kunwald welcomed my journal and my struggle against anti-Semitism, and thus appreciated me even before becoming personally acquainted with me. Yet thanks to our personal interactions, we were able to develop a relation of genuine friendship.

My evening political discussions had developed very nicely, attracting about a hundred twenty people. Allers and his wife were regular guests, Allers playing a major role in the discussions. Dr. Missong also came regularly. A particularly active participant was a very devout Protestant from Hermannstadt. He was a contributor to the *Ständestaat*, and I was always very pleased at the high level of his remarks. Klaus was of course one of the leading figures at these evenings.

Among the attendees were many aristocrats, as well as numerous respected personalities and senior officials, such as von Herrnritt, who was also a contributor with our journal. There were also various medical doctors, such as Dr. Liebl, a urologist, and also our family doctor, Dr. Pollaczek.

Another regular attendee was Reich, the music critic and friend of Alban Berg. He was particularly attached to me and expressed his desire to become Catholic. I no longer recall when he mentioned this for the first time. In any case, I recommended he see Fr. Alois Mager for catechesis. His reception into the Church did not take place until 1937.

Oesterreicher was a regular attendee, while Simon came frequently. Unfortunately, I no longer remember the numerous other participants by name.

1936

During the winter I had an audience with Chancellor Schuschnigg. He took this occasion to complain about Friedrich Wilhelm Foerster, from whom he had received a letter urging him to dismiss all of his ministers and to replace them with people suggested by Foerster. "Much as I value Foerster as a pedagogue," Schuschnigg said, "his suggestions are completely unrealistic and impossible. I am completely informed about his sources concerning the situation in Austria, as the entire correspondence of Görgen is being monitored."[*]

I could sense his irritation over Görgen, which I understood only too well, even though I myself was also very unhappy with Schuschnigg's politics. Görgen was excessive in his polemics and had a strong tendency to exaggerate. But this was also embarrassing for me because I did not know the extent to which Görgen invoked me in his letters. In fact, I had to assume that he mentioned me, and that Schuschnigg spoke in this way to admonish me. Schuschnigg would have had no reason to say anything had he not assumed I was somehow connected with Görgen and Foerster. Perhaps Foerster, who was a very good friend of mine, had made some mention of me in one of his letters.

All this was quite uncomfortable for me and greatly strained my relationship with Schuschnigg, which admittedly had already deteriorated. He knew that I remained a strict adherent of the Dollfuss policy toward Germany and that I did not agree with his pan-German sympathies. I

---

[*] Hermann Görgen (1908–94), German Catholic social scientist, historian, and politician, had served as Foerster's assistant, and was teaching in Salzburg in 1936.

could sense that there had been a great deal of agitation against me with Schuschnigg. I had attacked many unreliable figures in Austria, including some in the very circles in which Schuschnigg moved. But as he remained blind to the dangers posed by these people, he increasingly saw in me the embittered emigrant who has become suspicious of everyone.

Two decisions in particular signaled Schuschnigg's withdrawal from me. The university was to host a series of lectures on fundamental issues of philosophy, with a certain emphasis on politics. It would have been quite natural to assign these lectures to me. This was entirely in keeping with Dollfuss' intentions and would have fulfilled his expectations of me when we discussed my appointment at the university. Now that people at the university had gotten used to my teaching position, there would have been no risk, no reason to worry about another scandal like at my inaugural lecture. And it would have been in Schuschnigg's best interests.

Instead, the lectures were entrusted to Knoll[*] who was neither a professor nor in any way suited to the task. Knoll completely changed his opinions in order to win this new appointment. He had been an enthusiastic legitimist and an admirer of Karl Ernst Winter. Now he completely abandoned his former legitimist position, instead adopting a stance of appeasement toward National Socialism.

The second decision was the appointment of Dempf[†] as full professor of philosophy. Dollfuss had promised me the full professorship. I had been told that for tactical reasons one could only give me the associate professorship for the time being and that at the first opportunity I was to be made full professor. When I visited Schuschnigg in January 1935 to thank him for my appointment as assistant professor, he said to me, "This is just the beginning," by which he made clear that the appointment to full professor would soon follow.

With Dempf's appointment, I would now be confined to the assistant professorship for the long term. Of course I was happy that it

---

[*] August Maria Knoll (1900–63), taught sociology at the University of Vienna.

[†] Alois Dempf (1891–1982), Catholic philosopher.

was Dempf, who was a pious Catholic and in no way a Nazi. Still, it was a great snub to me and also a heavy financial blow. I no longer recall when Dempf's appointment took effect, but probably it was not until the summer semester of 1936.

My friendship with Kern developed more and more and we saw one another frequently. Wherever I would give a lecture, he would accompany me for protection. I spoke often during this time, principally at legitimist gatherings and with particular frequency at Jewish gatherings thanks to extensive Jewish circles that adhered to a strict legitimism.

Two Jews I still remember especially. The one was a small, gentle human being, unusually attractive and very religious. His disposition to the Church was very reverent, indeed, very open, and I could have deep conversations on religious subjects with him. He came to see me frequently and was an avid reader and enthusiastic supporter of our journal. Regrettably, I no longer recall his name. I very much fear that he was later murdered by the Nazis. The other was a general by the name of Viktor Krones. He was a very pious orthodox Jew and an ardent supporter of the Habsburg monarchy. He was a truly reverent figure, the embodiment of the thoroughly upright Jew, of the "righteous" one in the Old Testament sense.

There was also Dr. Robert John, whom I already knew from Salzburg. Not only did he attend my evenings through the years, he also became a real friend of mine. He was half-Jew and looked quite Jewish. He was chaplain in the parish where Franz Domanig was the pastor. The parish was in Wieden, not far from the Ringstrasse, quite near the Palais Schwarzenberg.

Dr. John was an ardent legitimist and a great devotee of Dante. He was working on a major work on Dante. I must say that, based on what he told me, it seemed quite unsatisfactory, for he claimed that Beatrice was merely a symbol of moral theology. But what was most striking about Dr. John was his exceptional kindness, his deep piety, and his humility. He was one of those in Vienna on whose friendship I could absolutely depend.

Around this time, I wrote a letter to Fr. Richard Beron, OSB, who had spoken about me and my struggle against National Socialism in the most derogatory fashion to acquaintances of mine. He thought it was completely outrageous that I did not want to accept God's will. National Socialism was now here in full swing: *"Vox temporis, vox Dei,"* "The voice of the times is the voice of God." Like it or not, I had to accept that it was only a matter of time before National Socialism would come to Austria. To resist this was both wrong and futile. Thereupon I wrote to Fr. Richard, suggesting a discussion, yet he thought it superfluous to speak with me.

So I wrote him a letter in which I briefly explained that God calls us to fight the Antichrist regardless of whether we triumph, which ultimately is up to God. If God permits evils such as Bolshevism and National Socialism, then of course, as St. Paul says, it is to test us; it is precisely our struggle against evil that God wills, even when we suffer external defeat. I sent my letter on the feast of St. Peter Damian, February 23, making reference to this great saint, who was so uncompromising that he even opposed the Pope who sought to lead an army (despite the fact that it was a completely just war).

I have neglected to describe how Oesterreicher had established a journal called *Die Erfüllung (Fulfillment)*. He had written various very beautiful essays in it, profoundly religious in their style, and at a very high level. But the essays by the other contributors were also very good. The entire journal was on an unusually high level. Oesterreicher had also asked me for an article, which I probably wrote during the spring of this year.

He had founded an institute for the conversion of the Jews which he called Pauluswerk [Work of St. Paul]. Founding the journal had been the first step down this path. Conceived as a particular service to the Jews, the mission of the Pauluswerk was to present Christian teaching and also the Church in her authentic form and in all her splendor. This was also the purpose of the journal *Fulfillment*. In addition, the Pauluswerk was to care for the catechetical formation of Jewish converts and, following their baptism, to organize scriptural and liturgical evenings for them on an ongoing basis.

Abbot Peichl was the president, and Fr. Bichlmair* the vice president. Also on the board was Spitzer—ironically known as Monsignor Spitzer—whom I already knew since 1922. An industrialist named Spiegler was particularly active in some capacity or other. A Jewish convert, he was married to a Czech singer. Since becoming acquainted with Oesterreicher, many Jews had been baptized by him, often with me as godfather. The baptisms usually took place in the church entrusted to the nuns of Notre Dame de Sion.

I think it was this same spring that a book by Anton Stonner was published in which for reasons of opportunism he professed himself entirely for National Socialism.[1] I can hardly describe how much this book upset me. I could not believe my eyes when I read the passage where Stonner says that, in order to awaken a love for the swastika in children already at a young age, religion teachers should point out that mass vestments in the Middle Ages bore the swastika.

In another place Stonner cites the Gospel passage that he who wishes to lead must serve, and then says that this entirely describes our Führer. After all, does not Hitler keep saying that he simply wishes to serve and does not the selection of his subordinates prove this? Then in a passage about the role of education in fostering physical fitness, Stonner suggests that Christ was also perfect in this regard, considering the strength he showed in crying out so loud from the cross after all he had suffered. These are not exact quotations, yet they convey exactly what Stonner had written.

Dr. Missong wrote a lengthy, scathing review for the *Ständestaat* of Stonner's book. This was not my first experience of Stonner. His conduct on past occasions had revealed a boundless egocentricity and lack of character, yet this book surpassed everything. It was unbelievable that a Catholic theologian could write such things, all the more so because he had said to me in March 1933, as I was leaving Munich and Germany for good, "You absolutely must go. There is no limit to

---

* Georg Bichlmair, SJ (1890–1953), preacher and spiritual director.

what one can expect from these criminals." Obviously nothing in the developments since 1933 justified the reversal of his earlier assessment.

Following the death of Dollfuss, the Ständestaat *came into increasingly desperate financial circumstances.*

A serious prospect for preventing bankruptcy of the journal presented itself in the summer semester of 1936. Probably around June, Klaus introduced me to a German gentleman who was interested in buying the *Ständestaat*. Both of us, Klaus and I, were naturally very cautious. After all, this man could be a Nazi in disguise trying in this way to clear away an obstacle for National Socialism. He invited us to an opulent meal at an elegant hotel and we discussed the possibility. We made clear that the orientation of the journal would have to remain the same, and, I think, we may even have stipulated that we would continue to be the editors of the journal. Everything was still rather vague. After having met us a few times, the man told us he would draw up and then present us with a contract.

I had received an invitation from the League of Nations Committee on Intellectual Cooperation to participate in a symposium in Budapest that began on Trinity Sunday and lasted for eight days. The financial terms were very favorable, with each participant receiving not only free travel and lodging but also a sizeable daily sum of money by way of compensation for the time consumed by the symposium. Above all, I was extremely interested in the symposium, where I would be able to meet many significant personalities, and also to participate in discussions inevitably touching on the contemporary crisis of worldviews. In this way, I had the chance to act on behalf of my struggle and my work at an international forum.

We traveled to Budapest on Trinity Sunday. Upon arriving, we were picked up and brought to an extremely elegant room at the Hotel Jägerhorn.

We had received a program listing all the invitees. The well-known French writer Paul Valéry* was chairman of the symposium, which in turn was hosted by the Hungarian professor Pál Teleki,† who much later became the Prime Minister. Two among the participants I already knew. The one was Professor Huizinga, the important Dutch historian who as rector in Leyden had received me in 1933 when I had come to deliver a lecture. The other was the historian Professor Halecki‡ whom I had gotten to know well in 1931 at a meeting of the Pax Romana in Fribourg.§

Of the other participants, I still remember Thomas Mann,¶ the Milanese journalist Ugo Ogetti, the Spanish historian Madariaga,** Professor Joan Estelrich from Catalonia, a French writer named Duhamel,†† a Hungarian historian Professor Edgar Alexander,‡‡ a German professor and his wife whose names I have forgotten, and Baron Montinaque whom I probably also knew from the Pax Romana.

At the reception that evening, there were naturally many Hungarians who had been invited, even though there were not official members of the Committee. I surely must have seen Count Széchenyi, who had come to visit me in Vienna and with whom I was so much of one mind, as well as Baron Kornfeld, a very wealthy industrialist who had great intellectual interests and surprisingly knew my books, for example, my *Metaphysics of Community*.

The theme of the symposium was almost entirely on the battle

---

* Paul Valéry (1871–1945), leading twentieth-century French poet.

† Count Pál Teleki (1879–1941), geographer and politician, Hungarian foreign minister, and later prime minister.

‡ Oskar Halecki (1891–1973), a Pole teaching at Warsaw University.

§ An international Catholic organization of university students.

¶ Thomas Mann (1875–1955), poet and author.

** Salvador de Madariaga y Royo (1886–1978).

†† George Duhamel (1884–1966).

‡‡ Pseudonym for Alexander Emmerich (1902–70), who initially worked for collaboration between the Catholic Church and the Third Reich but later became a resolute opponent.

between worldviews, be it fascism and socialism, communism and liberalism, and above all the antithesis between National Socialism and a Christian vision of reality. There was a markedly liberal contingent represented chiefly by Madariaga. Paul Valéry sympathized with him, Duhamel probably as well. Ugo Ogetti, whom Mussolini had appointed senator and invested with a title, represented fascism, while a few of the Hungarians, including the historian Valentin Hóman,* who was Minister of Culture at the time, somewhat sympathized with National Socialism. The Catholic contingent was made up of Halecki, Prof. Alexander, Estelrich, and me. Huizinga also represented a Christian conception of the world.

I spoke against National Socialism in very sharp terms, pointing to its utter immorality and foolishness, which naturally left no uncertainty about my Catholic standpoint. Curiously enough, as I later learned, Thomas Mann liked my lecture especially well. For my part, I was very happy about Thomas Mann's lecture in which he declared himself fully in favor of a worldview built on the foundations of antiquity and Christianity.

I was very surprised to hear this from someone like Thomas Mann, the author of *Joseph in Egypt* and *The Magic Mountain*. He was, after all, so influenced by Freud and so far away from all religion. But apparently National Socialism had awakened him. He now saw, if only in part, where the disavowal of Christianity can lead. In any case, our encounter after the session was very genial, also because he had known several of my sisters. I myself did not recall ever having spoken personally with Thomas Mann. So this was the first time.

I remember especially a fierce dispute between Madariaga and Ugo Ogetti during one of the sessions. Though of course I was an opponent of Fascist tenets, in this controversy I did sympathize with Ogetti more than Madariaga. Beyond his liberalism, Madariaga was also fiercely anticlerical, which naturally set me at odds with him more than anything else. This was still at the time when Mussolini's position toward Hitler

---

* Valentin Hóman (1885–1951), actually the minister of education.

was one of reserve. Nor could I forget Mussolini's conduct in 1934: his friendship with Dollfuss and then his mobilization of Italian troops at the Brenner Pass after the murder of Dollfuss.

Mussolini had also published two essays that poured a great deal of water into the wine of Fascist doctrine. In the first, he defended the full sovereignty of the church and the state, notwithstanding that Fascist doctrine holds that the church is subordinate to the state. The second article was about Austria as the bulwark of Catholicism. Both articles were quite positive. Against this backdrop, I naturally felt much greater solidarity with Ogetti than with Madariaga, who was closely affiliated with the very leftist Spanish government thanks to his extreme liberalism and anticlericalism.

Paul Valéry did not speak a great deal during the sessions; he presided and made occasional remarks. Count Teleki, who I think was a professor of astronomy,* was a pious Catholic, as I later found out, yet he did not make his Catholic position known in the discussions. The Danish professor was a socialist but also a very likeable person with whom one could have a good discussion. His wife was very animated and interested in intellectual matters. She too was an ardent socialist. But we were united in the condemnation of National Socialism, and they were respectful of my Catholic standpoint, while making clear that they themselves did not share it.

On Wednesday I was invited alone (without my wife) to a luncheon with the former prime minister Esterházy.† It was a private invitation totally unrelated to the symposium. I had been invited simply as a private citizen. I met various interesting people at this meal, which took place in the beautiful Baroque palace of Count Esterházy.

The leader of the small land-holders party, Tibor von Eckhardt,‡ had also been invited. I had heard a great deal about him and the word was that he was rather sympathetic to National Socialism. Thus I sized him up through the narrow lens of strong prejudice, making no effort

---

* Of geography, in fact.

† Móric Esterházy (1881–1960).

‡ Tibor von Eckhart (1888–1972).

to engage him in conversation or to really get to know him. Much later in America, where I came to know him very well, I realized how unjust I had been to him. He never sympathized with National Socialism. Above all, he was an unusually intelligent man, especially in political matters, and a very dignified and cultivated Hungarian aristocrat. I will still have more to tell about him. But at the time I did not notice any of his qualities because I simply ignored him.

On the feast of Corpus Christi, all of the participants of the symposium went to Esztergom. The weather was beautiful, as it was throughout our sojourn in Budapest. We rode in a car together with Ogetti. The drive to Esztergom, the old episcopal city on the Danube northwest of Budapest, was very beautiful. I was particularly delighted to see all the little places where Corpus Christi was being celebrated. We saw numerous processions, houses decorated with rugs and flowers. Frequently we came across large quantities of flowers that had been strewn onto the street. We also saw many of the faithful returning from the processions.

Ogetti had described my father, perhaps after his death, as the last of the great Italian Renaissance artists. This was not only an allusion to the fact that my father, like the Renaissance sculptors, was also an architect and even a painter, but above all to his spiritual kinship with them. Upon arriving in Esztergom, we gathered for a meal on a terrace with a beautiful view. Paul Valéry gave a speech on this occasion which he ended by saying "Eljén" ("Viva")—the only Hungarian word he knew.

This trip to Esztergom allowed for more personal conversations with other attendees. I was able to speak with Baron Montinaque, an especially congenial person who was also an exceptionally handsome man. But what drew me to him most was that he was a deeply devout Catholic. When one is surrounded by a mix of nonbelievers and lukewarm Catholics, it is always a unique and profound joy suddenly to encounter someone who is deeply devout and Catholic to the core. And so it was with Montinaque in this setting.

The participants were invited to a lunch on Margaret Island, where von Hildebrand met both the culture minister and the philosopher Béla von

Brandenstein (1901–89), both of whom sympathized with National Socialism. One other professor from Vienna attended the forum, the eminent historian Alfons Dopsch (1868–1953). "I was happy to meet him in this context," von Hildebrand wrote, "and not just during the faculty meetings in Vienna which provided me a mixture of sheer torture and boundless boredom." Von Hildebrand and Gretchen "returned to Vienna, very satisfied by our time in Budapest."

On July 11, 1936, the Schuschnigg government signed an agreement with Germany as part of a larger attempt to improve relations with their threatening neighbor. Schuschnigg sought to reduce German propaganda in Austria and also to have the Thousand Mark embargo lifted. Germany agreed not to intervene in internal Austrian affairs and also to lift the embargo in exchange for amnesty for Austrian members of the Nazi Party, which was illegal in Austria, and for inclusion of two high-level Nazis in the Austrian government. This was a source of "deepest sorrow" for von Hildebrand, for this "journalistic truce" meant a further constraint on his intellectual battle against Nazism.

Germany and Austria agreed to end all feuding between one another in the press. Naturally, this was a disastrous mistake. One can only defend a fortress under siege by resisting any act of appeasement. The moment one begins coming to terms with an opponent—which inevitably results from such a journalistic truce—one has already begun to aid one's enemy by throwing open the gates to the Trojan Horse.

Not only did this step reveal the unfortunate spirit now animating the Austrian government—the spirit of appeasement, which was also represented by Guido Zernatto*—it also meant we now had to fear that the censor would make great difficulties for our journal, even forcing us to alter our course which, of course, we would never have accepted. The

---

* Guido Zernatto (1903–43), poet and general secretary of the Patriotic Front.

journal only had a purpose if we could carry out the struggle against National Socialism with all our might and without any compromise.

I still remember how Klaus and I had been invited to the home of an Austrian aristocrat. We were sitting in the garden or perhaps the terrace of his house, and raising our wineglasses we toasted "to Austria and the return of the monarchy." We had begun by discussing the phony truce, and our sorrow and worry over the direction of the Schuschnigg regime weighed heavily on us as we looked out over our beloved Vienna on this beautiful and still very bright summer evening. Our toast to Austria was marked by an inner "perhaps." For there are moments when, precisely because everything is going so badly, one can only muster a spirit of *spes contra spem*, of "hope against all hope." This spirit filled us in that moment and is the reason that toast remains so unforgettable for me.

Thank God, our journal was not subjected to censorship, as we had feared. At the same time, the indirect persecution became far more aggressive. Attempts were made to shut us down, but we were not censored. We were able to carry on our struggle against National Socialism without compromise until the very end, that is, until our flight from Vienna.

Yet from the moment of this so-called journalistic truce, we became a thorn in the side of the government. They only did not dare to shut us down for the simple reason that doing so would have given scandal in the eyes of the French, Italian, British, and American embassies. This would have created the impression that Austria had fundamentally abandoned the battle for its independence. This of course was not the policy of the Austrian government, which had in no way renounced the independence of Austria. The government did not wish to be "Nazified," yet its leaders wrongly thought one could live in peaceful coexistence with Hitler, and that through concessions one could induce him to greater friendliness. With the exception of Italy, this was the fundamental error of all the European nations at that moment, for they had not yet grasped the spirit of a totalitarian state.

· · ·

In Salzburg, to my great joy I met Franz von Hoesslin[*] in the court-yard of St. Peter's Church. We greeted each other very warmly. Some acquaintance of mine wanted to take a picture of me, so Franzl and I were photographed together. Franzl laughed and said, "I'm lost if this photo falls into the hands of the Nazis. If I'm seen standing arm in arm with enemy number-one of National Socialism, then surely I'm ripe for the concentration camp." He laughed as he spoke and seemed to be unafraid. Hoesslin was a very courageous person to begin with.

He told me on this occasion (perhaps he had already told me previ-ously?) that he had spoken about me with Eva Wagner-Chamberlain[†] in Bayreuth. She had asked about me and when Hoesslin laughed and told her I had become a very dangerous and feared man, she cried out full of pity and horror, "So he is not a Fascist? Poor man! How unfortunate!" Nevertheless, she said "Fascist" rather than "National Socialist," which revealed a little remnant of reserve in the face of National Socialism. Being far less bad than National Socialism and lacking the senseless racism, Fascism struck her as being in better taste.

Annette Kolb,[‡] who had left Germany in 1933, came to visit us in Vi-enna. Fedja painted a portrait of her. It was always a joy to see Annette again. There was something stimulating and totally original about her. She delighted me through all the memories she embodied for me. Her presence brought back the world of 1908, of Mottl,[§] of Berlioz's *Beatrice and Benedict*, of her parent's home on the Sophienstrasse. This was the backdrop against which I saw her. I kept meeting Annette in the most varied of life circumstances, in St. Moritz after the war and now again in Vienna. Naturally, we very much agreed in regard to National Social-ism, which she rejected just as totally as did I. She had been living in Paris since 1933.

---

[*] Franz von Hoesslin (1885–1946), conductor famous for his interpretations of Wagner and a longtime friend of von Hildebrand. Hoesslin's wife was Jewish.

[†] Daughter of Cosima von Bülow (1837–1930). Cosima married Richard Wagner (1813–83) in 1870 following her divorce from conductor Hans von Bülow (1830–94). Eva von Bülow (1867–1942) married Houston Stewart Chamberlain (1855–1927), whose writings influenced Nazi racism.

[‡] Annette Kolb (1870–1967), German writer, pacifist, and friend of von Hildebrand.

[§] Felix Mottl (1856–1911), well-known conductor in Munich.

A particularly great joy for me was the visit of Ludwig Derleth[*] and his wife. They just turned up one day at our apartment on the Habsburgergasse. It was the first time I had seen him since 1920, that is, since his marriage. He had been in Rome for a long time and then in Switzerland. Now he had moved to Vienna and was living outside the city in Perchtoldsdorf, along the way to Mödling. I was overjoyed to see him again and to experience once more his noble character and his extraordinarily spiritual makeup. He said to me, "To me, you are 'Monsieur Colonna,'" by which he alluded to my unflinching struggle against National Socialism.[†]

During this time, we also had a controversy with the well-known specialist in German studies, Nadler,[‡] who was a professor in Vienna. He had a theory in which he divided German literature according to the various Germanic tribes, itself an unfortunate idea. He had written a book in which he suggested among other things that a particular distinction of the Austrian tribe was that it had given Hitler to Germany. Nadler himself was not a National Socialist—in fact, he presented himself as a Catholic—and so we were very surprised by his remark. He did not speak in an effusive way, nor did he include any adulation of Hitler. Still, he presented it as a service rendered by Austria.

Klaus wrote a very good review of the book in our journal. In an effort to elicit goodwill on Nadler's part, Klaus wrote that surely he could not possibly have meant that Hitler was a blessing for Germany. On the whole, the book received a very positive treatment, expressing just the one regret that Nadler's remark could be misunderstood. Nadler, however, sent a reply in which he explained that he had meant exactly what he had written, namely that Hitler was to Austria's great credit. We printed his letter, yet this time with a stronger expression of regret over such a blunder.

---

[*] Ludwig Derleth (1870–1948), writer and poet.

[†] The Italian word *colonna* means "pillar."

[‡] Josef Nadler (1884–1963), Austrian literary historian.

It must also have been during this summer semester that we were invited for dinner at the exquisitely beautiful apartment of Coudenhove-Kalergi and his wife, Ida Roland. They lived in a building on a beautiful courtyard—probably once belonging to a monastery—located in the section of the Inner City between St. Stephen's Cathedral and the Danube Canal. Not only was their apartment of particular architectural beauty, it was also magnificently decorated with beautiful furniture.

The deputy mayor, Lahr, had also been invited that evening. He told various Jewish jokes, imitating the wheeling and dealing ascribed to Jews, yet with a certain trace of anti-Semitism. I found him very unattractive and his anti-Semitic jokes made him even more so.

Something had just happened at the time which had been a great embarrassment for the Nazis. I regret that I no longer recall what it was, but there was a photo in the newspaper showing Ribbentrop* in London with a dumb look on his face because of the embarrassment. As we looked at the newspaper and the photo, I was quite vocal about my satisfaction over the disgrace for the Nazis and over the look on Ribbentrop's face. To my great surprise, the deputy mayor declared that he could no longer tolerate my hostile stance toward Germany, my intolerable gloating.

It is difficult to describe how upset I was by his remarks. I responded in the sharpest of terms, countering that it was not Germany that was at issue but the criminal regime of Hitler and National Socialism. It was a very tense and awkward situation. Coudenhove said to Lahr, "To my mind, what stands between us and these people is the dead body of Dollfuss. And that is an unbridgeable gulf."

It was very discouraging to see the naïveté of the various foreign ambassadors (with the exception of the American) toward National Socialism. I noticed this when I pointed out to [the French ambassador] Viscount de Montbas that Nazi Germany was every day becoming an increasingly serious danger to the rest of Europe. He said to me, "You exaggerate. Mussolini is presently far more dangerous. We are much

---

* Joachim von Ribbentrop (1893–1946), Nazi ambassador to England in 1936, later served as German foreign minister. Ribbentrop was executed at Nuremberg in 1946.

more worried about him than about Hitler. After all, Hitler is only interested in Austria. He does not want anything from the rest of Europe."

I was deeply discouraged by his political blindness and his failure to understand Hitler's character. In 1936, Hitler had remilitarized the Rhineland. In 1935, he had introduced military conscription. Both were clear violations of the Treaty of Versailles. It was sheer blindness not to see that Hitler would never allow France to keep Alsace-Lorraine and that once he had taken Vienna, Czechoslovakia would also be in greatest danger. Naturally, Viscount de Montbas thought of himself as far more competent in political matters, and so all my attempts to convince him, to open his eyes, were of no avail.

Von Hildebrand spent the summer of 1936 in Italy.

Through Don Mario, I had already made some attempts to get an audience with Pope Pius XI. However, I soon realized that it would be fairly difficult given that a private audience indicates a friendly interest, even a personal initiative, on the part of the Holy Father (in contrast to public audiences) and also because politically speaking I was a very controversial personality. The German embassy at the Vatican would immediately have protested that such an enemy of the Third Reich had been received. Moreover, I did not represent Austria in any official capacity, which according to diplomatic code would have entitled me to a private audience.

To the Nazis I was guilty of high treason and hostile to National Socialism, while in the eyes of the Austrian government I was *persona non grata*. For this reason, Don Mario thought that the audience would in any case not be granted very quickly. I was also asked why I had requested an audience and whether there was anything in particular I wanted to bring to the Holy Father's attention. I replied that I was only seeking his blessing for my difficult work.

By contrast, I did not have to wait to receive an audience with the Cardinal Secretary of State, my beloved friend Monsignor Pacelli. Once again he received me with great kindness and once more I experienced the irresistible charm of his unique personality. I spoke to him on this occasion about the cause of legitimism in Austria and its aspirations for the return of the Habsburgs. His reply, "*magari, magari,*" "if only, if only it could be so," made clear how much he would welcome this and simultaneously how difficult and unlikely he considered it.

Yet we were in complete agreement about Nazi Germany. After all, the Church's relationship to the Hitler regime was worsening by the day, with violations of the Concordat everywhere to be seen. The situation between the Church and National Socialism was much tenser than at the time of my last audience with Cardinal Pacelli a year and a half earlier, in January 1935.

From time to time Count Caspar Preysing would visit me. He was the financial manager for Prince Josias von Hessen-Waldeck, who had large estates in Lower Austria. On one of his visits he told me that he had recently become quite friendly with Eugen Kogon. It had already been quite some time since Kogon had distanced himself from the *Schönere Zukunft*. He was now, according to Preysing, a completely resolute opponent of the Nazis. Preysing was sure I would get along with him very well. While this news made me very happy, still I did not entirely trust Kogon.

Another frequent visitor was Prelate Ohnmacht, the secretary of Bishop Gföllner. Prelate Ohnmacht was in fact a real friend. He shared my political stance completely and we were of one mind in many things. Of course I traveled to Linz variously, to visit Bishop Gföllner, but also to give lectures.

On December 2, 1936, the Nazis revoked von Hildebrand's German citizenship. Any property he still had in Germany was forfeit to the state.

1937

January 1937 saw various things come to pass. First Dobretsberger, who was professor of economics in Graz, was nominated by Schuschnigg to become Minister of Social Affairs. We, meaning Klaus and I, welcomed this appointment because Dobretsberger was a radical opponent of National Socialism. He was also completely free of any pan-German tendencies. A great friendship soon developed between him and Dr. Simon, who sometimes invited us over together with Dobretsberger. I cannot say that I was particularly drawn to him as a personality, nor did I admire his intelligence as much as Simon did. Yet because of his stance toward Nazi Germany, his appointment as Minister was a very welcome development.

A beautiful memory from January 1937 was the lunch to which Kunwald invited Gretchen and me. Kunwald was a significant personality and a very cultivated man. As I mentioned earlier, he had been Seipel's advisor on financial questions, while his student, Kienböck, had strengthened and stabilized the Austrian currency. But Kunwald was no longer in agreement with Kienböck's approach. He said to me that a bumpy table must be sanded so that it can be used. But once it is smooth, one will sand away the entire surface of the table if one does not stop sanding. This is what he thought Kienböck was doing. In combating inflation, it was necessary for the government to save money and limit expenditures, yet now it was essential to proceed differently in order to stimulate the economy.

Speaking with Kunwald was always interesting. On this visit, he told me that he knew Giraudoux[*] and that he played a role in choosing the German title for his work *The Trojan War Will Not Take Place*, which Annette Kolb had translated into German. His stories about Seipel were always especially interesting. Apparently Seipel would never ask his advice before making decisions in financial and economic matters, but he would always come to Kunwald after deciding and would ask him to critique what he had done. Seipel hoped to draw lessons from this critique for the next time. Kunwald was a noble man, kind and free of prejudice, yet at the same time a keen observer of human nature. To be invited by Kunwald was always very interesting and will ever remain a lovely memory for me.

Oesterreicher intended during the course of May to present four lectures at the Pauluswerk. The lectures were to address the question of Israel, and the speakers envisioned were Senator Pant, myself, Fr. Stratmann, and Oesterreicher himself. My theme was "Israel and the West." I began working on my talk far in advance, in part because I was fascinated by the subject, but also because Oesterreicher was constantly pushing me.

Every so often, von Hildebrand presents an episode out of chronological order. That happens in the following description of a crisis with Fr. Georg Bichlmair, SJ, which developed in the Pauluswerk already in late 1935 and early 1936. The lecture series von Hildebrand describes above and returns to below took place in May 1937.

During this time, a crisis broke out at the Pauluswerk. Fr. Bichlmair struck upon the unfortunate idea that one should tolerate a certain anti-Semitism in Catholics infected by Nazism to prevent them from falling away from the Church. This despite the fact that he himself was a

---

[*] Jean Giraudoux (1882–1944), French writer.

great friend of the Jews and directed many Jewish converts. It was just another manifestation of the disastrous old idea that compromise can keep people from falling away. The same logic had led to past compromises with nationalism in various points, just as it had with the idolization of science or with the Zeitgeist.

Fr. Bichlmair thought that by allowing for a moderate anti-Semitism one could prevent many people from making a break with the Church. And so he began presenting ideas much like those already introduced by Fr. Schmidt, SVD, who had made a distinction between Jews baptized "lying down" and "standing up," that is, baptized as infants and as adults. I already described that episode, which took place already in the fall of 1933. Being the vice president of the Pauluswerk, Fr. Bichlmair's position set off a great uproar within the organization. I was especially upset.

Having not yet committed his views to print, he read us the article he wanted to publish at a meeting of the Pauluswerk. Fr. Schmidt was there and, as far as I can recall, also present were Abbot Peichl, who was president of the Pauluswerk, Spiegler, Spitzer (nicknamed "Monsignor Spitzer"), Oesterreicher, who was director of the Pauluswerk, and myself. There were surely others, but I no longer remember them.

After he read his article aloud, I pressed my objections to Fr. Bichlmair in the most forceful of terms. I pointed to the objective falsehood of his proposal, the betrayal which it represented in light of the present rise of National Socialism, and how hopeless it was that it would prevent Catholics from falling away. For what good is obtained when people who consider themselves Catholic and who still receive the sacraments adhere to ideas that are incompatible with Christ? Is it not much worse when people who consider themselves Catholic, and present themselves so, have fallen prey to the heresy of racism? I pleaded with him not to publish the article.

Oesterreicher spoke far less sharply than I, yet he too advised against publishing the article. Spiegler said, "I am happily married to an Aryan woman. The ideas you have presented, Reverend Father, have deeply upset me and can only bring about harm." I cannot remember if Fr. Bichlmair responded to our request.

In any case, he did publish the article, which naturally meant that he could no longer remain vice president of the Pauluswerk. He resigned and Alois Wildenauer, the excellent provost of the Votive Church, was chosen to fill his position. We dedicated an entire issue of the *Ständestaat* in response to the position expressed in Fr. Bichlmair's article, which is to say, all the articles in our issue were focused entirely on the refutation of anti-Semitism. I wrote an article, as did Dr. Missong and others.

Von Hildebrand would respond to Fr. Bichlmair in his essay "False Fronts" in 1936: "Bichlmair's attempt to 'take the wind out of the sails' of National Socialism ... obscures the clear, classical, Catholic point of view," he wrote. "The only effect of this lecture will be to allow those Catholics who are infected by the errors of the present day to abandon themselves with a good conscience to their un-Christian attitude toward the Jews."

During the spring (I no longer recall exactly whether it was before or after Easter), a Hungarian journalist invited us to a meal together with Toynbee[*] and his wife. I was happy to get to know him, having heard about him, though I had yet to read anything by him. He had come to Austria to get a sense for the political situation, and also because of a book on church and state (or something along those lines) which he was supposed to publish. He was not writing the book himself; rather, it was a study being published by his department which one of his assistants was writing. Toynbee was just the official editor.

I was thus very interested to speak with him about Austria and also about National Socialism and the danger it posed for Europe. Both for the sake of the truth and also for the sake of Austria, it was very important that the English have an accurate perception of the Nazis, and Toynbee was a man who exerted a certain influence on public opinion

---

[*] Alfred Toynbee (1889–1975), English historian known for his twelve-volume *A Study of History*.

in England. His wife, I had previously been told, had become a Catholic. She was the daughter of the famous philologist Gilbert Murray.[*] I had a very good conversation with Toynbee, who told me that his assistant, who was working on the study, would be visiting Vienna. He added also that his assistant was a Catholic and that this would enable us to get along well and greatly facilitate our conversation. But this turned out not to be the case at all, as I will explain.

I invited Toynbee and his wife to my next political afternoon (or was it in the evenings at that time?). He came and was a lively participant in the conversation. He seemed to understand well the danger of National Socialism, and also how disastrous it was to believe that one could pacify Hitler with concessions or rely on any formal agreement with him. Despite seeming to understand all this well and sharing our perspective entirely, nevertheless on his return journey through Prague Toynbee said to Beneš,[†] that he should give another chance to Henlein,[‡] the leader of the National Socialist Germans in the Sudetenland. Beneš was quite right to notice that Henlein represented an increasing danger for Czechoslovakia and was thus looking for a way to fend him off.

Toynbee's "still give him a chance" revealed that he had not understood the true nature of National Socialism. He apparently believed it was possible to reason with people who belonged to a totalitarian party, approaching them, as it were, in a spirit of *noblesse oblige*. This, of course, was the classic misunderstanding of the nature of National Socialism and Communism.

After some time—perhaps three weeks later—I received a visit from Toynbee's assistant. He complained that he had had to wait so long for an audience, while Papen had received him in the friendliest manner without delay. He then told me how much Papen had helped him understand that Catholicism and National Socialism were in no way separated by an irreconcilable antithesis. How could a person possibly be at odds with Catholic teaching by having a strong sense of national

---

[*] Gilbert Murray (1866–1957).

[†] Eduard Beneš (1884–1948), then president of Czechoslovakia.

[‡] Konrad Henlein (1898–1945).

identity and by recognizing the undeniable significance of racial differ-ence? After all, he himself would be quite unhappy if his son were to marry a black woman.

It is not hard to imagine the distress I felt at his words. I tried to show him the incompatibility between Catholic teaching and biological materialism, which forms the foundation of National Socialism. I cited the words of Secretary of State Pacelli (I no longer remember whether the encyclical *Mit brennender Sorge* had appeared; if so, then I quoted from it as well*). I pointed to Paragraph 24 of the NS Platform, which states: we accept Christianity to the extent that it agrees with Nordic sensibilities.

Of course this paragraph was itself absolutely unacceptable, yet over the years the Nazi posture toward Christianity and especially toward the Catholic Church had totally changed. Or, to be more precise, Hitler had dropped his mask, and now his hatred for Christ and the Catholic Church, which merely for tactical reasons he had hidden, came into the open. The open persecution of the Church was already under way by this time.

Sadly, none of my arguments made much of an impression on Toyn-bee's assistant. Only one remark seemed to catch his attention. I said, "I have known Papen for a long time, and I must tell you that I would never shake his hand 'because he is no gentleman.'"

The spring saw much discussion around a "disastrous book" called The Foundations of National Socialism *by Bishop Alois Hudal (1885–1963), the Austrian Church's leading representative in Rome. (The book must already have been available in late 1936 given that von Hildebrand wrote a critical review in the November 15 issue of the* Ständestaat.[1] *In 1920, the historian Ludwig von Pastor had warned von Hildebrand, "Do not trust this man. He is consumed by ambition. He is a devious and untrustworthy person."*

---

* Pope Pius XI issued the encyclical on March 14, 1937.

. . .

Hudal had published a book in which he sought to demonstrate that National Socialism and Catholicism were in principle entirely compatible. Only in a few minor points did Hitler need to improve his understanding. The book gave the impression that there was 95% agreement, or at least harmony, while only 5% in National Socialism needed modification.

To grasp the true monstrosity of the book, one has to realize that it appeared after the publication of the encyclical *Mit brennender Sorge*, and that the persecution of the Church in Germany was already in full swing. Naturally, we responded in our journal in the most energetic way. We devoted almost an entire issue to this book, which we rejected in very sharp terms. Hudal ended up having no success with the book. It was prohibited in Germany because the Nazis did not deem it sufficiently "orthodox."

Thus, his betrayal turned out to be entirely ineffectual. The excuse that through this book Hudal would ease the situation of Catholics in Germany also proved to be completely mistaken. Obviously, Hudal's book was a totally illegitimate attempt to serve the cause of "peace" between the Church and National Socialism. Its failure to have any public efficacy was thus a just punishment for what was truly a betrayal of Christ. Of course, the excuse for the book was itself an expression of "the end justifies the means," yet even from a purely utilitarian perspective the whole thing proved to be fruitless.

About this time, von Hildebrand's brother-in-law Fedja Georgii came under suspicion with the Nazi authorities. He had in fact done nothing to oppose them, though he had never made a secret of his principled rejection of National Socialism. The suspicion could have "catastrophic consequences" for Fedja and his family. To clear things up, Fr. Alois Mager suggested they visit Franz von Papen, whom he knew.

. . .

Fr. Alois saw through Papen just as I did, and Papen must have known that Fr. Alois was not a Nazi. But the personal acquaintance with Papen made it possible for Fr. Alois to call on him with Fedja and to ask him to clear Fedja of the false suspicion. They went to Papen and everything was satisfactorily resolved.

The meeting was also very gratifying for me. Fr. Alois told me that, among other things, the conversation touched upon me and my journal. Papen said, "That damned Hildebrand is the greatest obstacle for National Socialism in Austria. No one causes more harm." This made me very happy because it meant that my work and my battle in Austria had not been for naught.

The Kulturbund was very active in Vienna. I rarely managed to attend the always interesting lectures which regularly took place there. I did go when Berdyaev came to speak. I had met Berdyaev in Paris and knew that he was a significant and profound thinker. He spoke very beautifully, yet in the middle of the lecture, just as he was speaking about God (it sounded liked "Good" in his very heavy Russian accent), he began making his grimaces. These grimaces were a nervous affliction, which I had already noticed when I first met him in Paris with Count Pange.*

I invited Berdyaev to my political evenings where he made many beautiful and interesting contributions to the discussion. At one point he said, "The world is anthropocentric, yet man himself may not exist like this. He must be theocentric." This thesis was both beautiful and deeply true. But it was also particularly salutary at a time defined by collectivism and materialism in so many different forms. Overall, Berdyaev made a great impression on the guests.

I remember one occasion in 1937 when Dempf came to visit me. Whether he came before or after Easter, I no longer recall. He was very nice and friendly. He must have known that he had received the professorship which had been promised to me. Of course he could not help

---

* Count Jean de Pange (1881–1957), French historian.

that his appointment had been an injustice to me. But how totally different it was to speak with him than with any of my other philosophical colleagues!

What could I have discussed with Reininger?[*] Certainly, Reininger was a friendly, proper old gentleman, but we had nothing to say to one another. Schlick was very friendly to me on a human level, and he was an outspoken opponent of National Socialism, yet as a logical positivist it would be hard to imagine someone philosophically more antithetical to me. He was also completely unreligious.

Against this background, Dempf was a true consolation. His noble face, his deep piety, his kind and unostentatious manner, his philosophical openness, and his sincere opposition to National Socialism, all of this set him worlds apart from my other philosophical colleagues in Vienna. I still remember Dempf being moved to tears as he spoke about the resistance to National Socialism by various circles of German Catholic youth; the feeling that he had abandoned them by coming to Vienna filled him with emotion. Much as his disposition won me for him, we never managed to develop an ongoing relationship.

Meanwhile, Klaus Dohrn and Eugen Kogon had become very good friends. Klaus had gotten acquainted with Kogon through Count Caspar Preysing who worked together with Kogon in managing the properties of Prince Josias von Hessen. Kogon had totally changed his political stance and had become a complete opponent of National Socialism. He was also interested in the *Ständestaat* and eventually emerged as a potential buyer.

The reunion with Fr. Stratmann was a great joy for me. I had last seen him in Rome, where he served in the Sacred Penitentiary at Santa Maria Maggiore, probably in 1935 or perhaps even in 1933. He had undergone a great deal. At the very beginning of the Hitler regime, he had been arrested and, to make a point of humiliating him, had been locked up in a prison ward for troubled girls. This turned out to be quite fortunate for him because the ward was under the authority of a woman

---

[*] Robert Reininger (1869–1955), professor of philosophy in Vienna.

who was Catholic. She treated Fr. Stratmann with the greatest respect and reverence. He said, "She was like a mother to me."

He was then brought before a court because his pacifism was deemed to be treasonous. The judge treated him shamefully, yet luckily this took place early in the Nazi regime when everything was still much less drastic and strict. It was impossible to prove anything more than his principled pacifism, which in those days was not sufficient for a conviction. He was released but threatened with more drastic consequences if he did not abandon his pacifism in the future.

Von Hildebrand now returns to his description of the four-part lecture series at the Pauluswerk in May 1937.

Sadly I no longer recall the sequence and the spacing of the lectures. One of the lectures was given by Senator Pant—unfortunately rather disappointing, for he did not have any special interest in the topic. What he said was certainly correct, but it was neither deep nor original nor particularly well delivered. I had the impression that even then his health was no longer so good.

Then again, his distinction lay not in being a significant thinker, but in his courage, his readiness to make sacrifices, his moral integrity, his refusal to make compromises, and his piety. He fought for all that was good and true, which itself was far more important than being able to contribute deep and interesting ideas. But obviously this lecture was not really suited to draw out his great qualities. It was, I think, the last time I saw this noble man. Overall, the lectures were quite a success and Oesterreicher was very pleased.

A few days after my lecture, Gretchen and I were invited by a certain Baroness Pereyra. There I met Baron Zessner-Spitzenberg,* and also a young aristocrat who attacked me because of my lecture at the

---

* Hans Karl von Zessner-Spitzenberg (1885–1938), leader among the legitimists, incarcerated at Dachau where he died.

Pauluswerk.* He had only read about it in the newspapers. "How can you approve of this awful Jewish lot being taken up into the Church? You should be glad that they are not in the Church."

I replied to him, "If you are arguing that the conversion of disagreeable people is undesirable, then you would also have to consider as undesirable the presence of any Prussians in the Church." Apart from addressing his terrible argument, I said to him, "How can you pass such a sweeping judgment against the Jews? Hebbel says so truly, 'The Jew is neither better nor worse than the man.'† The noblest people I met in my life were Jews." It was a fierce discussion which simply showed again how even people who wanted nothing to do with the Nazis could be incredibly clueless and infected by Nazi poison.

One evening we heard on the radio the awful address of Goebbels against the clergy. It was in response to a speech by the cardinal of Chicago‡ who referred to Hitler as a "paperhanger," adding humorously, "and I've heard, not a very good paperhanger." Goebbels responded with a dreadful speech in which he made "revelations" about the alleged moral degeneracy of the clergy in Germany. He began by quoting the Catholic press from 1906/07 at the time of the famous Eulenburg trial.§ Prince Eulenburg, who was *persona grata* at the court of Emperor Wilhelm, was accused of homosexuality. The Catholic press at the time insisted that everything be revealed and prosecuted in court, regardless of Eulenburg's social position.

Goebbels read this aloud and then added the following, "Oh you angel of premonition! What was said back then must now be applied to the shocking moral degeneracy of the clergy." This was followed by a stream of totally ridiculous slanders. Finally he cried out, "I would never allow my daughter to go to confession because I have no way of knowing what might happen to the poor innocent girl." The whole speech was delivered in a tone both terrible and melodramatic. But what really

---

* Entitled "The Jews and the Christian West," von Hildebrand's lecture was first published in Oesterreicher's journal, *Die Erfüllung*, in 1937. A portion is featured in this volume on p. 270ff.

† Friedrich Hebbel (1813–63), German dramatist and poet.

‡ George William Cardinal Mundelein (1872–1939).

§ Prince Philipp Eulenburg (1847–1921), diplomat and friend of Emperor Wilhelm II.

stood out in an awful way was the spirit of untruth and of hatred for Christ, along with the brutality and baseness of Nazism.

In May, Professor Schlick was shot by a student at the University. The student was mentally ill. I was deeply shaken by this murder. Although I considered Schlick disastrous from a philosophical perspective, I had great regard for him as a kind person and for his courageous rejection of Nazism.

Sometime after the murder his son came to me and asked me to take up the defense of his father in my journal. He wanted me to respond to the outrageous article in the *Schönere Zukunft*, which claimed that the shooting of Schlick was simply a primal protest of the people against the anti-metaphysical Jewish stance of Schlick. While Schlick was not himself a Jew, he was taken to be a representative of the Jewish spirit, which was supposed to be profoundly anti-metaphysical and destructive. The shooting of Schlick was not a murder but in itself a healthy protest against the Jewish spirit in Schlick.

The son of Schlick asked me to rebut this article. Naturally, I immediately agreed. It was a curious situation for me to have to defend Schlick, whom I completely rejected as a philosopher. On the other hand, the terrible article in the *Schönere Zukunft* demanded an absolute repudiation. So I wrote an article in the *Ständestaat* in which I began by showing that the murder of Schlick was based entirely on personal reasons, having no connection to his philosophy. But then I also showed how completely false it was to claim that the Jewish spirit is anti-metaphysical. Maimonides[*] and Spinoza[†] were Jews, and both of them metaphysicians. Bergson,[‡] Husserl, and Cohen[§] were all Jews, yet one certainly cannot accuse them of developing a destructive philosophy. But I primarily emphasized how grotesque it was to connect the murder of a non-Jew with anti-Semitic propaganda, to use the murder as an occasion for such propaganda.

---

[*] Moses Maimonides (1135–1204), most significant medieval Jewish philosopher of religion.

[†] Baruch Spinoza (1632–77), Dutch philosopher.

[‡] Henri Bergson (1859–1941), French philosopher and Nobel Peace Prize laureate for literature.

[§] Hermann Cohen (1842–1918), German philosopher and influential representative of neo-Kantianism.

ESCAPE FROM VIENNA

March 1938

The memoirs of Dietrich von Hildebrand break off in late August 1937 at a moment of high drama. In that same year, his brother-in-law Theodor (Fedja) Georgii was told by Franz von Papen, the Nazi ambassador to Austria: "That damned Hildebrand is the greatest obstacle for National Socialism in Austria. No one causes more harm." What Georgii could not have known at the time was that von Papen was then hatching a plot to assassinate von Hildebrand.

The evidence of this plot is documented by historian Rudolf Ebneth in what remains the definitive history of von Hildebrand's journal, *Der christliche Ständestaat*.[1] Ebneth quotes a secret dispatch from von Papen to Hitler himself, dated April 30, 1937, and marked "top secret." Here are the key lines:

To: The Führer

From: Ambassador Franz von Papen

As the *Essen National Times* has already reported, a National Union for German Liberation was recently established here. This organization seeks to overthrow the Nazi regime and is trying to unite the enemies of Nazi Germany under a single leadership. The mastermind behind these intrigues is the all-too-well-known expatriate emigrant Professor Dietrich von Hildebrand, editor of the weekly journal, *Der christliche Ständestaat*. . . .

Because of the importance of this matter and fearful that

the suspects might be warned and their tracks covered, I have immediately sent copies of the enclosed documents to the Director of the SS, Himmler. . . .

We may be able to strike a severe blow against these extremely evil and dangerous enemies of the Reich working in Austria.[2]

This was not the first time that Hitler had received reports about von Hildebrand's journalistic activities. In a lengthy dispatch to the Führer dated June 13, 1935, Papen had written: "In speaking with the [Austrian] Foreign Minister, I took the opportunity to express the sharpest possible protest against the rhetoric of various [Austrian] publications. Among these *Der christliche Ständestaat*, published by the emigrant Hildebrand, is the worst offender."[3]

Some years ago, the FBI was able to locate a number of documents that show how von Hildebrand's intellectual resistance was noticed even in the United States. The most remarkable of these is an undated memorandum (likely from the early 1940s) apparently signed by FBI director J. Edgar Hoover himself. Hoover writes:

> Hildebrand and his son Franz are engaged in operating the "International Catholic Office for Refuges' Affairs" at 11 West 42nd Street, New York City. This report from the New York Field Division indicates that [sic] subject is a "famous foe of Nazism."
>
> The file further reflects that Hildebrand was dismissed in 1938 [actually in 1933] from the Munich University because of anti-Nazi activities and that his good friend, Chancellor Dollfuss of Austria, was instrumental in bringing subject to the University of Vienna, where in addition to his professorship he edited the most violently anti-Nazi publication in Austria. Von Papen reportedly made repeated requests of the Austrian Government for the suppression of this newspaper.[4]

These are just some of the most impressive documents mentioning von Hildebrand that have come to light. Ebneth cites numerous documents in his study,[5] yet there is good reason to believe there are more waiting to be discovered. Historians should take up the important task of assembling a complete record of von Hildebrand's activities as mirrored in the remembrances of his contemporaries, in the press of the day, and also in government archives.

While the memoirs trail off in 1937, von Hildebrand's story certainly does not. The fullest published account of the period extending from 1937 to his arrival in New York City in 1940 is found in the thrilling final chapter of Alice von Hildebrand's biography of her husband, *The Soul of a Lion*,[6] which she bases on outlines and on extensive notes von Hildebrand had made for these years. We also have the accounts of two eyewitnesses who describe his flight from Vienna in 1938. There were in fact two flights from Vienna, and the first is related by his friend Hellmut Laun (1920–81), as we shall see momentarily.

In early 1938, as the Anschluss gained momentum, von Hildebrand realized that he would soon have to leave Vienna. From the chief of the secret police in Vienna, he had learned already in January 1935 that the Gestapo were spying on him; they had even rented the apartment directly across the street to watch his every move. But the danger to him was more acute. As a result, he had arranged with friends in Salzburg, which is very near the German border, to notify him the moment there was any sign of German mobilization. Since the telephones were presumably tapped, the caller was simply to say, "If Anna still wishes to see her grandmother, she must leave immediately."

On February 12, 1938, Austrian chancellor Kurt von Schuschnigg went to Berchtesgaden, just across the border in Germany, to meet with Hitler. Schuschnigg had clung to the notion of "peaceful coexistence" with Nazi Germany and hoped still to preserve Austria's independence. Among many demands, Hitler told Schuschnigg to curb the journalistic activities of Dietrich von Hildebrand and other German émigrés fighting Nazism from Austria.[7]

Schuschnigg's last move was to hold a referendum in which he hoped to secure a clear mandate for continuing Austrian independence in full view of the international community. Voting was scheduled for March 13, 1938. When Hitler learned of this, he decided to act preemptively.

Of course, von Hildebrand was unaware of Hitler's plan and so he continued to believe that he was safe until the referendum.

Here we come to the remembrance that Hellmut Laun has left of von Hildebrand's last days in Vienna. The date is Monday, February 28:

> It was Mardi Gras 1938 and we had decided to have a light-hearted get-together in my apartment, so as for once to forget for a while the daily concern and agitation that we lived with. There were about thirty of us, the inner circle of von Hildebrand's friends, and the party lasted into the early hours of the morning. Von Hildebrand stood at the center of this happy group; he was as lively and entertaining as anyone could be in such a social setting. He told us many funny stories from his life, and as many jokes as the Viennese comedian Karl Farkas, and at the end of the evening he read to us from his beloved Molière. My guests departed in a very happy frame of mind. During this joyful evening we had forgotten about the storm clouds that were forming on the horizon.[8]

One cannot fail to be impressed by von Hildebrand's freedom of spirit. It surely gives evidence of his deep trust in divine providence that he was able, even in the lengthening shadow of catastrophe, to celebrate like this with his friends.

The following evening, Laun was settling in for an early night, exhausted from the previous night's celebration. No sooner had he laid down than the telephone rang. Laun recounts:

> [Theodor] Kern was on the line. His voice was somber and changed as he asked me to come immediately with my car to the Hildebrand's apartment in the Habsburgergasse. I got no answer out of Kern when I tried to probe him about what was going on. I quickly realized that something had happened that he could not mention on the telephone.

Arriving in his small car, Laun found the von Hildebrand family and some of their closest friends in a state of highest tension. The call had come from Salzburg, "If Anna still wishes to see her grandmother, she must leave immediately." The sudden departure was especially difficult for Gretchen, as von Hildebrand describes in his notes:

> The situation was terribly dramatic. My wife Gretchen had to be persuaded to leave. For her this exodus meant another adventure. She had lived under such tension for the last few years that it was very difficult for her to make up her mind. Finally I succeeded in convincing her that it was only flight which could save my life and hers.

The sun was already setting as Laun's car, with von Hildebrand and his wife, headed toward the small town of Marchegg on the Czech border, where they hoped to catch a train to get out of Austria. The route would take them through a sparsely populated portion of Austria which was completely unfamiliar to Laun, who continues:

> It was pitch black with a clear starry sky above. I had been driving straight for quite some time and I was on the lookout for lights on the assumption that we would soon be arriving in Marchegg. Suddenly the engine stalled and would not restart. What could I do in the dark, without light, and without proximity to nearby houses? We were dismayed since each of us was conscious that von Hildebrand's life would be in greatest danger if we missed the train! As I opened the hood, without any hope of discovering the problem, I heard my passengers begin praying the rosary. Wearily I closed the hood and tried again to start the car. The engine started running as if nothing had been the matter. We breathed a sigh of relief, but after another hundred meters we had again come to a stop. This routine repeated itself dozens of times. It was a terrible ordeal for poor Professor von Hildebrand as we only made very slow progress in small stages. Finally we saw lights coming from Marchegg in the distance, but we had to admit defeat. It would no longer be possible to reach the train station in time.

Again, we have von Hildebrand's own description:

> There are moments in life in which everything seems to be
> collapsing: our head-over-heels departure from Vienna, which
> seemed to guarantee our safety, turned out to be an illusion.
> Why should Hellmut's car develop troubles just when its good
> performance was essential to our escape? We prayed ardently, and
> finally decided to spend the night in the small town of Marchegg
> and take the very first train in the morning. We found a room in
> a small inn on the main road; and it was there that we spent one
> of the most terrible nights of our lives: trucks were constantly
> passing and every time I imagined that they were German tanks
> which had already advanced all the way to the northern border of
> Austria.

The next morning, they continued with their plan and rode together
to the train station by bus. Laun again captures von Hildebrand's remarkable freedom of spirit:

> We took our seats on the bus. Along the way—and this I
> will never forget—von Hildebrand recited his favorite poems by
> Mörike. Outwardly he seemed completely composed.

But the pressure was obviously enormous. Even after von Hildebrand had boarded the train with Gretchen, Laun, standing under their
compartment window on the platform, remembers how von Hildebrand
kept looking anxiously toward the border:

> I could see from the tension in his expression that he feared the
> news of the invasion could still arrive before the departure of the
> train and that this would lead to the closure of the border. Finally
> the all-clear was given! We waved and waved until in the distance
> the train passed over the March Bridge and then disappeared from
> sight. I knew at that very moment the terrible fear of death had
> suddenly lifted from my beloved friend and he was now saved.

Laun returned to have his car repaired. The source of the stalling turned out to be a broken gas line. As he burst into the apartment of his friends, he learned that there had been a false alarm from Salzburg. To the surprise of Laun and the circle of friends, von Hildebrand and his wife returned to Vienna a few days later. Laun comments:

> Of course we knew that a final farewell was quite imminent. We sensed that the occupation of Austria would have the effect of making a war even less avoidable. Thus our final gatherings took place under a shadow and an uncertain and threatening future drew near. We knew how much von Hildebrand loved Western Europe, especially Austria and Vienna, whose beauty he knew and admired in all its particulars.

In fact, Hitler's invasion came just a few days later, and so did von Hildebrand's final escape from Vienna. Here, in addition to von Hildebrand's notes, we have an account written by his nephew, Michael Braunfels, who was then a music student living in Vienna. Braunfels sheds further light on why von Hildebrand hoped to stay in Vienna, despite the fact that his friends in Germany were increasingly calling to urge his departure—in guarded tones, of course. Braunfels recounts:

> In the Kärntnerstrasse people expressed their opinions boldly through swastikas and the red, white, and red [of the Austrian flag] which they wore on their lapels or on the arms. Toward the end of the week, it became ever more clear that the swastikas were hopelessly in the minority—which again encouraged Gogo's* optimism and relative lack of worry. If my memory is correct, I still saw Gogo on Wednesday or Thursday of that week and though being somewhat nervous he was still quite optimistic.[9]

---

* Von Hildebrand's lifelong nickname.

March 11 was for Braunfels a day like any other:

That evening, I went over to Gilbert Schuchter's to prepare a
rice pudding. We engaged in much lighthearted banter. Just as we
were expecting a Mozart symphony on the radio, we were stunned
when instead we heard the voice of [Arthur] Seyss-Inquart.[*] He
admonished the public to remain calm and announced that he
had taken control of the government in order to welcome Hitler's
troops. We immediately left and ran to the von Hildebrands' in
the Habsburgergasse. Naturally it was not easy to make our way
through the crowds that were gathering. We saw many shady
characters who were now brashly, arrogantly, and aggressively
displaying themselves as Nazis. There were also faces, pale and
shocked, eyes wide with terror, and many elderly women standing
in their doorways with eyes red from crying.

Finally they reached the von Hildebrands' apartment:

When I saw Gogo, his hands were trembling from the
agitation. Gilbert and I implored him to leave everything and
to flee at once. In the background I could see Gretchen already
packing their suitcases.

Von Hildebrand might have been able to save his possessions:

I still wished to try to save my beautiful furniture and works
of art, and it occurred to me that I could sell them pro forma to
George Shuster (the president-to-be of Hunter College [in New
York City]) and his wife, Doris, who were in Vienna at the time.
They would then become American property and be saved. A
young Jewish attorney expressed himself willing to draw up

---

[*] Arthur Seyss-Inquart (1892–1946), Austrian Nazi politician, appointed to Schuschnigg's cabinet at Hitler's demand.

the deed, and I still see myself going from room to room, and declaring that I was selling my property to Dr. Shuster. . . . But the awareness that the Jewish attorney was endangering his life by drawing up this deed, and the terrible pressure under which we found ourselves, made me give up the whole project. It was getting late, and the tumult on the streets was increasing.

Von Hildebrand's ability to show concern for the Jewish attorney, even in a moment of looming mortal danger for himself, reminds us that his struggle against Hitler was above all carried out on the battlefield of conscience.

Braunfels' account continues:

I told Gretchen that once I had helped Gogo find a taxi I would come back in a second one to pick her up. Gilbert and I stood on either side of Gogo as we prepared to leave. He had dressed to make himself as unrecognizable as possible, allowing his hat to sit low on his brow. Not for the world would he be separated from his old-fashioned walking stick with its silver cap, by which everyone knew him (he insisted it was absolutely necessary in case he needed to defend himself!). It was not at all easy to find a taxi. There were just too many people who needed to flee!

Could it be that von Hildebrand's humor did not desert him, even in this dire moment? Braunfels reports, "When we finally got a taxi in the vicinity of the opera house, Gogo bowed before the taxi driver, as if before the Kaiser himself!" Schuchter continued on with von Hildebrand to the train station, while Braunfels soon found a second taxi and returned to the apartment to fetch his aunt Gretchen. This was not without its own drama:

As I stepped onto the street with Gretchen, the car was surrounded by a curious and—to my perception—rather rowdy crowd. For this reason it seemed prudent and safer if Gretchen rode alone to the train station, so that the crowd would not bother

her. I bid a heartfelt farewell to "Mama." The meter popped up in the taxi, and the crowd no longer paid heed to Gretchen, who rode off undisturbed, while I walked slowly toward home. They followed me for a brief while, but as I did not turn around, they eventually went their own way.

Already at the train station, von Hildebrand waited for Gretchen's arrival with great anxiety. He writes:

> The anguish I went through while waiting at the railway station cannot be described; time was pressing and I had firmly decided not to leave without Gretchen, whose life was certainly also in danger. What a prayer of gratitude came to my lips when I saw her! We rushed to the train that was leaving for Pressburg [Bratislava] shortly afterwards.

But they would not be safe until they had crossed into Czechoslovakia. Von Hildebrand continues:

> The trip from Vienna to the Czech border is not a long one; but it was a terrible one. The train was full of people, mostly Jews, hoping to escape at the very last minute; they all had an agonized expression on their faces; one felt as if they were terrified by the sight of a snake about to devour them. There was a gruesome Nazi on the train, who was gleefully looking at his victims in all the compartments. When the train finally arrived in Pressburg, the conductor announced that only those who had a foreign passport could leave the country; all others were to go back to Vienna. The expression of despair visible on people's faces was so terrible that one had the feeling of a sort of apocalypse.

This would have been a death sentence for the von Hildebrands had they been using Austrian passports. Dietrich had in fact automatically become an Austrian citizen the day he began teaching at the University of Vienna in 1935, but he had never acquired an Austrian passport and instead traveled on the Swiss passport he had inherited from his grandfather. By marriage, Gretchen was also a Swiss citizen:

> I had this precious document with me. In the Swiss passport, the place of birth is not indicated; it only states the Canton to which one belongs, and one's profession: in my case, the only things stated were Zurich and Professor. The guard asked me whether I was a professor in Zurich; without answering I nodded, and we went through.

A few hours later, the border police would have been equipped with the arrest warrants and photos of Dietrich and Gretchen that were posted at all Austrian border crossings. Von Hildebrand continues:

> Practically all the other passengers were sent back to their horrible fate. The train started moving again, and all of a sudden we saw the sign indicating that we had reached Czech territory. We were saved. What a hymn of gratitude we prayed! Of course, the future was dark: we had lost everything, and all my fears about the spreading of Nazism had been confirmed; I knew with absolute certainty that Austria was to be the first victim, but that the invasion of this noble country was only a first step that was to lead inevitably and mercilessly to another terrible world war.

"Five hours after our departure," he writes, "in the middle of the night, three Gestapo agents came to my apartment to arrest me, and found it empty. I had the honor of being the first on their list of arrests, after the heads of the government." Some have suggested that he would not have been arrested but simply shot on sight:

> I made a telephone call to Vienna, to find out that three Gestapo officers were in my apartment. The maidservant who answered the phone was sly and clever enough to make me understand that we had undesirable guests by asking them *sotto voce* whether I was to know that they were there.

I found out later that my devoted friend Marguerite Solbrig had had the presence of mind to burn my address book, containing the list of all my friends, acquaintances, and collaborators in Vienna. She certainly saved lives by this loving and intelligent gesture.

It would have been fascinating to hear von Hildebrand himself describe how he and Gretchen made their way from Czechoslovakia, then to Hungary, and then to Fribourg in Switzerland, where they would live for eleven months, and from Switzerland to Toulouse in southern France, where he taught for most of 1939 at the Catholic University of Toulouse. It would have been gripping to hear him tell how they experienced the German invasion of France in 1940 and the German advance toward the south of the country, and about their struggle to find a way out of France through Spain into Portugal.

Not only would he have told of the horrors of flight and hiding but he would have given particular attention to the many people who overwhelmed him with their generosity as he ran from one place to another, seeking safety for himself and his family. He would have singled out for a special remembrance the saintly Edmond Michelet, to whom he was referred by the Catholic philosopher Yves Simon; only through the heroic services of Michelet and his wife was von Hildebrand able to get the false documents he and his family needed to remain hidden in France until they could escape to Spain and then to Portugal.

He would have told how, once he arrived in Lisbon, he learned that he had been put, through the mediation of Jacques Maritain, on a list of one hundred Jewish German intellectuals to be brought to the United States by the Rockefeller Foundation. He was one of just two Catholics who were included on account of their outspoken battle against anti-Semitism.

Had he finished his memoirs he would have let us see not just the witness but the refugee, the man of faith who in desperate circumstances kept alive his hope in God and his gratitude for every helping hand extended to him and his family.

Perhaps nothing sums up so deeply the spirit of Dietrich von Hildebrand's witness as what he confided to his wife, Alice, in his final years.

It is fitting that we give her the last word, for Dietrich's memoirs, remarkable as they are as a historical document, were first and foremost a love letter and a labor of love:

Having spent a blessed sabbatical year with my husband at the family villa of San Francesco in Florence, and having seen the von Hildebrand mansion in Munich, I once asked my husband,

> Was it not hard for you, having spent much of your life in these beautiful and noble houses, to live for years totally dependent on the help of others and in slummy apartments?" He looked at me in *utter amazement*. "How could you ask such a question?" he exclaimed. "For *nothing in the world* would I have traded the joy of tasting the sweetness of Christian charity!"

PART II

WRITINGS AGAINST THE NAZI IDEOLOGY*

God is offended regardless of whether the victim of a murder is a Jew,
a Socialist, or a bishop. Innocent blood cries out to heaven.
—DIETRICH VON HILDEBRAND

We know from the memoirs that the main instrument by which Dietrich von Hildebrand fought against Nazism and for the independence of Austria was the journal he founded in Vienna, *Der christliche Ständestaat*. He fought as a philosopher; he fought at the level of first principles. Despite the lengthening shadow cast by Nazi Germany on Austria,

---

* Some of the texts that follow are complete essays, some are excerpts. With two exceptions the essays were all first published in *Der christliche Ständestaat*.

despite the approach of the world war, despite the fact that he lived in Vienna in constant danger of assassination, he did not withdraw from his vocation as philosopher. He did not think that the time for examining first principles was past; he did not think that making fundamental distinctions was irrelevant to the needs of the time.

We have heard in the memoirs the story of how he launched the journal with the help of the Austrian chancellor Engelbert Dollfuss. We want now to hear the voice of von Hildebrand speaking in the pages of the journal, speaking as his contemporaries heard him. It is one thing to hear von Hildebrand recalling in his memoirs a quarter of a century later the tumultuous years in Vienna, but it is something else to hear him speaking *in* those years, in the midst of the tumult. Thus the essays that follow complete the memoirs.

AUSTRIA AND NATIONALISM

Der christliche Ständestaat
December 16, 1934

*In April of 1921 von Hildebrand was invited to Paris as a German repre-
sentative to an international peace conference organized by the eminent
French Catholic pacifist Marc Sangnier. This eventful trip is vividly described in the opening portion of the memoirs. At one point during the
conference, von Hildebrand was asked what he thought about the German
invasion of Belgium in 1914. His answer, "It was an atrocious crime." This
earned him great respect among his French hosts, yet he set off a controversy
in the German press back home, for nationalism and militarism were alive
and well in Germany. Von Hildebrand was an archenemy of nationalism.*

*When Hitler began to rise in German political life, von Hildebrand
thought that he was appealing (among other things) to the worst kind of
German nationalism. Hence one great theme in his anti-Nazi writings
is the evil of nationalism. He abhorred the saying "My country, right or
wrong."*

*He was glad that he could conduct his opposition to Hitler from Vi-
enna, the Austrian capital, since the multinational structure of the old
Austrian Empire of the Habsburgs, he said, secured Austria against nationalism. He felt that he was calling Austria back to its multinational
roots and to its true identity when he urged it to become a bulwark against
German nationalism.*

*In this essay he explains some of these ideas, and he also lays out the im-
portant contrast between nationalism and patriotism by drawing a parallel
with the contrast between egoistic self-love and a rightly ordered self-love.*

• • •

Since the very beginning of its existence, Austria has embodied an antithesis to nationalism. As the eastern district of the Holy Roman Empire, which was itself the worldly representation of Christianity and thus free of all national narrowness, Austria exercised a purely Christian and Western European mission before the period of the Christianization of Hungary. Later, as the head of the Holy Roman Empire, it had a supranational character, not only because it always embraced non-Germanic nations such as the Bohemians, Hungarians, and southern Slavs, but also because it was interiorly united and formed by an ideal that was religious, multi-national, cultural, and dynastic in character. This was even more true of the Austro-Hungarian monarchy. And although the population of present-day Austria is almost entirely German, it nevertheless retains its mission of opposing nationalism. Through its independence and autonomy vis-à-vis Germany, Austria embodies an emphatic denial of the great heresy of the nineteenth and twentieth centuries: nationalism.

What is nationalism? This terrible error exists in many degrees, starting with the identification of nation and state and reaching all the way to committing idolatry toward a nation, that is, making the nation the highest criterion for the whole of life and making it the ultimate goal and highest good. We will content ourselves here with pointing out the distinction between nationalism and genuine patriotism, without going into all the other possible forms of deifying a nation.

Genuine patriotism and nationalism are as different from each other as the true, divinely ordained love of self is from egoistic self-love. Genuine patriotism and genuine love of the nation to which one belongs— two concepts that are by no means identical—are both morally positive and indeed, obligatory attitudes, like every divinely ordained, well-ordered love. To begin with, this love affirms the value that resides in the national community as such, considered as a spiritual space with an individually distinctive cultural character, a space into which the individual has been placed (usually not as a result of any effort on his own part) and which sustains and nourishes him like spiritual soil.

The affirmation of the general value that lies in the nation as such, and takes on a vivid, concrete form for each person with regard to his own nation, includes a special sense of belonging to the nation of which one is a member, love for the "divine idea" which this particular nation represents, a special familiarity and solidarity with it, gratitude for everything that one receives from it, a special understanding one possesses for it, and finally the task that one is given through belonging to it. All of these elements are contained in genuine patriotism as well as in true love of one's nation.

This attitude also entails that one acknowledges every foreign nation in its particular character as something justified and valuable. Certainly, a person's love for his own nation will be greater, more intense, and of a different kind. But every person who refuses to grant other nations the right to develop freely, who holds that he can ignore their rights and justified wishes, and who imagines that he may trample them underfoot if it should be advantageous to his own country, thereby contradicts the very foundation that validates his love for his own country. He is, to put it bluntly, incapable of truly loving his own country. His behavior is no longer the result of love, but of collective egoism—indeed, of nationalism.

The first characteristic of nationalism is thus a collective egoism that disavows respect and concern for foreign nations and evaluates the rights of one's own nation according to criteria different from those applied to other nations. It fails to see the beam in the eye of one's own country, while only seeing the splinter in the eye of the foreign countries. This fundamental error fails to recognize that nations need one another, even from a purely cultural perspective; that nations are created for each other's sake; and that pitting one's own nation against another and indulging in the delusion of every nation's cultural self-sufficiency actually hollows out and sterilizes the genius of one's own nation.

Nationalism is also present wherever the nation is ranked above communities of even higher value, such as larger communities of peoples or mankind as a whole. The German nationalist, for instance, maintains that the well-being of his own country is more important than the *bonum commune* of Europe or even of mankind. Here too, collective egoism is evident. This perversion reaches its culmination when the nation is ranked above the highest community of them all, namely the supernatural community of the Church understood as the mystical body of Christ. This phenomenon has occurred again and again throughout history, from Barbarossa, Louis of Bavaria, and Philip the Fair, down to our own days.

Another expression of nationalism manifests itself when the individual is regarded as a mere means for the nation to exploit. As soon as the good and ill of a nation, or even its mere existence, is ranked higher than the immortal soul of a human being, his immortal soul, and his salvation, the true hierarchy of values has been reversed and one falls prey to the heresy of nationalism. Whoever regards the unity of the nation as the ultimate and most vital bond of community and does not maintain that the unity of the living members of the Mystical Body of Christ constitutes a more authentic, more profound, and more living unity has also committed the error of nationalism. Anyone who does not see in other persons first and foremost a soul created by God and for God has already succumbed to this heresy, and the same is true of the one who sees a German, Frenchman, or Italian first, rather than a human being with whom he shares a profound connection through their great shared destiny, which encompasses birth, death, personal creatureliness, and the ordination toward eternity.

Finally, anyone who holds that state and nation are so interrelated that every nation requires the existence of a corresponding state, and who therefore sees a disvalue in the situation where either one and the same nation is present in several states, or various nations are joined together into a single state, is also a nationalist. He fails to see that a national bond of unity is not the only factor that contributes to the formation of a thriving state. He does not understand that, in order to be able to develop fully, it may make sense for certain nations to be present in several states. This is because he confuses the true value of his own nation with an imperialistic need to command the attention of other nations.

This brings us to the decisive point: the nationalistic ethos. No act of idolization originates in a real recognition of value; in fact, it necessarily blocks a recognition of the value proper to a good, for it does not recognize how this good is an image of God. The same is true of nationalism. Nationalists never see the true values of their nation, its cultural nobility, or the deeper significance of its national genius. All they see is its power, its *gloire*, its political influence. The decisive point, which makes the nationalist's breast swell with pride, is not the sublimity of his culture, but the number of square kilometers in his country and the size of its army.

The nationalist's love is not a greater love, but an inferior and impure love. Fundamentally, it is not love at all; it is self-assertion, the will to power, the drive for prestige, and self-glorification. No amount of sacrifices made on behalf of the nation in a time of war can in any way change this. The nationalist is incapable of genuine love, for love of a good is always genuine only to the extent that it participates in the love with which God loves it.

The horrible heresy of nationalism not only destroys the unity of the West, but also corrodes each individual nation from within. It is a terrible misfortune for any country, but for Austria, it is the negation of its very meaning and essence. . . . The meaning of Austria's present mission is to be an outright repudiation of nationalism. Even today, although Austria has a population that is almost entirely German, it is not a mere branch of the German nation, nor a mere portion of the German cultural sphere; still less is it simply Germany's outpost in the East. Austria constitutes a cultural space all its own, a totally unique form of German character that differs as greatly from Germany as America does from England. As I have already shown in these pages, Austria embodies the noblest and most authentic development of the German spirit.

And Austria still retains its abiding mission of universality today. It must always continue to be an organic marriage between the essence of East and West, between the spirit of North and South, between Germanic and Latin culture. Its purpose and meaning has never been simply to Germanize its neighbors; every imperialistic, centralizing, or colonizing attitude contradicts its very essence and mission. Its policy has never been militant subjugation, but rather the organic unification of different cultures. This is why the old saying applies to the cultural sphere as well, *"Bella gerant alii, tu felix Austria, nube!"* (Let other countries wage war, you, O happy Austria, expand by marrying.) Even the Austria of today, small as it is, has been charged with the mission of being a bastion against National Socialism and Bolshevism and to remain the West in microcosm, a building block for the reconstruction of Europe in the Catholic and Western spirit. Austria must lead Europe in its return to Christ and its liberation from the heresy of nationalism. Austrian patriotism has always consisted in avowing those principles of unity which rank higher than a purely national principle. Above all, it has embraced these three crucial elements: the Catholic idea, the Western idea, and the idea of a universal, federative, and dynastic bond among peoples.

Even today, every true Austrian who loves his country, who knows its tradition and history, and who understands its meaning and mission, must profess his allegiance to supranational principles of unity and possess the universal Western spirit. Genuine patriotism and nationalism are always mutually exclusive, but *Austrian* patriotism and *Austrian* nationalism contradict one another in an especially egregious manner. The patriotism of the Austrian, if he has understood anything at all of Austria's genius, must be relaxed, harmonious, and well-ordered for it is necessarily more than the mere expression of his self-assertion or will to live: it is his profession of allegiance to the supranational, Catholic, and cultural idea which unites peoples. An affirmation of Austria and a commitment to its existence and flourishing always entails an affirmation of even higher values as well. This glorious country, which lies at the heart of Europe in more than a merely geographical sense—this unparalleled microcosm of the West, with its radiant, gentle, reconciling, unifying, Catholic atmosphere that surrounds us on all sides and elevates all whom it envelops—this nation at the heart of Europe gives birth to a consciousness of community that offers the true antidote to nationalism.

The political orientation of Austria must always do justice to its mission. If Austria wishes to remain true to its innermost identity, it must never conduct nationalistic politics in concert with Germany—not even with a Germany freed of National Socialism. Rather, its politics must be always and exclusively European. Austria will always side with those countries whose politics are inspired not by nationalistic dreams of power, but by the *bonum commune* of Europe; for one is a true Austrian only if one is also a European. And it is precisely loyalty to this universal character of political action and to the true legacy of the old imperial idea that gives rise to the great mission which the independent nation of Austria has taken up on behalf of German culture as a whole, namely the inner liberation of Germany from an un-German, Prussian hegemony. . . .

GERMAN CULTURE
AND NATIONAL SOCIALISM

Der christliche Ständestaat
June 3, 1934

We saw in the introduction to this book that von Hildebrand, as the son of a great German sculptor, was a man of profound artistic sensibility. Here he denounces Nazism on the basis of his artistic culture. In the essays that follow we will see him usually speaking as a personalist philosopher, but here he speaks as a man of culture. We are reminded of the moving passage in the memoirs where he hears his wife Gretchen playing Bach on the piano and is overwhelmed by the contrast between the world of Bach and the world of Nazi Germany.

This essay is important in another respect: it shows that von Hildebrand's antinationalism, as expressed in the previous essay, did not prevent him from having a particularly deep understanding for and ardent love of his own German nation. He never adhered to the cosmopolitan mentality of those who feel themselves to be "citizens of the world" with no particular attachment to their native nation. The talk of "German culture" in the title of this essay encompasses both Austria and Germany, and it does not refer to Germany in distinction to Austria, as in the previous essay.

Again and again, one encounters the fatal error of equating the battle against National Socialism with a battle against Germany. Only a confused, short-sighted way of thinking could identify one particular government with an entire people, much less a nation. It has not, for instance, occurred to anyone to identify the Austrian Social Democratic government of 1920 with the Austrian people, thereby construing all attacks on socialism and its spokesmen as attacks on the Austrian people. . . .

The un-German character of National Socialism can be seen not only in its basic blindness and hostility to other nations, but also in the following points.

Anyone who can appreciate the nature of the great, noble German nation sees that its particular strength lies entirely in the realm of the spirit. Germany's greatness resides not only to an eminent degree in the realms of theoretical knowledge, art, and especially sublime spiritual music; it also boasts a remarkable wealth of geniuses and outstanding individual personalities. But the particular strength of the German nation is not the culture of daily life, nor the formation of the vital-psychical sphere that is so appealing in the English, nor the enchantment of comportment and demeanor, the grace and charm of temperament that is so striking in the Romanic and Slavic peoples. The German strength lies in specific expressions of the spirit.

Perhaps the Germans are often less loved than people of other nations because, in order to grasp their unique value, one must penetrate all the way into the hidden sphere of the spirit—a requirement not especially apt to make a people outstandingly likeable. To transfer a nation's center of gravity to the vital sphere generally entails a misconception of its genius, quite apart from any distortions that may have arisen from an ideological heresy. In the case of the German genius, however, it entails a very specific error. If the glorious treasures of German culture are to be brought to light, the German must turn all his attention to the sphere of the spirit.

For the German, the cultivation of the vital sphere is much more embarrassing than for the Englishman or the Italian. Though he is disposed to be more dualistic than the other two, he is also constrained to master everything (including the vital-psychical realm) precisely by first anchoring himself in the sphere of the spirit. Yet for this very reason, we also encounter a spiritual alertness and richness in the German that is otherwise rare in such large groups of persons: and in this respect, there is something to be said for the hackneyed expression about the Germans as a people of "poets and thinkers." This specifically spiritual trait of the German nature is also revealed in the German's undeniable longing to see the whole of life as anchored in the spirit. The German is specifically "unfrivolous": the sub-spiritual sphere never suffices for him. Thus he becomes especially prone to creating idols. For even when he loses his way in the lowlands of life, he always tries to undergird baser things spiritually and, whenever possible, metaphysically.

The extremely brutal atmosphere of National Socialism, the hostility to the spirit we encounter in the style of its spokesmen, its terminology, its songs, its public manifestations, and its institutions—in short, in its entire ethos—is thus a terrible defection from the German essence and destiny. Anyone who has read *Faust*, who has listened to the works of Mozart and Beethoven, or who has felt the unique nobility and the deep, distinguished preciousness of the German nature, need cast only a single glance at the shrill, demagogical mentality of National Socialism, which aims only at producing external effects, to see that nothing less German could possibly be imagined. It is no exaggeration to say that not a single word in all the speeches of the representatives of National Socialism is even remotely related to German literature. Anyone who regards the programmatic text *Mein Kampf*, so full of slogans and pseudo-education, as a product of the German spirit, has never sensed even a hint of the genius of the glorious German nation. In this book, demagoguery and slogans are, in fact, elevated to the level of principles.

Anyone who has immersed himself in the calm and lovely world of the fairy tales of the Brothers Grimm; anyone who has been embraced by the chaste poems in *Des Knaben Wunderhorn*; anyone whose soul has been expanded by the radiantly golden richness of spirit found in a poem of Goethe's; anyone whose heart has been moved by the angelic, sublime beauty of Mozart's music, can feel nothing but deep revulsion at the sound of the Nazi *Horst Wessel Lied*, and must inevitably feel that here two irreconcilable worlds have confronted each other. Anyone who wants to know what the German essence and spirit are should contemplate Grünewald's altarpiece in Colmar, or Schlüter's statue of the great Elector, Frederick III; he should read the poems of Walther von der Vogelweide and Wolfram von Eschenbach, or the works of Goethe, Kleist, and Hölderlin; he should open himself up to the thoughts of Leibniz, Adam Möhler and Scheeben; he should quench his thirst with Bach, Gluck, Mozart, Beethoven, and Schubert; he should look to figures such as Kepler, Otto the Great, Maria Theresia, and St. Albert the Great.

Then he will understand that the hysterical mixture of brutality and sentimentality, the rattling clang of sabres, and the endless flood of spiritually vapid slogans in the Third Reich constitute the most extreme denial of the German spirit and nature. No true German could fail to weep and blush with shame over the fact that the people privileged to call this radiant, kingly fullness and nobility of spirit its own should be handed over to such an un-German, half-baked torrent of slogans and such a clamorous sham, such trivial, such wretched kitsch. The one who is unmoved by all this should keep silent about German culture and the "national feeling," since he has clearly never understood what undeserved fortune he enjoys by being German.

It is also totally in keeping with the un-German ethos and spirit of National Socialism that a great number of its spokesmen repeatedly declare that the glorious two thousand years of German history is irrelevant. They instead attempt to establish direct ties to a nebulous Germanic culture which existed prior to the birth of the German nation. But this "German culture" of Hitler is as little related to true German culture as the female mannequins in a hairdressing salon are related to real feminine beauty.

THE DANGER OF BECOMING MORALLY BLUNTED

Der christliche Ständestaat
November 10, 1935

Von Hildebrand saw that many people who began with a strong oppo-
sition to Nazism could not persevere in this stance; as time passed the
force of their opposition weakened and their sense of the evil of Nazism
became blunted. They "got used" to the Nazi regime. They did not neces-
sarily change their judgment about Nazism, but they ceased to feel the evil
of it. Von Hildebrand tries in this essay to rally his troops by alerting them
to this danger of human nature. He admonishes his readers to cultivate
a certain inner awakedness with regard to goods and evils—not to take
them for granted and not to fail to feel them. He speaks to them as a kind
of spiritual master teaching about the interior discipline needed in the
encounter with monstrous evil.

Habit is a sort of beneficial adaptability in human beings that can make
their lives more bearable, yet it is also a force that can diminish the
spiritual alertness of a person, which is the foundation of all true moral
and spiritual life. Under certain circumstances, it can even eliminate
this alertness entirely.

As long as we are dealing with sufferings that derive from objective
disvalues (such as sickness, physical pain, or impoverishment), the fact
that a person becomes somewhat accustomed to the suffering is a salu-

tary aid, for it frees him to be responsive to more important and more essential things. Of course, a saint will not rely exclusively on habit: he will first experience the oppressive character of an evil fully and accept it with resignation as a trial. He will not become numbed toward it. The saint will do justice to the meaning of every suffering and allow its purifying effect to unfold completely. The apathy of Stoicism is in no way his ideal. But as long as it is a question of sufferings that are not caused by the destruction of something of objective value, even the saint will get used to them to some extent. And this must be recognized as salutary, for once his resignation and peaceful acceptance of the suffering as coming from God's hand has had its purifying and deepening effect, he becomes free for more important and more essential things, whether in the sphere of the active life or by becoming more capable of appropriately responding to greater and deeper "words" that God speaks to him.

But even in the case of an ordinary person who is not yet capable of this highest affirmation of all sufferings, it is a salutary gift if he does not become continually absorbed by such suffering or constantly oppressed by bitterness, but instead is adaptable enough to grow accustomed to the suffering and thus to become relatively free for other, more important things and to endure the suffering more and more as a matter of course and without noticing it.

But the situation is very different when it is a question of joy rather than suffering. Human beings should never grow accustomed to any gift from the "Father of lights": the sun shining for us, every drink of water that refreshes us, or the physical health and external means that enable us to lead a tolerable life. In such cases, habit has an exclusively negative effect, for the grateful appreciation of all things that are good should never diminish; nothing should ever be simply taken for granted. Here our task must be to restrain the power of habit and to take care that we never become blasé. We must remain grateful for all goods, great or small, with an undiminished alertness.

Even in the case of responses to evils that stem from the loss of a great value, we must never get used to them—for example, the death of a beloved person or a situation in which we are cut off from religious support. The response God wants from us here is a resigned and peaceful endurance of these evils, not our getting used to them. The magnitude of the loss in such cases needs to be felt in an undiminished fashion.

Most importantly, however, we must not concede any power to habit when it is a question, not of goods or evils *for us*, but simply of positive or negative *values*. We must never grow so accustomed to the beauty of the Ninth Symphony of Beethoven, for example, or to the beauty of nature, that we are no longer impressed by them. *A fortiori,* we must never become accustomed to the moral goodness of a human being, and still less to the splendor of Christ's holiness. On the contrary, the flame of His holiness ought to be emblazoned upon our hearts more and more. The spirit of *gratias agimus tibi propter magnam gloriam tuam* ("We give you thanks for your great glory") must never wane within us; indeed, it ought to increase unceasingly. Otherwise, as Plato says in the *Phaedrus,* "the wings of our soul" will wither.

Nor must we ever get used to sin—for then moral disvalues such as infidelity, injustice, mendacity, or brutality will no longer make any impression on us. Our consciences become numbed all too easily, not only when we ourselves sin repeatedly without truly repenting of the sin each time, but also when we put up with the injustices of others and so accustom ourselves to a morally poisoned atmosphere.

Whoever habitually consorts with persons who are morally perverted in their basic outlook will, as a result of putting up with their attitude, slowly become poisoned himself, even if he had initially rejected it with indignation and never given it his approval in any way. If he does not "break" with the others, his initial indignation will soon subside and turn into a mere regret; he will become more and more desensitized by getting used to the base moral atmosphere they inhabit. Similarly, if a state, employing the fullness of its inherent dignity, and by means of its divinely ordained authority, enacts laws that profoundly conflict not only with all natural law, but even with the commandments of God; if deeds which must be called criminal are perpetrated on a daily and hourly basis in the name of this state authority; and if the spirit that fills this state is a spirit of brutal force, unparalleled injustice, diabolical hate, and mindless impurity, there will be a much greater danger of demoralization, even for all those who do not live within its borders.

The tendency to put up with such a state grows stronger, as time goes by, than it would in the case of a single wicked individual. Every new murder committed by an individual occasions the same sort of revulsion in us. The countless crimes of which we hear in the course of our lives fail to desensitize us precisely because we never resign ourselves to them. Each crime remains isolated, and despite their frequency, we never grow so accustomed to them that our criteria change and we tacitly tone down our moral demands. The murderer of Düsseldorf, or the crimes of a man like Harmann, do not make a "common" murder any less horrific in our eyes, or lessen the justified indignation it arouses in us.

But if a state slowly descends—in its official statements, in its legislation, and in its day-to-day conduct of affairs—ever more deeply into immorality and barbarism, then there is a tremendous risk that the populace will gradually become accustomed to its ethical level, that their initial indignation will subside, and that they will imperceptibly lower their own ethical criteria when they see that all the crimes committed by the state go unpunished as it continues to exist with the dignity of its own inherent authority and the formal recognition of other states.

At the time, the laws passed by the National Socialist regime in the year 1933 provoked great indignation everywhere in the world. Since then, however, so many even more terrible things have happened that the events of 1933 no longer make much of an impression on most people. They have gotten used to the Third Reich by means of an imperceptible process of acclimatization that has led to its increasing acceptance. Their own moral sensitivity has suffered harm. The Third Reich is fortunate there is no effective judicial decree that identifies and condemns the kind of spirit that motivates it (although such judgments are often applied to the private murderer and criminal), and this lack allows the force of habit to have its full effect, even with regard to moral issues. How accustomed the world has become to the rivers of blood, the countless instances of oppression, and the flood of the most terrible injustices perpetrated by Bolshevism!

People generally remain indignant only for a short while. After a certain time, a person tends to become weary of disapprobation, even if the deed that occasioned his revulsion goes unpunished and the sin continues to cry to heaven. If he cannot find relief for his indignation by doing something himself, and he is powerless in the face of the continued existence of evil, he will soon revert to everyday living. On the other hand, his ability to make ethical distinctions would not be weakened in any way if he were to arrive at an inner peace by enduring, as something permitted by God, an evil that he cannot effectively combat—not in any way resigning himself to it, nor wavering in his inner rejection of it, but enduring it with the awareness that he does not have the power to remove every evil from the world. For that can be done only by the Lord God, who says: "Vengeance is mine." If, however, a person simply permits himself to get used to an evil, if he simply "comes to terms" with it because it exists *de facto* and he cannot change it, then his soul will suffer harm. It is imperative that we recognize this danger and take up the battle against the desensitizing effect of habit.

As Christians, of course, we must never succumb to any embittered attitude of hatred. We must always retain a profound compassion for those who have gone astray, and we cannot allow ourselves to be poisoned by our indignation. Yet we must remain alert. Our indignation and profound sorrow over the fact that a state officially proclaims, propagates, and puts into effect things that make a mockery not only of God's commandments, but of the most elementary principles of humanity, must not be permitted to abate. There are some monstrosities we must never forget, much less accept, such as the racial materialism of the National Socialist ideology, the policy of sterilization, the legislation regulating marriage, the denial of an objective law, the murders of June 30, 1934, the unparalleled persecution of the Jews (which repudiates any and every human solidarity), the pharisaical trials on trumped-up charges related to foreign currency (leading to draconian sentences that mock any notion of natural law), and the arbitrary defamation of countless individuals. Nothing should diminish our inner judgment, our unconditional rejection, our consciousness of the horrific immorality of it all, and our determination to fight it with every means available.

This is completely different from a politically motivated attitude of rejection and disavowal (such as occurs, for example, in connection with a revolution). This attitude may well be justified: for we should not "put up" with something we regard as incompatible with the "genius" or tradition of a country. But the rejection of moral and religious disvalues is in an entirely different category. For here we face a threat to the integrity of our moral standards, where "habituation" means that we no longer use our original moral standards to assess measures implemented elsewhere, but instead regard them against the background of the Third Reich. We owe it to ourselves, to our neighbors, and to our homeland to guard ourselves against such moral blindness. As soon as we clearly grasp the threat that the mere existence of the Third Reich poses to our moral vision, much has already been gained.

This may strike many readers as unbridled obstinacy, as riding a hobby-horse or even as personal embitterment. But no such consideration can prevent us from calling attention again and again to this danger or from being resolute in challenging people to alertly judge and resolutely reject the National Socialist ideology and morality. For here too, the words of St. Peter that the Church prays every evening are eminently applicable: "*Fratres—Sobrii estote, et vigilate: quia adversarius vester diabolus tamquam leo rugiens circuit, quaerens quem devoret: cui resistite fortes in fide.*" (Brothers: Be sober, be watchful. Your adversary the devil prowls around like a roaring lion, seeking someone to devour. Resist him, firm in your faith) (1 Pt 5:8–9).

AGAINST ANTI-SEMITISM

Free World
November 1941

We know from the memoirs about the anti-Semitism that von Hildebrand encountered in Austria. Many people who agreed with him about the evils of Hitler and Nazism still harbored animosity toward the Jews. Recall his 1933 lecture at the seminary in Vienna: when he exposed as un-Christian the anti-Semitism widespread in Austria, half the seminarians left in protest. Or recall how he fought against the anti-Semitism that broke out in 1936 on the occasion of the murder of the philosopher Moritz Schlick. Some people wanted to excuse the murder on the grounds that Schlick embodied "the Jewish spirit," even though he was not Jewish himself. Very few Catholics, and indeed very few bishops at that time, fought against anti-Semitism as resolutely and as relentlessly as von Hildebrand did. One has only to read about von Hildebrand in the recent study of the historian John Connelly, From Enemy to Brother *(Harvard, 2012), in order to see how extraordinarily independent von Hildebrand was from his milieu and his times, and how radically he lived out of his Catholic faith and his Christian personalism.*

He wrote much in his journal against anti-Semitism, but the following essay, though just like the essays in his journal, was written in 1941 in the United States. It gives a particularly good recapitulation of his stance against anti-Semitism.

The absolute incompatibility of anti-Semitism, as an element of racism, with the democratic ideal and with Christian doctrine is obvious. Adolf

Hitler said in Nuremberg in September 1933: "Between a man of a higher race and a man of a lower race there is a greater difference than between a man of a lower race and an animal." This conception, denying the essential difference between the human being and the animal, denies also the spiritual nature of man and the unity of humanity. The foundation of all authentic democracy, on the other hand, is the dignity of every person and the fundamental rights which every man possesses as a human being. Democracy thus presupposes not only the essential difference between man and animal but also the common spiritual nature of all human beings regardless of race.

The contrast of racism with Catholic doctrine is still more radical. Every man, whatever his race, is created by God after His image. Every man has an immortal soul destined for eternal communion with God. Race, according to Catholic doctrine, is a quite secondary and accidental biological factor, having no effect on the possibility of man's attaining his eternal end, since the values he is called upon to exemplify are by no means determined by race. Men as such are all equal before God: all are fallen in Adam, all are redeemed in Christ. St. Paul says: "There is neither Jew nor Greek. There is neither bond nor free. There is neither male nor female. For you are all one in Christ Jesus." The racial doctrine of Adolf Hitler was condemned by the Holy See in March 1938, along with seven other propositions characteristic of the Nazi regime.

There is another kind of anti-Semitism, however, which is much more widespread than the racial variety. It does not refer to this pseudo-philosophic approach; in fact it even emphatically rejects it. This brand of anti-Semitism simply affirms that the Jews are a disastrous element for any constructive culture, for the healthy life of nations. Anti-Semites of this variety accuse the Jews of infecting occidental philosophy and art with a destructive, disintegrating spirit. Some pretend that the Jews are responsible for the demoralization of business life, that they are racketeers; now seeing in them the creators of a ruthless capitalism, now accusing them of being the spearhead of Communism, of spreading revolution and dissension wherever they go and destroying all genuine patriotism. All agree that as a foreign element in the body of a nation the Jews are parasites. This kind of anti-Semitism, although not expressly based on the Nazi philosophy, is at the present time a consciously employed and dangerously demagogic weapon of Nazism.

The rising tide of anti-Semitism in the United States should serve to remind us that in the tragedy of Europe, where one country after another succumbed to Axis invasion, anti-Semitism was the forerunner of Nazism. In gaining sympathizers within such countries as Austria, Holland, Poland, Hungary, and France, anti-Semitism served to weaken the resistance toward Nazism. Charles Lindbergh's speech at Des Moines and the attitude of the Senate subcommittee investigating war propaganda in the movies are reminiscent of the well-known tricks of Nazi propaganda. Today anti-Semitic propaganda in the United States, conscious or unconscious, means helping Hitler and breaking the moral defense line against Nazism. The more one who calumniates the Jews assures his hearers that he is not an anti-Semite, the more we must distrust him as a dangerous demagogue. Using the well-known formula of Mark Antony—"Brutus is an honorable man"—he lulls his hearers into a sense of security, the more readily to introduce his poison.

This demagogic brand of anti-Semitism is just as incompatible with genuine democracy as the racial variety. It invokes, in the first place, a limitation of the rights of certain citizens in order to diminish their influence. Now a limitation of rights, or any unequal treatment, is admissible in a democracy only if the individual in question is mentally or morally irresponsible or if he has been proved lacking in loyalty to the country. The anti-Semites, in contrast, would place restrictions on individuals solely because they are Jews.

Some of them—and they are the great majority—believe that the simple fact of Jewish descent is enough to justify a limitation of rights, and feel themselves very generous and free from prejudices if they concede that there may be some persons of Jewish descent who may be excepted from this general restriction. They do not see the injustice of vilifying an individual because of his descent, of presupposing that he is morally unreliable in consequence of a fact for which he is by no means responsible. To concede exceptions for Jews who overcome their "disadvantages" by special merits is to reveal still more clearly the obvious injustice of the whole concept. There is a certain irony in the fact that the same people who claim that democracy is in danger when the President exercises certain extraordinary powers in an emergency do not hesitate to violate by anti-Semitic propaganda the most elementary principles of democracy.

Some anti-Semites limit themselves to fighting only against those Jews who belong to the Jewish religious community. Obviously any restriction of the rights of a citizen in consequence of his religious conviction is contradictory to the democratic idea. It was surely a thoroughly undemocratic attitude that inspired Hohenzollern Germany, secularized France, and, above all, England before the Emancipation Bill to deprive the Catholics of many rights and to treat them as second-class citizens.

But, anti-Semites will object, shall we stand inactively aside while the Jews conspire to poison our morality and culture and use us for their selfish purposes? Certainly we should fight all immoral influences from whatever source, but no reasonable and serious man can pretend that all evil comes from the Jews, or even that there are more Jewish racketeers, more Jewish philosophers and artists of a destructive nature than may be found among the "Ayrans." As the German poet Hebbell puts it, "A Jew is neither better nor worse than any other human being." Moreover, certain bad characteristics that are common among the Jews are a result of the immeasurable injuries which non-Jews have inflicted upon them. Rather than incite our indignation, those defects should awaken our conscience and call forth a *mea culpa*.

The myth of a conspiratorial Jewish clan ruling the world is as ridiculous a fable as the widely spread tale of world domination by the Jesuits. Great masses of people have always been susceptible to such fantastic illusions and are always glad to have a scapegoat. They willingly swallow propaganda to the effect that some Jewish world center is responsible at one and the same time for Communism and capitalism, for wars and pacifistic defeatism—for whatever, in short, is regarded as a particular danger in a given country at a given moment. But it seems incredible and disappointing that in our day such ridiculous old myths as the *Protocols of the Elders of Zion* and one about "ritual murders" are again revived by certain so-called scholars. This kind of "science" reminds us of the fantasies of Ludendorff [a famous World War I German general] and his wife, who pretended that Bolshevism was a product of Jews and Jesuits working together.

When we consider this popular anti-Semitism from the Catholic point of view, we find it even more incompatible with Christian doctrine than with democracy. We do not intend here to enter into a full theological examination of the mystery which according to Catholic doctrine is connected with Israel. Israel, once the elected people of God, Who, in the Catholic concept, calls upon it above all to profess the faith in Christ, is regarded as the prodigal son by the Holy Church and its conversion is the deepest desire and hope of Christianity. The words of St. Paul in his Epistle to the Romans (Chapter 11) express this position toward the people of Israel in so far as the religious question itself is concerned. . . .

The concept of Christianity excludes any prejudice against a race, a people, or a nation. Every human being, having an immortal soul, is, when baptized as a member of the Corpus Christi Mysticum (Mystical Body of Christ), a child of God, regardless of his descent. All the liturgy is penetrated with the consciousness of a community which transcends all nations, races, and peoples. And all men who do not belong to this Catholic—that is to say, universal—community are considered, no matter what their race or nationality, as catechumens *in spe* or as beloved errant brothers. Monsignor Saliege, Archbishop of Toulouse, declared some years ago: "I cannot forget that the root of Jesse flourished in Israel and gave there its fruit. The Holy Virgin, Christ, the first disciples were of the Jewish race. How could I not feel myself bound to Israel as the branch to the trunk, which bore it? Besides this I know only one morality and it has universal validity. In every man I see and esteem the sublime dignity of human nature. Catholicism cannot admit that belonging to a certain race should deprive a man of any of his rights. Catholicism proclaims the essential equality of all races and all individuals. A universal religion, Catholicism does not acknowledge differences in the scale of human values that are based on blood or race."

The most hideous element in modern anti-Semitism is the ambiguity in the definition of "Jew." Sometimes one opposes Jew to Christian, sometimes Jew to Aryan. But in reality anti-Semitism today always has a disguised racial background; when a man who believes himself a Catholic is an anti-Semite, he pharisaically attempts to cover what is really a racial infection with a religious mantle. This is obviously the most hideous hypocrisy. Instead of desiring the conversion of the Jews, as the Church does, he prefers to have them remain far from Christ because his antipathy is in reality nourished from sources quite different from religious zeal. These anti-Semitic so-called Catholics, having become a prey of prejudices and racial passions, want to silence their Catholic consciences by pretending that they fight the Jews because they have crucified our Lord. Are they not aware that they themselves crucify Him again by their anti-Semitism? Do they forget that the crucifixion of Jesus Christ was not exclusively the specific answer of the Jewish people to God but the answer of fallen humanity? Do they believe that the Romans or the Germans would not just as readily have crucified Him? . . .

Every real Catholic understands that the present persecution of the Jews and anti-Semitism in general is a part of the anti-personalism, the collectivism, which must be considered the most anti-Christian revolution the world ever witnessed. Every Christian must understand that anti-Semitism is not a problem that exclusively concerns the Jews, but that the dignity of the individual is at stake and that he must therefore feel, in the face of anti-Semitism: *Tua res agitur!*—This concerns you!

For in the long run anti-Semitism always ends in anti-Christianism, as the development of the Nazi doctrine so abundantly proves. This connection between anti-Semitism and anti-Christianism is not accidental but is determined by an inner logic. . . .

THE JEWS AND THE CHRISTIAN WEST*

Die Erfüllung
1937

In the memoirs for 1937, von Hildebrand tells about writing and delivering this lecture. In this excerpt from it we see him seeking out the theological foundations of "the Jewish question." He develops the idea of the Jews as the "Menschheitsvolk"—the "representative people of humanity." Even though he holds, as do all Christians, that the Old Testament is fulfilled in the New Testament, he also holds that the Jews still have a central place in salvation history. Of course he affirms that Christians ardently desire the conversion of the Jews, but this does not prevent him from speaking with the greatest reverence for the "mystery of Israel," nor from acknowledging the wrongs that Christians have inflicted on the Jews over the centuries, nor from feeling a profound solidarity with the Jews, movingly expressed at the end, nor from protesting against anti-Semitism even in its "subdued" forms.

The battle for the Christian West, which is raging furiously today, draws the question of the nature and spiritual roots of the West into the center of intellectual analysis and debate. It is therefore not coincidental that

---

* This essay was translated by John Henry Crosby and first published in *Logos* (2006), 9/4, 145–72.

the question of the Jews and the Christian West is presented first in this lecture series on the Jewish question. It is a matter of equal concern for Jews as well as Christians, and its resolution contains significant consequences for both sides. . . .

Israel—Representative People of Humanity

The Old Testament is divine revelation. Yet it is also the history of the Jewish people, an expression of its essential character, its ethos, its poetry; and these elements too have a deep share in the inner formation of the West, one that cannot simply be thought away, even if these elements are of course incomparable with the purely revealed content of the Old Testament.

Like no other people, Israel was a classical representative of humanity. I do not say that it possessed this role on the basis of its natural disposition but that it became this by divine election. This election is a free act of God, requiring no human or natural justification. And yet, this election and the special revelation so deeply bound up with it, formed and molded Israel and its history in the deepest and most interior way. The spirit of Israel as we find it in the Old Testament is inseparable from the fact of this election and from the light of revelation given to the Jews, just as the cultural expressions of the Christian Middle Ages are inseparable from the fact of Christian revelation.

Israel was the classical representative people of humanity (*Menschheitsvolk*) on two grounds. It was this, first of all, through the unique spirit that it radiated and by which it was permeated: Israel was the only people conscious of man's metaphysical situation before God, the only people whose life unfolded *in conspectu Dei*—in the sight of God. If we think of Abraham, Isaac, and Jacob, or of Moses and David, we never encounter just one or another ethnic characteristic (*völkische Eigenart*) but man *qua* man in his direct confrontation with God. Man stands before us in all of his heights and abysses, man in his yearning for God and in his apostasy from God, man caught in the surge of his disordered passions, and man in his need for redemption. Sin is never considered harmlessly and lightly, as in certain phases in the history of another people (by which I mean the Greeks, who also, in a completely different sense, can be described as a classical representative people of humanity). The abysses of human nature that at times open in the Jewish people are terrifying, and yet they are experienced as abysses, they are seen for what they really represent *in conspectu Dei*. Let us recall the instance of David with the wife of Uriah, of the scene with Nathan the prophet, and of David's repentance. Again and again we encounter the quintessential tragedy of man. Everything is filled with an ultimate solemnity, with the seriousness of the situation of man, suffused by the breath of God.

All that is human can be grasped in its true greatness and depth only when seen in the light of God, in whose image man is created. Every attempt of an anthropocentric humanism to see man in himself and cut off from his ordination to God leads to a complete flattening and hollowing of everything human. Every pure humanitarian idealism is weak and pretentious, like the attempts of Icarus to fly. The true seriousness, the uplifting greatness and importance of human existence, only becomes apparent against the backdrop of the great dialogue between man and God, where the need for redemption and the dependence of man on God is clearly grasped. . . .

Israel was the only people to whom, before the fullness of time, God showed his countenance, the only people he called by name, in such a way that they came into full consciousness of the need for redemption and cried out to heaven for two thousand years: *"Ostende nobis, Domine, faciem tuam et salvi erimus"*—"Show us your face Lord and we will be saved." Objectively, the entire world at that time stood in a state of advent, but Israel alone was aware of this. Of course, Israel still walked in a state of semidarkness, for the full light of divine truth had not yet been illuminated. Yet while the others still walked about entirely in the darkness, unaware of their situation, Israel was conscious of its state of semidarkness and longed for the full light.

The history of Israel—which, as Theodor Haecker says, alone among the nations had a sacred history—has to do not just with the concerns of a particular people but with what is of real and ultimate significance for every human being. One would have to be blind to read the Old Testament without being deeply moved by the grandiose, indeed, the classical humanness (*Menschlichkeit*) by which everything is suffused, yet which follows solely on the fact that everything is filled with a sacred breath of eternity. "*In lumine tuo videbimus lumen,*" says the Psalmist, "In your light we see light," and this applies to the entire greatness of humanity that the Old Testament brings before our minds. Mighty and fearsome, like the waves of the sea, are the passions that rage in this people; exalted and of inexorable clarity, like the light of the sun, is the consciousness of sin whence arises the spirit of deep repentance.

In the Old Testament, we encounter all of the decisive and most important human stances in their classical forms: the faith and "Here I am Lord" of Abraham; the trust in God of Isaac; the powerlessness of man and his surrender to God in Job; the struggle of man with God in Jacob; the repentance of David; the most ardent earthly love in the Song of Songs, so classical in its setting that it could become the symbol of the love of the Church for Christ; the pride and falling away from God with Solomon; the dance around the golden calf, just as the Israelites had left Egypt; and the holy reverence before God of Moses, surely the most fundamental stance of all authentic human existence. Certainly, the Church and its saints point us in the direction of a world of incomparably deeper and more sublime human stances; in those who are redeemed, the fundamental human stances appear in a much loftier way, and above all we find in them a fullness of supernatural life, which we could seek to no avail in the Old Testament. Yet given the situation of advent, which at the time was still objectively the case, the fundamental stances that fill the Old Testament are the classical responses.

While the world of Greek culture and thought is the fountainhead of Western intellectual life and culture, while this people shines into human history like a bright spiritual light, while one finds among the Greeks the home of authentic philosophy and art, Israel is the home of a universal humanity in which quite other depths of human existence are illuminated. Here the drama of man as such is played before our eyes; here we have to do with realities—arrogance and concupiscence, persecutions and sorrows, love and hate, yearning for God and immersion in mundane things, true faith and idolatry, sin and repentance, rebellion against God and adoring reverence, apostasy from God and love of God—realities that are of ultimate relevance to anyone bearing a human countenance, whether cultivated or uncultivated, talented or untalented, master or slave.

Israel was the only people whose inner point of unity lay not at a racial or cultural level but on the religious level. True belief in the one God and the awaiting of the Messiah constituted the "form" of Israel's unity. The knowledge of that which for all of humanity is the one great, ultimate, and decisive concern held Israel together interiorly. Israel was the representative people of humanity because it was the religious people *par excellence* and because the religious question is the question of humanity as such, because God is the absolute concern for all human beings, the concern that addresses each human being individually, whatever his particular characteristics may be: *Tua res agitur!*—This concerns you!

Israel was the representative people of humanity in yet a second respect. It is the people to whom God spoke, among whom he revealed himself to humanity, the people he chose to be representatives of all humanity, to whom he addressed words that are the concern of all humanity. Although he bestowed upon the Greeks a unique capacity for arriving at genuine knowledge of creation, and although the Greeks were called to discover the world of natural values for humanity, he unveiled himself to the Jews, he revealed to this people that which is of real and ultimate significance for every human being. He himself spoke to Abraham and Moses, he announced through the prophets him who would become not only the Messiah for Israel but the redeemer of mankind.

And he chose this people—which through revelation became the representative people of humanity more than merely extrinsically—in order to bestow human nature upon his only begotten Son. The fact that Christ in his human nature was a Jew, that in being born a Jew of the Virgin Mary he took on human nature fully, forms the character of the Jewish people's representation of humanity in the deepest and clearest way. Christ spoke to humanity when he spoke to Israel, and

Israel's response to his manifestation was the response of humanity. The apostles and disciples who recognized and followed him were representatives of humanity, as were the Pharisees and all who crucified him. It is more than naïve to see the crucifixion of Christ as a specific response of the Jewish people exclusively, as if his fellow countrymen would not have crucified him had he been Roman, Greek, Persian, or Germanic. The "let him be crucified" was the voice of fallen humanity, which Israel represented here as in every other situation. But the response of the apostles and disciples, "Lord, where shall we go, for you have the words of eternal life?," was also the voice of humanity in its searching and yearning for God. And is not the denial of Christ by Peter and the sleeping of the three disciples on the Mount of Olives a prototype of our bearing toward Christ, does not Christ in the liturgy speak to all of us each year when he asks—"*Sic non potuistis una hora vigilare mecum?*"—"Could you not watch with me for even just one hour?" Israel is the representative people of humanity; therefore its fate must touch us more, must concern us more, than that of any other people.

Israel's Influence on the Christian West

The spirit of this representative people of humanity, which finds expression in the unique poetry of the Psalms and the Song of Songs, and which is so thoroughly formed by God's grace, has had a tremendous influence on the formation of the Christian West. When once I was speaking with Theodor Haecker (who in his book *Virgil, Father of the Christian West* has given us one of the deepest books on the Christian West) about the elements that formed the spiritual countenance of the Christian West, he said to me very emphatically, "Do not forget Israel!" The influence of Israel on the thought, imagination, and feeling of the Christian West occurred above all through the liturgy. The liturgy is largely comprised of materials taken from the Old Testament, as in the Psalms and in many readings and antiphons, thereby absorbing much of the spirit of the Jewish people as representative of humanity. . . .

Of course, the Old Testament was always transmitted to the

Christian West in the light of the New Testament, and this light reveals the true meaning of the books of Moses and the Prophets, of the Psalms, and of all the other books of sacred Scripture. In it the true and authentic image of the Old Testament becomes visible, which, after all, is essentially ordered to the New Testament. For the Christian West, the Old Testament has always represented divine revelation in a state of advent, and its eternal content lives on as a part of the New Testament.

Israel—the Lost Son

Thus far we have only discussed the influence of the Jewish people on the Christian West insofar as it is expressed in the Old Testament, that is, before Christ. Through the rejection of the Messiah, however, the status of the Jewish people was substantially altered. The role of representative of humanity, once that of Israel, has now passed over to the Church of Christ. The head and heart of humanity, the link between God and man, is no longer in Jerusalem but in Rome.

Nonetheless, Israel has not ceased to have a certain primacy of place among the peoples (*Zentralvolk*). Just as belief in the true God and expectation of the Messiah once provided the source of unity for Israel, so its rejection of Christ has fused it together over the past two thousand years and placed its mark on its being and destiny. Israel is perpetually formed by the religious: positively at first, and then negatively. For, willingly or not, Israel is always concerned with the great question of human destiny, namely the stance toward Christ: initially in its longing expectation of the Messiah and today in its compulsive hardness toward Christ. Yet even in its apostasy, in the lapsing of its vocation, Israel continues to be a metaphysical representative people of humanity. The continued existence of the Jews as a unified people as well as their dispersion throughout the whole world are a consequence of their rejection of the *lapis angularis,* the cornerstone. The present unity of the Jewish people and their difficult fate are not caused by a particular religion but by their rejection of the true religion. Thus, they continually bear witness to Christ indirectly. The Jews in their many sufferings and in their continuing existence are, like no other people, the expression of the mysterious dispensation of Providence. They are the "pedal point" of human history, and an abiding mystery surrounds them. A pedal point is, after all, an underlying voice that, without entering directly into the musical event, in its very separation and through its mere presence nevertheless belongs deeply to the whole, lending color to everything, and which in the end joins in the overall harmony of the piece of music.

The destiny of the Jews and their attitude toward Christ has always possessed a unique importance. St. Paul, in his Letter to the Romans, expresses this most emphatically: "In respect to the gospel, they are enemies on your account; but in respect to election, they are beloved because of the patriarchs. For the gifts and the call of God are irrevocable" (Rom 11:28–29).

Israel is unique among the nations in every respect. Throughout most of its history, Israel has dwelt in isolation from all others, like no other people, not in its own land but scattered about the world in the most varying of countries, always in a segregated corner under foreign authority and under severe laws discriminating against Jews (*Ausnahmegesetzen*)—put simply, in the ghetto. In the midst of the Christian West and without taking part in its formation, Israel has lived its separate existence. Its direct influence upon the Christian West during this time has been slight. Even so, Israel does not stand within the Christian West as a foreign body but as a providentially intended element of central importance. The lost son too belongs to the family and cannot be considered as just another foreigner. Indeed, the conversion of all people and all nations is a central and immediate concern of Christians. Yet the conversion of Israel, the people of God, is the special concern of Christianity in quite another sense.

The first reason for this rests upon the fact that this representative people of humanity, through whom God spoke to mankind, was called to recognize Christ before all others. In other words, since, as we know through revelation, the conversion of the people of Israel is of such paramount importance in the eyes of God, it must also find a special place in the heart of every Christian.

Second, Israel's role in the spiritual formation of the Christian West is too great and deep to be considered like that of the Chinese and Indians (who in their own right are not and ought not to be considered far from our hearts). The Jews are the "beloved for the sake of the fathers," they are as a people so interwoven into salvation history that they belong to the Christian West in the deepest spiritual way, even if exteriorly they remain cut off. . . .

Tua res agitur!

There is one thing above all that we must not forget, namely that the present attack on the Jewish people is not just about a minority problem, as important as these problems are in themselves. As we saw in the beginning, Israel was the representative people of humanity and God addressed man as such when he spoke to Israel. Hence the current attack on the Jews targets not only this people of fifteen million but mankind as such. Each one of us must perceive the present degradation of the Jews as an attack on human nature. . . .

Above all, Catholics must all perceive the present-day attack against the Jews as something that directly threatens them. Did not Christ the Lord say, "What you have done to the least of my brothers, you have done to me"? Is not the defamation and degradation of the Jews a direct attack against the incarnate God, against human nature sanctified by the Incarnation? Indeed, what is happening today is not the special concern of a particular people. No, true for us all are the words, *Tua res agitur!*—This concerns you!

THE DANGER OF QUIETISM

Der christliche Ständestaat
March 10, 1935

In von Hildebrand's memoirs we often read about Austrian and German Catholics who were overeager to build bridges between Christianity and Nazism. But there is another group of Catholics who failed in a different way to join in the struggle against Hitler, namely those who thought they had good religious reasons for not getting involved. These Catholics thought that they could live their faith in a purely interior way and that they need not give it any more of an external expression than celebrating the liturgy in church. They did not feel impelled by their faith to bear witness in the public square. Von Hildebrand says that these Catholics run the risk of "quietism," and in this essay he challenges them to take their faith outside the church sanctuary and into public life, especially when public life has been taken over by criminals.

The Center Party to which he refers at the beginning was the Catholic political party in Germany. Von Hildebrand wants to say that through the political involvement of this party in an earlier generation, German Catholicism became too worldly and lost some of its religious luster. He warns his readers not to react so strongly against that politicized Catholicism as to fall into the opposite danger of quietism.

The period of political Catholicism in Germany and Austria (now a thing of the past) had certain merits, and though these positive aspects are sometimes unjustly forgotten or denied today even by Catholics, such a movement did undoubtedly harbor dangers from a religious point of view. After the great period during which the Center Party* was founded—a period in which fundamental religious motifs determined the politics of the party—it was increasingly taken over by the autonomous laws of party politics. This process of secularization went hand in hand with a threat to properly religious formation. A tactical attitude also gained too much influence in the properly religious sphere. The religious significance of the Party's external organization was overshadowed, and political tasks were given too much prominence at the expense of the full development of the divine life implanted in individual believers at baptism.

For many, working on behalf of Catholic schools, state support of the clergy, and equal treatment of Catholics employed by the state, and even the augmentation of the Center Party's power took precedence over evangelization and the purely religious transformation of the individual in Christ. Many saw membership in Catholic organizations or parties as the mark of being fully Catholic. What is more, the spirit of compromise—which is inevitable in politics—frequently played too strong a role in the religious sphere of life.

This is why many committed Catholics were calling loudly for a depoliticization of Catholicism even before the era of National Socialism. Once National Socialism came to power, however, and the Catholic political organization broke down, the watchword for many German Catholics became "withdrawal into the purely religious sphere." In many Catholic circles, some even in Austria, one encounters the view that the lesson to be learned from the defeat of political Catholicism in Germany is that Catholics should turn away from politics in order to concern themselves exclusively with religious matters and adopt a passive attitude toward political events. Indeed, one may sometimes hear even the clergy in Austria voice the opinion that one must already mentally adjust now to the possibility of a National Socialist regime and

---

* The Center Party was the dominant Catholic political party from its founding in 1870 until its suppression by Hitler in 1933.

should be on one's guard against cultivating excessively intimate ties with the present regime.

However, there is clearly something ambiguous about this call to depoliticize Catholicism and to concentrate solely on religious matters. When it entails a due regard for the primacy of the purely religious sphere, disavows an excessively intimate relationship between religion and party politics, and aims to put an end to the politicizing of religion, it is undoubtedly good and justified. The bankruptcy of political Catholicism in Germany does indeed teach us this lesson. But it is utterly impossible to expect Catholics to be indifferent to politics at a time when the debates in the political sphere concern not just political issues but, as our martyred Chancellor Dollfuss once stated, fundamental beliefs about the meaning of existence.

When today the Antichrist is rearing his head in Bolshevism and National Socialism, when Christ is persecuted with unprecedented hatred, and a revolt is raging not only against the sphere of the supernatural but even of the person in general, all Catholics must fight for Christ in the political sphere with full personal commitment, representing *importune opportune* (in season and out of season) the claims of the kingdom of God and thus, implicitly, those of morality and the natural law. They will feel called to this commitment to the extent that they live in Christ and see everything in the light of the supernatural, to the extent that they have interiorized their religious existence and are conscious of the primacy of the properly religious sphere as the *unum necessarium* (the one thing needful).

In a time when the state expressly advances totalitarian claims and incessantly seeks to overstep its divinely ordained sphere of competence, indifference to the political sphere on the part of Catholics constitutes an outright desertion of duty. It is precisely the rootedness of genuine Catholics in a realm that transcends politics, their freedom from the inner dynamism of political practice, and their consideration of all things *in conspectu Dei* (before the face of God) that requires them to erect a dam against every encroachment of the state.

In point of fact, the real lesson to be learned from the bankruptcy of politicizing Catholicism is this: rather than politicizing Catholicism, one must instead Catholicize politics. For the human being is an integral whole, and true religiosity will inevitably induce him to regard all areas of life in their orientation to God and to work, always and everywhere, for the kingdom of Christ. This begins in one's own person, in the *induere Christum* (putting on Christ) and the full development of the supernatural life implanted in us by holy baptism; it entails "radiating Christ" not only in the apostolate of being, but also in the apostolate of the word; and, finally, it requires a commitment to Christ in the earthly public sphere and in political activity, in order that there, too, everything may be formed in the spirit of the natural law and of Christian teaching.

Naturally, the principal contribution of the Christian in this sphere is his personal transformation in Christ. But that must not be his only contribution. It is of course true that, for the Christian, the transformation of the face of the earth does not proceed primarily from without by means of laws of the state, but rather from within by means of the conversion of the person. Naturally, the Christian rejects every form of earthly messianism and remains ever aware of "how great is heaven and how small the earth." Nevertheless, he makes use of all legitimate earthly means in order to shape the *polis* (the political community) in such a way that the kingdom of Christ may be built up within it.

Thus "Catholic Action," in accordance with the intentions of the Holy Father [Pope Pius XI], is indeed apolitical in the sense that it must not be understood as a political party or engage in party politics itself; but it certainly extends into the political sphere, since Catholics who are active politically have the same obligation to carry the spirit of Christ into this domain that they have with regard to any other sphere of life. Anyone who does not admit this is not thinking as a Catholic, but in the manner of pietistic quietism. This is undoubtedly a danger today. . . .

The professed goal of Catholics calling for their own "depoliticization" is, in itself, quite ambiguous and misleading; but at the present moment it entails a particular danger. Bolshevism and National Socialism are primarily worldviews. They neither are, nor wish to be, mere political systems. Apathy toward the political sphere on the part of Catholics easily leads, therefore, to apathy toward National Socialism as a whole. Many say, "Why should we always simply attack and criticize? Let us depart from the political sphere; let us search out and convert those who have gone astray. Let us, who stand aloof from politics, spread the spirit of love and reconciliation."

This is, at bottom, a cowardly flight from the battle to which God is calling us. It is our obligation as soldiers of Christ to wage war against the Antichrist and to rip the mask from his face. The "apolitical" disposition cultivated by certain Catholics, which induces others to refrain from exposing and relentlessly fighting against National Socialism, is an evil sophism. What is at stake in the position one adopts toward National Socialism as a whole—not merely toward some of its theoreticians such as Rosenberg and Bergmann, etc.—is nothing less than the question: Are you for Christ, or against Him?

Here too, Christ's words hold true: "He who is not with me is against me" (Mt 12:30). The soldier of Christ is obligated to fight against sin and error. His battle against the Antichrist is prompted by his love for Christ and for the salvation of souls; he fights this battle for the salvation of those who have gone astray. His attitude is one of true love. But those who flee from the inevitable battle and treat irenically those who have gone astray, obfuscating their error and playing down their revolt against God are, fundamentally, victims of egoism and complacency.

Ceterum Censeo . . . !

Der christliche Ständestaat
October 14, 1934

Von Hildebrand takes as his title the famous advice that Cato the Elder kept giving the Roman Senate about how to conduct the war with Carthage: "ceterum censeo Carthaginem esse delendam," which means, "Moreover, I think that Carthage should be completely destroyed." Von Hildebrand wants to say the same thing about the Nazi regime: it cannot be corrected or reformed; it is so fundamentally unsound that it can only be destroyed. He addresses here the type of person who often appears in the memoirs, namely the person who cannot discern this fundamental unsoundness and who harbors illusions of influencing Nazism in a Christian direction. Just recall the two German Dominicans whom von Hildebrand encountered over dinner in 1933 in Paris (see page 70). In this essay he shows how we discern the incorrigible evil of Nazism: by examining its first principles, that is, its understanding of truth, of the human person, of the unity of the human family.

Notice his particularly significant statement at the end that even if the Nazi regime treated the Church well for tactical reasons, Nazism would remain an Antichrist and a deadly enemy of the Church because of the first principles on which it is built. We are reminded of this striking passage from the memoirs, 1933: "It is completely immaterial if the Antichrist refrains from attacking the Church for political reasons, or if he concludes a Concordat with the Vatican. What is decisive is the spirit that animates him, the heresy he represents, the crimes committed at his behest. God is offended regardless whether the victim of a murder is a Jew, a Socialist,

or a bishop. Blood that has been innocently spilled cries out to heaven."
He is thus warning against a certain egocentric way of opposing Hitler—
opposing him because he is a threat to me or to my people or to my church,
and not in the first place because he shows the face of the Antichrist.

Some Catholics who with growing concern and regret see the increasingly manifest trend in National Socialism toward an outspoken rejection of Christianity pin their hopes on statements the Führer repeats from time to time to the effect that he opposes "neo-paganism" and adheres to "positive Christianity." This hope betrays not only a naïve optimism, but also a complete failure to recognize the authentic essence of National Socialism. Indeed, it betrays a general ignorance of how one goes about discerning the spirit or essence of a movement.

The question whether a movement, tendency, or party is compatible with the spirit of Christ and the teaching of His Church cannot be answered simply by looking at the positions explicitly adopted by its representatives in their public pronouncements regarding Christianity and the Church. Most heretics initially presented themselves not as enemies of the Church but rather as "reformers." Yet they articulated statements which materially contradicted the true teaching of Christ and fostered an ethos that was incompatible with His spirit. They presented these things as true Christianity; indeed, they frequently presented them as the authentic and original teaching of the Church. The mere fact that heretical theologians (or heretical laymen involved in religious matters) subjectively think that their theses are compatible with Christian doctrine offers no guarantee that they really are dogmatically unobjectionable.

Much less, therefore, does the assurance of the leaders of a political movement—who know and understand as much about the teaching of the Church and the spirit of Christ as an ass does about playing the harp—have any significance whatsoever for the attitude a Catholic must take toward these movements. At most, the assurance of the Führer of the National Socialist movement that he adheres to "positive Christianity" and opposes the endeavors of neo-paganism could be taken as expressing a political intention with regard to the Church. It could be interpreted as an assurance that he will not pursue a policy hostile to the Church, but it could never be taken as an indication that National Socialism as such wants to be Christianized, or could be Christianized. For the declaration, upon the lips of the very man who has called into being a movement that is anti-Christian in its profoundest essence, that he rejects neo-paganism and adheres to positive Christianity, merely proves that he has not the slightest idea of what is Christian and what is not.

The question whether a movement is or is not compatible with Christianity can never be decided by the subjective assurances of its "leaders," but only by comparing the ideas which constitute its substantive core with the teaching of the Church, and by comparing the typical ethos of the movement with the spirit of Christ. It is surely not difficult to recognize that National Socialism is thoroughly and explicitly anti-Christian in every element of its substance. There are some who doubt the compatibility of National Socialism with Christianity only because of the books of Rosenberg, Bergmann, Gebhardt, etc., or because of the movement of the [aggressively Nazi] "Deutschchristen" and the "Deutschgläugiben," and indeed hold that only these parts of the National Socialist movement are un-Christian. Such persons are truly to be pitied for the poverty of their *sensus catholicus* (sense for what is truly Catholic). Even if all these elements did not exist in National Socialism, someone with a clear view of the matter would not fail to recognize the Antichrist as the spirit informing the entire movement.

First of all, as I have frequently shown in these pages, the article in the Party program that reduces religion to a function of the feeling of the Nordic Germanic race not only negates Christianity, but the religious sphere as such. An innerworldly and thoroughly subjective factor thus becomes the criterion for the attitude that must be taken to religion. Since religion is essentially the revelation of God, it cannot be measured by any innerworldly standard. This point of the Party program is enough to place an unbridgeable gulf between National Socialism and religion in general, and *a fortiori* the Christian Catholic religion. Even if the National Socialist platform made no other substantial affirmation regarding Christianity, this point alone would be a sufficient warrant for all the bishops of Germany to pronounce a justified *anathema* on National Socialism.

Second, the statement made by Hitler himself at the Party convention in Nuremberg in 1933 that "the difference between a human being of a higher race and one of a lower race is greater than the difference between a human being of a lower race and an ape" constitutes a formal negation of Christian teaching. To begin with, Hitler implicitly denies the spiritual nature of the human being when he regards differences among spiritual persons as greater than the distinction between spiritual persons and mere non-personal forms of life. The failure in principle to recognize the essence and value of the human being and to take into account the fact that a human person, regardless of race, is a being endowed with an immortal soul, capable of consciously knowing and loving God and called to eternal fellowship with Him, means the denial of one of the fundamental presuppositions of Christianity. For the entire Creed unconditionally presupposes the spiritual nature of the human being and the unique value of each immortal soul. Moreover, this basic constitutive difference between human beings and even the most highly developed of animals cannot find a more elementary expression than in the fact that the second divine Person not only took on human nature, but even died for all human beings on the cross.

Third, Hitler's statement denies the primacy of the spiritual sphere in the human person over the vital sphere. In contrast to Catholic teaching, which St. Thomas Aquinas summarizes with the phrase *anima forma corporis* (the soul is the form of the body), in National Socialism the human being is degraded to a mere function of the vital sphere. Linked with this is its logically consistent denial of the Catholic doctrine that each soul (unlike the body) proceeds immediately from the hand of God and is not a product of physical generation. National Socialism thereby characterizes itself unequivocally as a "materialism of blood," and no thinking person can doubt its complete incompatibility with Christian teaching any longer.

Finally, Hitler's declaration denies the unity of human nature, and thus also the community of mankind. Christianity does not merely teach the descent of all human beings from Adam and Eve, nor does the Church only teach that human persons constitute one family. Rather, the totality of all persons—all those who have ever lived, who are living now, and who are still to be born—form such a close community that it was possible for everyone to fall in Adam and Eve and for everyone to be redeemed and raised up in Christ. The unity of all human beings, the totality of mankind, is an indispensable presupposition of Christian doctrine.

Furthermore, the totalitarian claim made by National Socialism runs into an irreconcilable conflict with Christianity. The doctrine of the omnipotence of the state is heretical in every form, and most of all in its most extreme form, National Socialism, which in this respect far surpasses anything that has ever existed before. According to Church teaching, the state is a community with a sharply circumscribed sphere of competence. A person belongs to it only insofar as he is a citizen; but his membership in the state does not constitute the totality of his being. His final destiny transcends the sphere of the state by far: he is created by God, destined for God, and belongs "totally" to God alone. He is, moreover, primarily destined to be a member of the Mystical Body of Christ, and only secondarily to be a citizen of the state.

What, then, is a Catholic to say in response to a doctrine which not only demands a state monopoly on education, but even gives the state a right to determine which human beings are permitted to procreate, and thus which human beings may or may not be born? Only one response to such a doctrine is possible: *Anathema sit* (Let him be anathema).

Let no one object that National Socialism has not developed on the basis of such a definite theory, or that its intellectual formulations are vague, or that it is a movement which could still "develop in a very different direction." No: every movement has an inner idea which determines its outward manifestations and shapes its life and ethos. We must therefore carefully observe the outward manifestations of a movement in order to grasp its ethos. Only then will we recognize which statements are typical and characteristic of it, and which are only a demagogic bluff. Anyone with the slightest sensitivity to the spirit of a movement cannot fail to recognize the nature of National Socialism:

naturalistic, antagonistic to things of the spirit, and based on a material-ism of blood.

The idolization of virility—that is, the "heroic military ethos" which is the leading image of the Third Reich and is unequivocally expressed in all its public declarations, speeches, songs, poems, decrees, and edicts—represents the most extreme antithesis to the spirit of Christ and the Catholic ethos. In its idolization of the brutal "masterful" or "noble, Nordic" man who relies solely on himself and his own strength and who arbitrarily disposes over his own country (and others' as well), we encounter not only a pagan ethos alien to Christianity, but the pur-est form of an utterly arrogant rebellion which rejects the spirit of the Sermon on the Mount. We need only see for ourselves the physiog-nomy of any National Socialist leader, or listen to any of their speakers' tone of voice and cadence, or observe the megalomaniac hubris which permeates all their pronouncements, with all their strutting displays of brutality and ruthlessness, all their glorification of arbitrariness and power, and all their explicit elimination of objective law! Is it possible to find anywhere in history a mentality more radically opposed to the spirit of Him who said: "Blessed are the meek, blessed are the peacemakers, blessed are those who hunger and thirst for righteousness?"

The deeds of the National Socialists truly correspond to the spirit of the Antichrist. From their sterilization laws and their attitude toward the destitute and the incurably sick to the sadistic torture of those lan-guishing in concentration camps; from the unprecedented murders of June 30 [1934], which were subsequently "legalized," to the prepara-tions for the murder of our unforgettable Chancellor Dollfuss, every-thing exudes the unmistakable spirit of the Antichrist.

Only the one who lacks all *sensus catholicus,* all spiritual-intellectual clarity, and all capacity for judgment could still doubt today that Na-tional Socialism is a thoroughly anti-Christian movement which oper-ates with a frightening logical consistency, a movement that draws its very life from its intrinsic antithesis to Christianity!

These factors—racist materialism, anti-personalism, naturalism, and totalitarianism—are not merely accidental elements, as is the case, for instance, with socialism's ideological opposition to culture. Rather, they are profoundly rooted in the very spirit and essence of National Social-ism. As we have seen, Hitler's pronouncements against neo-paganism cannot in any way alter the anti-Christian nature of his party. It there-fore betrays an enormous political naïveté when people believe that his declarations should be interpreted as expressing a sincere intention to take a politically friendly stance toward the Church. For in the long run, the creator of National Socialism will not be able to avoid coming into greater and greater conflict (even on a strictly practical level) with the Church and its demands.

Anyone with even a modicum of political literacy will clearly see that these pronouncements are merely a political stratagem. First, one sends other persons ahead who so appall Catholic circles in their public and unrestrained attacks on Christianity and the Church that the Füh-rer's subsequent disavowal of these people almost makes his behavior appear to be a sign of hope, indicating a friendly disposition toward Christianity. "Aha," say some, "the Führer is against 'neo-paganism'; so, when those groups are eliminated, National Socialism and the Church can make their peace."

But does a movement come into conflict with the Church only when it attacks the Church outright? Is not everything that is opposed in any way to the spirit of Christ also incompatible with His Church? Is someone an enemy of the Church only when he attacks her openly, and not as soon as he denies the truths of Christianity? Is he not an enemy of the Church who not only tramples underfoot the commandments of God in practice, but also avows that he rejects them in theory, and is imbued with an ethos as incompatible with Christianity as fire is with water?

In truth, even if Hitler were to burn all the neo-pagan books; even if he were to condemn Rosenberg, Bergmann, and Gebhardt to the same fate as Roehm [whom Hitler had executed]; even if he were to forbid all direct attacks on the Church; even if he were not merely to ratify favor-able concordats, but also abide by them—even then, as long it refused to dissolve and liquidate itself completely, National Socialism would remain every bit as much the Antichrist against which we must fight relentlessly. For the constitutive intellectual content which holds it together as a movement, as well as the ethos which informs its outward manifestations, are loathsome in the eyes of God, and do not become the slightest bit more pleasing to Him when camouflaged and veiled in phrases that are friendly toward Christianity. Rosenberg, Bergmann, and the "Deutschgläubigen" are merely the overt consequences of the deepest essence of National Socialism, and we must be grateful to all those who help to expose its real essence and work to eliminate all the obscurity which surrounds it.

Here, as with physical illnesses, the more clearly the presence of the sickness is revealed by its symptoms, the better it will be for the patient. No suppression of the symptoms, no palliative treatment, no weak attempts to make peace with the spirit of the Antichrist (for to make such a peace would be to repeat Judas' betrayal of Christ), no deal-making or obfuscation of antitheses—nothing can free either Christianity or the world from this horrible danger. The only remedy is a clear recognition of its true nature and the complete annihilation of this brown [Nazi] plague. There can be only one attitude for all Christians toward National Socialism, the one expressed in the Church's prayer: "*Hostium nostrorum, quaesumus, Domine, elide superbiam: et eorum contumanciam dexterae tuae virtute prosterne.*" "We beg Thee, O Lord, break the pride of our enemies and humble their insolence by the power of Thy right hand."

"*Ceterum censeo Carthaginem esse delendam*—Moreover, I think that Carthage should be completely destroyed."

FALSE FRONTS

Der christliche Ständestaat
September 27, 1936

Though von Hildebrand spoke as a fervent Catholic, he also knew how to appeal to a wider audience. In this essay he appeals to those who, while they may not belong to any church or even consider themselves believers, nevertheless still share the heritage of Western Christian civilization. They may have, for instance, a respect for truth yet without tracing this respect back to the God who is Truth. These people stand with von Hildebrand and other committed Catholics in forming a common front against both German Nazism and Russian Bolshevism.

Von Hildebrand sharply contests here the Nazi claim that the principal struggle in the world is the struggle between Nazism and Bolshevism. These two movements are in reality kindred spirits; their differences lie on the surface, but in their ideological substance they are cut from the same cloth. The real struggle of the age is between the totalitarian regimes, whether Nazi or Bolshevist, and the Christian West, including regimes and individuals who simply live by its light even though they may not profess the Christian name.

At the National Socialist convention in Nuremberg, Minister Goebbels declared that only two great fronts still exist in the world today: the Bolshevist front, including all those who countenance Bolshevism; and the anti-Bolshevist, Fascist, and authoritarian front. National Socialism stands at the head of the second and has saved Germany from

Bolshevism. Every conscientious person must therefore take his stance unequivocally in favor of the anti-Bolshevist front.

Understandably, this rhetoric has made a great impression on many people. The terrible events in Spain, the assassination of the clergy and religious, and the destruction of precious cultural treasures have rightly led to reactions of terror and horror everywhere, and have made many aware of the fearful dynamic set in motion by the passions of the masses that have been unleashed.

We are not interested here in the question of how far Moscow can be held responsible for the events in Spain, nor whether the Spanish phenomenon is truly Bolshevism rather than anarchism. The Spanish atrocities were not needed in order to recognize the terrible nature of Bolshevism. Its materialistic ideology, its disregard for all personal freedom, its collectivism and anti-personalism, its mortal hatred of Christianity and indeed of all religion, are sufficient grounds for every true Catholic to reject it unambiguously and to oppose it unconditionally.

Nevertheless, the ideological division of the present-day world into Bolshevists and anti-Bolshevists that Goebbels proclaimed at the Nuremberg party convention is false. The real battle lines drawn at the level of ideas are, in fact, very different. I have often pointed out in these pages that there is only one real antithesis to all errors, namely, truth itself. For errors, no matter how different they may be among themselves, are not truly antithetical to one another. Traditionalism and ontologism, Pelagianism and the Protestant doctrine of *sola fide* (by faith alone), collectivism and liberal individualism, socialism and capitalism—these pairs do tend in opposite directions, but because one error never counteracts what is specifically false in another, opposite error, none of them constitutes a genuine antithesis. In every case, the two are fundamentally related; they both proceed from the same initial falsehood, even though they move in opposite directions. Only the one truth opposes all errors, whatever their nature, both in their most decisive point and in their specific disvalue. One error can never be overcome by another, opposite error; the devil cannot be cast out with the help of Beelzebub.

In reality, there have been only two fronts in the world for the past two thousand years: the front for Christ and the front against Christ.

He is the cornerstone which separates all spirits. All other antitheses bypass the decisive question and thus remain superficial.

The question "for or against Christ" can be understood either in a more specifically religious sense or in a broader cultural and intellectual sense. In the former case, the question of the true Christian faith is the criterion of being for or against Christ; in the latter, it is the question of how much someone still holds fast to the foundations of the Christian West in a moral, legal, sociological, and cultural sense.

The contemporary intellectual crisis in Europe divides people into two camps: the enemies of Christian Western culture and those who somehow still hold on (in greatly varying degrees) to the foundations of this culture. The latter group may also include those who cannot be designated as Christians in a religious sense.

So what, then, defines the Christian West in this broader cultural and intellectual sense? In what respect does the Christian West form the real front against both Nazism and Communism? The first decisive element is the stance toward the question of truth. A profound reverence for truth is an integral aspect of Christian Western culture, as is a clear consciousness that the question of truth stands at the beginning of all decisions and cannot in any way be subordinated to practical considerations.

The view that [German] Minister of Culture Schemm expressed in an address to professors of the University of Munich in 1933 is diametrically opposed to this reverence for the question of truth: "From now on, what matters for you is not to ascertain whether something is true, but rather whether it is in line with the National Socialist revolution." The same holds for the following words in the National Socialist program: "We confess allegiance to Christianity insofar as it is in keeping with the Germanic racial sensibility." Here, the decisive question is no longer whether the doctrine of Christianity is objectively true, but whether it is in keeping with the subjective sensibility of a race and conforms to a certain racial ethos.

It must be noted that this attitude is much more radically opposed to the spirit of Christianity than the typical form of atheism, for the latter acknowledges, at least in principle, the decisive role of the question of truth. In National Socialism, however, the question of truth as such is suppressed in favor of a purely subjective factor. The question of the truth or falsity of a worldview, which alone should be decisive for our positive or negative response to it, is deposed from its seat of judgment. This connotes a still deeper breach with any adherence to objective truth than is to be found even in radical skepticism. When the latter denies the existence of objective truth, it necessarily takes seriously the question of truth as such. Here, however, the question of truth has been trivialized. The faculty for discerning the seriousness of the question of truth has died; the interest in the elementary question "What is true?" has been extinguished. This signifies an irrevocable break with the whole of Christian Western culture, which rests on the foundation of reverence for truth.

A second foundational element of Christian Western culture is the conviction that there is an objective moral law which is independent of all subjective interests, arbitrariness, and mere power. Whether committed by individual rulers or democratic masses, breaches of the law have always occurred *de facto* in the history of the West. But there has always been some adherence to the idea of an objective law and the question of right has been regarded as independent of the sheer assertion of anyone's egoistic wishes. This belief in an objective law immune to the arbitrariness of individuals and nations is an inheritance of the Christian worldview, which is still preserved even by many enemies of Christianity (although this is illogical from a strictly religious point of view) and also underlies the concept of the League of Nations.

The frequently repeated declaration of the National Socialist leaders that there is no objective right or wrong, and that "what is right is what is useful for the German people," fundamentally breaks with this foundational element of the public life of the Christian West. The path for this National Socialist doctrine was prepared in the realm of philosophical theory by various forms of relativism and positivism, but only National Socialism has dared to draw out its basic consequence in praxis—that is, the conscious, programmatic renunciation of the foundation expressed in the words *iustitia fundamentum regnorum* (justice is the foundation of states).

Here too, an unbridgeable abyss opens up. On the one side stand all those who still hold fast to an objective law and believe that in individual cases of conflict, the question of right ought to take precedence over the question of sheer power; on the other stand all those who deny any such objective law in principle. It is absolutely impossible for these two sides to reach an understanding or meet on common ground. In cases of conflict, they cannot even appeal to a purely timeless, objective norm on the basis of which a decision could be made, for the one side denies that there is any authority higher than its own naked interests. We must not underestimate the depth of this difference, for here all spirits definitively part ways. With the denial of an objective law one not only stands outside Christianity as a religion but also outside the entire classical and humane cultural tradition of the West, which has received its decisive formation from Christianity.

A third fundamental element of Christian Western culture is the primacy of the spiritual sphere over the vital and, *a fortiori*, over mere matter. The divinely ordained hierarchy of the spheres of being has been denied by many philosophical systems, but Soviet Russia and the Third Reich were the first to deny this hierarchy in their official state ideologies and to draw the consequences of this denial in their laws and in the way they educate their youth. In Christian Western culture, the spiritual sphere is held to be higher than the vital and purely material spheres, the latter of which were bound to serve the former.

It is also considered to be ontologically superior. This position finds its classical expression in the wonderful words of St. Thomas: *anima forma corporis* (the soul is the form of the body). The composition of a person's blood is not decisive for his spirit; as a spiritual person, man proceeds directly from the hand of God, and his free will, his education, and his openness to the workings of grace play the decisive role in his development. Health is certainly a value, but what is it when compared to high intellectual gifts, to moral or religious values? Geniuses who were pitiful figures from a vital perspective have often kindled people's enthusiasm—and great intellects were so often such small, frail, and sickly men from a vital point of view. When a person possessed great intellectual capacities despite his deficiencies in the vital sphere, people grasped the tremendous victory of the spirit that he embodied. Two examples would be Kant and Prince Eugene; the latter, as is generally known, was physically deformed.

Both economic materialism, in which all spiritual values are merely a means to an end, and racial materialism, which idolizes the vital sphere, break in principle with this self-evident primacy of the spirit. The laws governing sterilization and marriage in the Third Reich and, above all, its racial doctrine—which reduces the individual spiritual person to a mere product of race—are clear expressions of a radical breach with this cornerstone of Christian Western culture.

A fourth factor—perhaps the most decisive of all—is connected with this last point. Since the Renaissance, various liberal theories have stripped the human person of his true nobility as the image of God. First, immortality was denied to the person, then freedom of will, then the capacity to make meaningful, intentional responses. Some saw the human being as a bundle of meaningless sensations, others saw him as a more highly developed animal. The practical consequences of this devaluation of the person were never drawn. A certain reverence for the dignity of the person, his inalienable rights, and his freedom of opinion lived on, though in reality such things logically presuppose the Christian concept of the human person.

It was left to Bolshevism and National Socialism to draw the ultimate consequences of this devaluation of the human person and to develop an anti-personalism which is radically opposed to Christianity. Here, the essential point is not whether the person is held to be a mere means for the state, the nation, a racial community, or an economic collective. What *is* decisive is the collectivism that subordinates the person in his very being and value to some natural community. According to the Christian conception, every human being has an immortal soul destined to be a vessel of grace and to enjoy eternal communion with God, which therefore possesses a higher value than anything else on earth. The fate of states, nations, and peoples as such is incomparably less important than the eternal salvation of a single immortal soul.

It is here most of all—in the position one takes toward the individual—that thinkers part ways. Anyone who advocates this anti-personalism has drawn the ultimate consequence of his breach with Christianity and has joined the irreconcilable enemies of Christian Western culture. Anyone who still holds fast to genuine reverence for the individual person is in some way drawing, albeit unconsciously, from Christian thought.

Closely connected with this is one's attitude toward the poor, the sick, and the weak. Christ says: "As you did it to one of the least of these my brethren, you did it to me" (Mt 25:40). The National Socialist morality of the master race views the sick and the weak as "faulty products" who are a tiresome burden on human society. The "hero ethos" of National Socialism and the ethos of the Sermon on the Mount constitute an utter antithesis. It is futile to attempt to combine them in any way; a choice must be made between these two worlds—separated, as they are, by an unbridgeable abyss.

If we take our starting point from these decisive philosophical antitheses in the contemporary political-social-cultural crisis, it becomes clear that the true demarcation of fronts turns out to be quite different from what the National Socialist party convention in Nuremberg would have us think. Purely political interests and exclusively tactical deliberations may lead to the formation of certain groupings, but the fronts that are based on worldviews—which will, in the long run, prove to be decisive in the political realm as well—are definitively sundered according to whether they make a radical break with the entirety of Christian Western culture or adhere to it, at least in its essential foundations. . . .

The ideological distinction between Bolshevism and National Socialism is not so very great, despite all the violent political animosity between them, which has totally different roots. One person might want to make an ally of Bolshevism while another may want an alliance with National Socialism, but the Catholic is separated from both by an unbridgeable abyss. He cannot choose between them, because they are essentially united on those critical points that separate them decisively from Christianity. All he can do is oppose both, pointing to Christ and the foundations of Christian Western culture, which alone constitute their true antithesis. He must see these ideologies as two equally dangerous, irreconcilable enemies of Christ.

THE PARTING OF WAYS

Der christliche Ständestaat
May 27, 1934

If the previous essay is addressed not only to Catholics but to all who live within the world of Western civilization, this essay is specifically addressed to Catholics. In particular, von Hildebrand wants to challenge those who adhere to a "merely theoretical, merely literary Catholicism" and who are therefore easily confused about the compatibility of Nazism and Catholicism. He admonishes them to a more strongly "lived Catholicism," for this will protect them from unreal theorizing and will enable them to "feel in their bones" the deadly antagonism of Nazism and Catholicism. In tranquil times, those who are merely Catholic on paper and those who are Catholic with their whole being mingle together and look alike, but a dramatic moment like the 1930s in Vienna has a way of revealing who is really who.

The present epoch is characterized by the fact that so many things once hidden are now being unveiled: both the good and the bad in people, which had remained concealed from others (as well as from themselves), is now coming to light. Hidden and base passions, brutality, ruthless violence, fanatical resentment, unprincipled behavior, cowardice, intellectual confusion, and weakness, on the one hand, and heroism, kindness, strength of character, noble courage, unwavering intellectual clarity, and a deep, indestructible religiosity, on the other—all these qualities are being revealed in many persons in whom one might never have suspected their existence. All this makes for a fearful trial, leading inevitably to a decisive parting of ways among persons: for the present hour leaves no room for liberal harmlessness, for just comfortably carrying on, for vacillation between good and evil, for a "classroom idealism" backed by no genuine commitment.

The present time, with its penchant for extremes, its tendency to absolutize positions, its fanatical idolatries, its unprecedented and ruthless propaganda, puts everyone to the ultimate test and compels the revelation of every person's true self. Even in the case of those who are merely confused and swept along by the tide, the present time reveals the muddled character of their thinking and how weakly they are rooted in the realm of true values.

For us Catholics, however, this time involves, above all, an exposure of our true convictions regarding Christ, His Church, and His Revelation.

The fact that National Socialism, in its content, its external power, and its broad dissemination, does not fail to impress certain Catholics reveals in a frightening way how theoretical and academic the world of religion has been for them, and how little the world of religion has actually possessed that status in their thinking and feeling to which it does, and indeed must, lay claim by virtue of its essence. Such idols would have long been rendered obsolete for any person whose life was truly nourished by the realm of the supernatural and the genuine hierarchy of values in the Christian spirit. Enslavement to an idol always proves that the soul of the person in question is not filled with true goods. When a disvalue is elevated to the status of an idol, it demonstrates that the person remained completely untouched by true values. If, on the other hand, a genuine good is elevated to the status of an idol by overestimating its value, it demonstrates that the person had not been sufficiently filled with higher values—and, ultimately, with God.

If a person has a deep relationship with the world of true art which fills his spirit with joy, he will not constantly wish he were going to the movies. If a man is filled with a great, profound love for a woman, the attractiveness of other women will not affect him. Whoever has really grasped the glory of the courts of the Lord, whoever has tasted the sweetness of the yoke of Christ, whoever has drunk of His living water, can no longer be intoxicated with blood and soil; such a person can no longer mistake stones for bread.

The fact that National Socialism possesses some kind of attraction for many Catholics starkly reveals that Christ has not reigned as King in their hearts, even if they are daily communicants and profess to be believing, convinced Catholics.

How is it even possible for the glorification of race to enthrall a person who has been born "not of blood nor of the will of the flesh nor of the will of man, but of God"? This whole sphere has long since lost its power to attract such a person—to say nothing of the horrible materialism of blood which, with its explicitly anti-Christian inversion of values, ought to awaken the impassioned protest of any Christian who is spiritually awake.

Racial identity—in its objectively proper place, free from all idolization—can never enthuse or excite the Christian, because it belongs to much too low a stratum. Unlike the bonds of family love, which are primarily based in the realm of the spiritual, the feelings of kinship or estrangement which originate in blood constitute a sphere that is triumphantly transcended by faith and the supernatural attitude. The person for whom the lower levels of motivation (such as the vital sphere) play a decisive role has not yet perceived even a hint of the world of spiritual values, let alone of supernatural reality. "Who are my mother and my brothers? . . . Whoever does the will of God is my brother, and sister, and mother" (Mk 3:33 and 35).

How could false earthly messianism and a belief in the transformation of the world by means of the form and laws of the state possibly find acceptance by a living member of the Mystical Body of Christ? No earthly messianism can make any impact upon one who has heard the words of Christ, "Behold, I make all things new"; who has grasped that only being "born anew" in Christ can transform the face of the earth; who has understood that only He can refresh those who "labor and are heavy laden"; and whose life is permeated by the sole great desire: *vultum tuum quaesivi, Domine,* "I have sought your face, O Lord."

Such a person is incapable of cloaking the state and the public sphere with a mystical aura, or of confusing it with an institution in which man can find salvation; he is incapable of absolutizing the political sphere and looking to it to provide the true fulfilment of life, for his heart says with the Psalmist, *Desiderium eorum attulit eis: non sunt fraudati a desiderio suo,* "So they ate, and they were filled: for the Lord gave them their own desire" (Ps 78:29). The Catholic who makes his own the slogan of "the totalitarian state" shows either that he is a thoughtless prattler, or that the truth of Christ has never become incarnate in him. The true Christian knows that only one thing can make a totalitarian claim, that there is only one thing which ought to give direction to our entire life, which must live in us at every moment, which has the ultimate say in everything, and to which we belong completely and unreservedly: the triune God and His incarnate Son, Jesus Christ. Only a soul that is starved and alienated from God could concede a "totalitarian" claim to earthly goods. Does not the very fact that it is possible for so many today to take questions such as those regarding the totalitarian state seriously (and even discuss them) demonstrate the existence of a horrible emptiness in their souls where Christ ought to reign as King?

How could a true Christian be impressed by phrases in which adherence to the "national community" is extolled as the conqueror of egoism and the experience of the national community is proposed as the true remedy against such egoism? For the true Christian knows, on the basis of his own living experience, that only by "dying to self" and "being reborn in Christ" can selfishness be overcome, and that any "losing of oneself" in a national community only replaces individual egoism with a collective egoism.

If someone has truly heard the words "I am the vine, you are the branches . . . apart from me you can do nothing" (Jn 15:5) and they have fallen on good and fruitful soil in him, how could he be in any way impressed by all the wretched counterfeits of those who are impotently caught up in vicious circles, falling prey now to one error, now to its opposite? The true Christian "sets his mind on the things that are above, where Christ is seated at the right hand of God" (Col 3:1–2). Can the sheer number of those who have gone astray, the fanaticism of their idolatrous devotion, and the ruthlessness of their methods avail to impress him with their deceitful offers of a purely earthly renewal of the world, with their false gods "that have eyes but do not see" and "ears but do not hear" (Ps 115:5–6)?

No—this only shows that these Christians have long since ceased to live in and for Christ. How could a true Christian regard even for a moment the submersion of the individual person into an earthly community as the ideal, confusing this act of subservience with that true gift of self to Christ in which, paradoxically, the person is given to himself anew and thereby becomes capable of the victorious love which is the foundation of authentic community? When a Christian hears statements such as "Marriage is not primarily a private matter, but the concern of the people," how can he possibly regard this as a form of selflessness, instead of reacting with horror? Even the noble unbeliever knows that marriage primarily concerns the ultimate form of communion in love between two persons and the coming into existence of a new human being out of this most intimate, loving union. For the Christian, this ultimate community of love is an image of the unity between Christ and His Church, and therefore a sacrament. The new human being who is to be born of this mysterious, holy union, this little person endowed with an immortal soul, is not primarily a new "citizen of the state," but a new citizen of the heavenly Jerusalem.

What an ignorant attitude toward the radiant virtue of purity is revealed when a Catholic priest extols becoming "parents and grandparents of a healthier and happier race" as the fundamental rationale of premarital abstinence! Has not every trace of the *sensus catholicus* been lost here?

And what about all the ludicrous respect for the "enthusiasm" of the National Socialist Youth in the Third Reich! Should not a true Catholic rather be gripped by horror and profound compassion when he sees how these youths, instead of listening to the words of eternal life and thirsting for the living waters of God, have become intoxicated with materialistic slogans and quench their thirst with rivulets of turbid water? Can we imagine St. Athanasius contemplating with admiration the "enthusiasm" of the Arians? The true Christian knows how easy it is to awaken a dynamically powerful, but qualitatively inauthentic and impure "enthusiasm," if one resolves to appeal to the lower human instincts. A Christian must really have lost sight of the clear picture of that pure and holy fire which inspired the saints, if this pitiful flash in the pan is able to make any impression on him!

There is no question that our reaction as Catholics to National Socialism constitutes an inescapable litmus test of our true attitude to Christ. In the many who oppose this horrible heresy with unequivocal courage, their response reveals a radiant heroism and a profound rootedness in Christ. We need only call to mind, for example, the [anti-Nazi] circle associated with the *Junge Front* in Düsseldorf. The opposite response exposes a religious vacuum in all those who have allowed themselves to be influenced in any way by the National Socialist movement, whether they defend it with apologetic zeal or hesitantly and tepidly approve of its so-called "positive aspects." The result of this litmus test cannot be altered merely by a visit to a church, no matter how fervent; nor by reception of the sacraments, no matter how frequent; nor by any profession of allegiance to the Church, no matter how emphatic.

We cannot close our eyes to the fact that some believing Catholics today (we may thank God that it is only a weak minority!) are bogged down in a merely theoretical, literary Catholicism, and no longer possess the *sapere Christum*, "knowing Christ." In a few days, we shall celebrate the holy feast of Corpus Christi—the feast which presents to our eyes the triumphant reality of the unfathomable love of God in the incarnation of His only begotten Son and the sacrament of the Eucharist. He who allows us to behold the glory of the Father and who once said to us: "Lo, I am with you always, to the close of the age" (Mt 28:20), He to whom alone we belong unreservedly, and for whom we exist, He stands in our very midst. He seeks each of us in merciful love, saying to us: *Gustate et videte, quoniam suavis est Dominus!* O taste and see how sweet the Lord is!" (Ps 33:9).

In light of this, how could false prophets still impress us? Have we forgotten that He said to us, "Beware of false prophets, who come to you in sheep's clothing but inwardly are ravenous wolves" (Mt 7:15)? Let us awaken to the light that envelops the Risen Lord. Let us break the spell that the false doctrines of a world alienated from God are spreading all around us, doctrines long since obsolete, disposed of, and discarded even before they arose again in our time. Let us open our hearts to the gifts of the Holy Spirit. "Jerusalem, Jerusalem, repent unto the Lord your God!"

THE STRUGGLE FOR THE PERSON

Der christliche Ständestaat
January 14, 1934

Von Hildebrand is known in philosophy for his Christian personalism, developed from his teachers Edmund Husserl and Max Scheler. It was, then, only natural for him to express his rejection of the Nazi ideology by showing that it is based on radical distortions of the human person. This essay is a good specimen of his personalist refutation of Nazism.

He begins the essay by speaking of the weariness felt by many people with "individualistic liberalism." By liberalism he means a certain approach to the human person that detaches man from God and has the effect of isolating men and women from each other. Von Hildebrand realizes that many people, weary of the bad fruits of liberalism, were being drawn into the Nazi orbit by thinking that Nazism was the true antidote to liberalism. They thought, for example, that the revival of German nationalism in Nazism restored the sense of community that they were missing. Von Hildebrand argues that the distorted image of the person in Nazism renders this ideology completely incapable of renewing authentic community. Only by setting the human person in relation to the personal Christian God can we overcome at its roots liberalism and its depersonalizing effects.

The spirit of the age is characterized by disaffection with individualistic liberalism. There are at least three positive elements in this trend, which can be summarized as follows: first, the subjectivism and relativism of the past few centuries have prompted a yearning for the realm of the objective: a longing for objective being, which rests in itself and cannot be reduced to a mere product of our imagination or thought; and for the realm of objective values, which possesses a significance and validity that is independent of our arbitrary will and subjective satisfaction.

Second, there is a yearning for the organic, and a growing aversion to the dominion of the mechanical, to the machine taken as the covert *causa exemplaris* ("paradigm") of all of life. In concert with such tendencies, there is also a rejection of the brutal construction of all things "from without," of the violent and artificial, and of the delusion that everything is doable. There is a longing for what is saturated with meaning, for what has developed organically and "from within," for what has grown instead of what has been made.

Third, there is a yearning for genuine community and a renunciation of any conception of the human person which fails to recognize his essential ordination to community and degrades community to a mere "means" which is indispensable only in a technical or practical sense. People are rejecting the dissolution of the essence and value of community, which reduces it to a mere sum of individual persons juxtaposed atomistically. They yearn for organic communities instead of merely artificial and arbitrarily constituted social structures.

This elementary craving for the objective, the organic, and community is the positive side of the coin of our time. The elementary breakthrough is the healthy, welcome response to the sins of liberalism and Enlightenment rationalism, the barren subjectivism and relativism of the nineteenth century, and the reduction of the cosmos—so saturated with meaning and illuminated by value—and the spiritual person, created in the image of God, to a bundle of sensations and sublimated drives (be it the libido or the drive for prestige).

It is a response to the reduction of the world of eternal truths, reposing in themselves, to merely subjective necessities of thinking. It is a response to the technological transformation and mechanization of the whole of life, to the excess of action at the expense of contemplation, to the bustling haste of the modern way of life, to the lack of reverence and understanding for the mysterious law of growth "from within," to the overgrowth of organization, and to the so-called "Americanism" in which the category of the quantitative suppresses the category of the qualitative.

Finally, it is a response to the uprooting of the individual from the community, to the atomistic juxtaposition of persons in social life, to the replacement of the social ranks by social classes, to the overgrowth of committees and associations, and to the dissolution of genuine communities into purely purpose-oriented associations, which possess a merely juridical reality but no proper value of their own. It is a response to a basic attitude which is not merely anthropocentric, but egocentric, because it sees the ultimate goal of life as the material prosperity of the individual, around which everything else revolves.

This reaction is, as such, good and healthy, but the paths to which it is presently leading are anything but good. Today the spirit and the spiritual person have been devalued, thanks to humanitarian liberalism's failure to understand the essence, destiny, and true dignity of the human person, and this discrediting is being preserved, not overcome. Out of weariness and disappointment with the image of the human person which, as developed by liberalism, has dominated non-Catholic Europe for centuries, many are turning to the subhuman and sub-spiritual for the fulfilment of the yearning described above.

But those who are doing so have not yet grasped the real cause of the trivialization of the cosmos, namely, the separation of the world from God, who is the epitome of all values and the archetype of all that exists, in whom all beings find their source, for whom they all exist, through whom all that exists has its meaning and value, and to whom all existence ultimately leads. When the light that "enlightens every man" was extinguished, every being was emptied of its meaning and value. Naturally, this has had radical and profound consequences, above all in the highest sphere of creaturely existence—i.e., in the sphere of the spirit and the spiritual person. For the greater the image of God in a being is, the more is its meaning and essence falsified when it is detached from God.

As I have already stated in these pages, nothing is more needed in the present-day chaos than a clear recognition of the hierarchy of being, as taught both by Revelation and the *philosophia perennis* [the tradition

of Greek and Roman philosophy]. We may add another task of immediate urgency: the rehabilitation of the spiritual person and the whole
sphere of that which is specifically spiritual. The following remarks
are meant, above all, to help overcome the pernicious anti-personalism
which threatens to undermine the whole of Western culture.

To begin with, we must grasp the causes of the discrediting of the
spiritual person brought about by liberalism. We must also recognize
that the true return to the objective, the organic, and to community
does not lead away from the spiritual person, but rather back to his real
essence and value.

It is entirely inadmissible to posit an antithesis between the person
and that which is objective. It is indeed true that only the human being
(insofar as he is a spiritual person) possesses the freedom which allows
him to deviate from the objective *logos* which governs being. Just as only
the human being can sin in a free revolt against values, so also only he
can go astray. Material objects, plants, and animals simply "are"; the
objective laws of matter and life operate in them. Only the spiritual person, as a conscious and free being, can behave "non-objectively," building up a world of mere outward appearances and denying the objective
order of being in his judgments, choices, and emotional responses.

Only the person is capable of behaving in a merely subjective manner which is not in accordance with the objective *logos* of being. But this
does not mean that the person as such is excluded from the realm of
objective being, or is incapable of behaving objectively—in conformity
with the objective *logos* of being. Insofar as he is a spiritual, personal
substance with a conscious existence that unfolds in meaningfully motivated acts such as knowing, willing, and loving, the human person is
not something "subjective" that stands outside of objective being. On
the contrary, the person is not even in the slightest less objective and
metaphysical in his being than the realm of matter or life; indeed, he
is a higher, much *more* potent being. Above all, he is a being who possesses an incomparably greater fullness of meaningful activity.

The human person did not create himself by his own power. He
discovers his personal existence as an antecedent gift of God, just like
the existence of his own body, of other persons, and indeed of the entire

cosmos created by God. In the same way, he discovers his freedom and his abilities to know, love, and will as an objective fact. In other words, neither he himself nor his abilities belong to the realm of the "subjective," of what is illusory, of that which exists only for the perspective of a subjective consciousness. The human person and his abilities, indeed his entire structure as a person, are objective *par excellence*. They are, in fact, a much more authentic image of God, the source of all objective existence, than all other created beings.

Furthermore, while the person's ability to gain knowledge and his freedom of response do entail the possibility of error and sin—i.e., the world of the merely "subjective" and "non-objective" which contradicts the objective *logos* of being—they also entail the possibility of a form of objectivity which is much higher (because it is more like God) than everything else in existence. Such is the objectivity that lies in knowing the truth and freely affirming the realm of objective values. True judgment and morally good behavior represent a highpoint of "objectivity," a kind of marriage with the objective *logos* of being.

Accordingly, true longing for the world of the objective need not lead away from the world of the personal; rather, it ought to lead *into* this world. To lose sight of the dignity and nobility of *ratio*, its classically formative power, and its illuminating fullness, simply because the rationalist intellect of the Enlightenment thinkers was flat and uninspired, would make for a lamentable misunderstanding.

The realm of the conscious, when it is wedded to the objective meaning of things and their place in the world of values, soars to spectacular heights far above all non-personal being, including the unconscious sphere to be found in the person.

Here we must also recall what we have written in these pages about the immense priority that the purely spiritual sphere in the human person has over the vital-psychical sphere. How much *more* objective and *more* "full-bodied" (because more similar to God) is the rational insight into the essence of some object than the obscure notions and impressions which arise in the vital-psychical sphere? How much *more* objective is the luminous, free, consciously sanctioned response to a clearly grasped and understood value than dark drives and strivings, or mere blind feelings of sympathy and antipathy? To claim that the latter are "more objective" (because devoid of freedom and consciousness) than purely spiritual acts would be as absurd as asserting that the inability to sin, which we find in purely material objects such as stones and mere creatures such as fish, is something higher than what we find in the spiritual person, who alone is capable of the true antithesis to sin— namely, morally valuable attitudes such as fidelity, justice, purity, and kindness.

The spiritual person, however, is not only objective in an even higher sense than all other beings; he is also a much more organic being than all other living things (e.g., plants and animals). How can we discern the hierarchy among organic beings? By grasping the degree of a being's inherent saturation with meaning, the extent to which the *materia* is governed by the *forma*, and the meaningfulness of its structural laws— all this constitutes the criterion of the organic.

Obviously, the spiritual person is, in this regard, enormously superior to plants and animals. In the person, we find a meaningfully conscious, "awakened" being that is aware of itself, but in plants and animals, we find either no consciousness at all, or merely a foggy consciousness bereft of the ability to perform meaningful acts. In the human being, there is a continuity of spiritual consciousness, a clear knowledge of self-identity in the sequence of individual experiences, and a continuous development of experience, but in animals, there is (at best) a discontinuous, momentary consciousness. The person is a rational being who is not only connected with his environment causally, but can touch it "intentionally" [that is, by being mentally present to it] and penetrate it in an act of knowing; he is capable of thinking, drawing inferences, and providing a meaningful motivation for his conduct. In an animal, however, we find, at most, mere sense impressions and instinctive reactions.

The person has freedom, responsibility, and the ability to possess moral values; but in the case of plants and animals, these are nowhere to be found. In the human person, there is a meaningful system of experiences: there is insight, emotional response, free will, and action; but in plants and animals, there is, at best, a merely causally linked sequence of impulses and modes of behavior. Although the word "organic" comes from the vital sphere, the real prototype of the organic among creatures is not any lower life-form, but rather the human being as a spiritual person. He stands much closer than plants and animals to the category of the *genitum, non factum* (begotten, not made).

The misunderstanding which gets in the way here is analogous to the one we previously encountered in the case of objectivity. Only the person is capable of producing the artificial. In the sphere of matter, the mechanical governs; in the sphere of life, the organic. In contrast to that which has grown, the artificial—or more specifically, that which has been "made" in an external way, such as machines or anything in the sphere of technology—necessarily presupposes a spiritual person. But this does *not* make the person into something artificial, neither the spiritual person himself, nor the real, essential depth of his inner life, nor even his behavior.

The predominance of the artificial in the epoch which was influenced by the liberalism of the Enlightenment; the triumphal march of technology during much of the nineteenth century and the beginning of the twentieth; the overgrowth of action when compared to contemplation; the primacy of a person's achievements over his being as person; the relegating of all of modern life to the periphery of existence—modern life, with its haste and its hurry, its inner impatience which no longer leaves any time for an event to develop from within; in a word, its so-called "Americanism"—all this has devalued the person, who is viewed as the origin of everything that is non-organic and artificial. But the real path out of the dead-end street of the artificial back to the organic does not pass via the cult of the vital. It passes via the rediscovery of the real essence of the spiritual person and what constitutes his true center of gravity.

It is of the utmost importance to see how much more organic the specifically spiritual sphere in the human person is than the vital-psychical sphere. The lucid, rational penetration into the essence of an object is incomparably more organic than ethnically linked beliefs and convictions which form themselves "anonymously." The freely sanctioned response to a value that is clearly grasped and understood is much more organic in its structure than the obscure, ethnically linked emotion of antipathy toward something that is perceived to be "foreign to the species." In the former case, there is an incomparably more meaningful union with the object. In reality, the organic does not constitute an antithesis to that which is luminous, conscious, and free—for otherwise the "Father of lights," who is the embodiment of all *ratio* and consciousness, would not be the *causa exemplaris* of all that is organic.

We must insist today with all possible emphasis that the true positive antithesis to the realm of the artificial and non-organic is not some obscure "stirring" of indefinable feelings and notions, but in fact the spiritual sphere in the human person—the sphere of the conscious "marriage" with being in a clear, lucid insight; in the value-response of a sanctioned love; in the free, meaningfully motivated will supported by the realm of objective values.

Similarly, to believe that the path to true community entails a rejection of the spiritual person, resulting in an affirmation of the cult of the vital and the vital-psychical sphere, is a pernicious mistake. First of all, we must note that community is possible only among persons, never among plants and animals. A community of dogs or cattle cannot exist. The specific structure of "community" as such necessarily presupposes the spiritual person. The notion that the appreciation of community rises in proportion to the debasement of the individual is a grave error which is wholly due to liberalism's devaluation of the spiritual person.

When the person was mutilated by being detached from God, and the meaningful, free, immortal person destined for eternity was reduced to a meaningless bundle of sensations, it inevitably became impossible to recognize the essential orientation of the human person to community. The same mutilation of the person has also led to further misunderstandings—not only to misconceptions of the essence and value of community, but even a supposed antithesis between person and community. In reality, the failure to understand true community is born of the failure to recognize the true essence and value of the spiritual person. Every form of anti-personalism necessarily ends by replacing genuine community with a mass or a pan-psychic totality.

It is also necessary, however, to see that the communities anchored in the purely spiritual sphere of man are much more authentic, typical, and organic communities than those rooted in his vital-psychical sphere. The "ethnic community" that arises out of mere tribal peculiarities, common living habits, and shared customs or practices is not more "full-bodied," organic, or profound than the nation which is anchored in the spiritual sphere, or the cultural and linguistic community which results from a consciously lived history. The nation not only stands much higher in value than the "ethnic community" which is anchored in the unconscious; it is also more organic in its structure because it encompasses a much higher realm of meaning.

This is true *a fortiori* of communities that are even higher than the nation, such as the family, marriage, and mankind. What a gulf separates the family from the clan. The clan is a community anchored in the vital-psychical sphere. It is based upon mere ties of kinship, certain common customs, and shared living habits. It is instinctive, sub-spiritual, obscure, and without content.

The family, however, is built upon the community of love in marriage, and the fact that children, as creatures endowed with immortal souls, have been entrusted to their parents by God—a fact which goes far beyond any mere ties of blood. It is built upon the task of educating children for life, and, above all, for God. It is built upon the creation of a spiritual milieu suffused with love and understanding, a milieu in which the human person can organically mature toward his vocation. But without an ultimate understanding of the essence and value of the spiritual person, and without recognizing that such a community must, by its very essence, be anchored in the spiritual sphere of the human being, the high dignity and value of this community simply *cannot* be grasped.

Only the rehabilitation of the human being as a spiritual person and the specifically spiritual sphere in him (as opposed to the vital-psychical sphere), only a radical overcoming of the anti-personalism we meet in Bolshevism and National Socialism, can fulfil the longing of a humanity disappointed by liberalism—the longing for genuine community, for the organic, and for the objective.

Anti-personalism, when carried through to its ultimate consequences, is always atheism—indeed, is the hatred of God. The assertion that the non-personal is higher, more comprehensive, and greater
than the personal constitutes an insurmountable obstacle on the path
to God. We encounter it in every form of pantheism, as well as in
pure atheism. It is the original source of all substitutes for God. Anti-
personalism is incompatible with all Revelation. Even in formal terms,
it revolts against the person of the God who speaks to us, and still
more against the God who loves us with an infinite love. Thus anti-
personalism necessarily bars the way to knowledge of the true God, in
whom the yearning for the ultimate foundation of all that is objective
and organic is satisfied at last.

That only God can provide such satisfaction becomes most obvious
when we consider that all human yearnings to be set free of error and
perversion must, in the end, lead to Christ. "Christ is the solution to all
difficulties," says one Church Father. As long as we rely on ourselves
rather than the God-man, Jesus Christ, absurdities of every kind—
including the perversion and violation of the hierarchy of being—
cannot be avoided.

The starting point for supernatural life in the human person—both
for an objective, ontic community with Christ as well as a personally
lived and experienced community with Him—is the spiritual person,
the purely spiritual sphere in us. "But to all who received him, who believed in his name, he gave power to become children of God; who were
born, not of blood nor of the will of the flesh nor of the will of man, but
of God" says the Gospel according to St. John (1:12–13).

Thus, anti-personalism signifies a separation from God and the
supernatural link to God through Christ. Furthermore, it denies the
highest and most authentic community of human beings with each
other, the unity of the members of the *corpus Christi mysticum* (Mystical Body of Christ). For this ultimate objective community, which is
possible only through a free gift of God, comes to the human being *qua*
spiritual person; that is to say, it presupposes the specifically spiritual
nature of the human person. All sanctification of the vital-psychical

and purely corporeal sphere of human beings is secondary, insofar as it presupposes a human nature formed by the Spirit or, to put it another way, insofar as it presupposes that grace attaches first of all to the spiritual person.

The incompatibility of everything connected in even the remotest sense with anti-personalism, everything that is in any way influenced by the present-day revolt against the spirit in National Socialism and Bolshevism, must be relentlessly exposed and unmasked. What, then, is the great imperative of the present hour? We must overcome the devaluation of the spirit. We must put the vital sphere and "blood" in their proper place. And we must rehabilitate the spiritual person in his true essence and value. In the night of contemporary anti-personalism, the words of the Psalm on the human person shine brightly: "Thou hast made him little less than God, and dost crown him with glory and honor" (Ps 8:5).

THE CHAOS OF OUR TIMES AND THE HIERARCHY OF VALUES

Der christliche Ständestaat
January 7, 1934

Here is a short excerpt from one of the essays that adds something impor-
tant to the previous essays: von Hildebrand speaks about the need people
feel to get beyond a way of living that is overly mechanized and controlled
and to recover a more organic and abundant way of living. He argues here
that the Nazi ideology is completely incapable of meeting this need, and
that its teaching and practice is in fact opposed to the more abundant life
that people long for.

The same persons who reduce the spirit to a mere function of one's
racial pedigree, who maintain that personality is a result of membership in an "elevated" race, and for whom physical health constitutes the
ultimate standard of judgment, also display a shocking ignorance of the
true meaning, value, and mystery of life. It is not just that the individuals who proclaim this cult of the vital sphere exhibit markedly psycho-
pathic traits. They also attempt to mechanize life in accordance with
a typically rationalistic attitude—an attitude whose ramifications are
on display for all to see in their mad idea that they can "breed" human
beings, in their arbitrary interference with human procreative capacity,
and in their "rationing" of human reproduction.

Do we not encounter, in such measures of the Third Reich, the spirit of mechanistic rationalization, so antagonistic to life; the spirit of irreverent arrogance, as depicted by Goethe in the character of Faust's assistant, Wagner; the spirit that reduces the world to an insurance agency; the spirit that strives to remove all risk from the world—despite that fact that life's deepest gesture, life's most profound and intimate act, is precisely the taking of a risk in which the person gives himself superabundantly? And does not the idea of a "total" state, one which interferes in every area of life and sets up commissions to "regulate" its mysteries—thereby suffocating all freedom—represent a total failure to recognize the true essence and value of life as something that, by its very nature, flows and pulsates freely? Truly, the present-day trend that pits life against the spirit, fancying itself to be the conqueror of rationalism, is in fact thoroughly permeated by mechanistic materialism and the very irreverence which characterized the Enlightenment.

AUTHORITY AND LEADERSHIP

Der christliche Ständestaat
December 10, 1933

This excerpt continues the thought of the previous excerpt.

Underlying these aberrations is a false belief in the power of the state to transform the world, a belief which is the foundation of socialism, of Bolshevism, and of National Socialism. Once man has become estranged from God he all too easily makes the state into a means of salvation.

It is at this point that we see the fundamental antithesis to the Christian view, which is also the view of Plato in the *Republic*. According to the view of the Church, the face of the earth cannot be renewed "from without" through laws of the state, but only "from within" through the transformation of each individual in Christ, through full and completely personal membership in the Mystical Body of Christ. Socialism believes, on the basis of its materialistic view of history, that a change of the economic order would transform earth into a paradise. Bolshevism wants to use blood and terror to replace the bourgeois type of human being with a new type. National Socialism thinks that it can create a "Germanic" type of human being with the brutal means of power available to a totalitarian state, through racial breeding, and through propaganda, and that it can call a new culture into life.

It is the old story of the search for the Philosopher's Stone. Quite apart from the various ideals which these movements hope to attain, and their substantial incompatibility with the ideal of the Christian, they all share, formally speaking, a naïve, mechanical conception of the process through which the world can be inwardly transformed. They want to bring on changes by force "from without," but these are possible only through the individual's free will, which is supported by the Church's stream of grace, guided by the Magisterium of the Church, and formed by Christ. They expect of the state things that by their essence are reserved to the Church.

MASS AND COMMUNITY

Der christliche Ständestaat
January 12, 1936

One main focus of von Hildebrand's philosophical research throughout the late 1920s was political and social philosophy. This research culminated in many publications, most notably his 1930 book, Die Metaphysik der Gemeinschaft *(The Metaphysics of Community). This philosophical work was the ideal preparation for the task that he undertook in Vienna by means of his journal. He often draws on this work whenever he analyzes the depersonalizing collectivism of Nazism and Bolshevism. In this essay he explains what it is to be absorbed in a mass, in contrast to living as a person in an authentic community.*

It is a fact that people react very differently when they are alone and when they are in a mass gathering. How easy it is for harmless people, who would never be capable of brutality on their own, to get carried away to the point of violence in mass gatherings! Certain slogans that have no effect on single individuals can "trigger" enthusiasm, emotion, or rage in a mass gathering. How much more volatile and unstable is a mass of people than an individual!

It seems that the individual abandons himself to much more irresponsible and uncontrollable passions and instincts when he is part of a mass. This situation robs him of his perspective, suspends the rule of reason, and hands him over to irresponsibility. We need only think of threatening situations that involve some imminent danger. If a mass of people is present, panic breaks out so easily; people who would behave much more reasonably if they faced the same danger alone or only in a small group lose their heads and become irrational. The war psychosis and the mass movements in the political upheavals of recent years offer sufficient examples of such irresponsible mass reactions, and show us clearly how low the individual's behavior patterns sink when he acts as a mere part of a mass gathering.

We consider it necessary and timely, therefore, to ask how the effect of becoming part of a mass on an individual is related to the essentially different elevation and inspiration that he experiences by being sheltered in a genuine community. Many confuse mass and community, and think that they see a return to genuine community in the growing tendency to make the individual part of a mass.

A mass is quite distinct from the various forms of genuine community like the family, the state, the nation, and the Church. First of all, in a mass, individuals are accidentally and un-organically lined up next to each other; they are thrown together without any inner principle of unity. In every community, on the other hand, there is a definite principle of unity, based on the realm of meaning at its core in the context of which individuals encounter one another.

Each community has a definite theme that forms it interiorly and gives it its particular countenance. Individuals belong to communities in a variety of ways, depending upon its theme. The family appeals to one aspect and stratum of the person, the state appeals to another, and the nation to yet another. A mass, however, lacks the structure provided by such an element of meaning; it is an accidental, unformed conglomeration of people which does not constitute any definite spiritual space in which each person has an ordered function comparable to that of citizen or subject, father or mother, brother or sister, and so on.

Second, linked to this distinction is the fact that the individuals in a mass possess a uniform role. Each person is, so to speak, the same as everybody else. In contrast to this, each individual in the community possesses a different, definite, and clearly delineated function. The community does not impose uniformity upon the individual, but rather (all solidarity notwithstanding) preserves the individuality of each person untouched. A mass, however, robs each person of his individuality, categorizing everyone as "average."

Third, a mass has a destructive effect on the human being as a spiritual person: it makes him irresponsible. The individual loses himself in a mass; he loses his head; he surrenders himself to something dark, intangible, and anonymous. In the community, he is dealing with something constant and tangible, something which appeals to him as a spiritual person, gives him a definite responsibility, and confers upon him rights and obligations. In communities structured with authority, the authority can relieve the individual of the responsibility for certain decisions. His position is one of conscious obedience, which he puts into practice as a free spiritual person—he does not simply "let himself go."

If we ask which aspects in the human person are awakened by being in a mass and how the individual is influenced as an element of a mass, the answer will always be: by sub-rational aspects and illegitimate forms of influence. The individual does not react with his own spirit when he is a part of a mass. He is not convinced by sound arguments or evident intuitions, but is instead swept along by suggestion and purely dynamic influences. A certain sensational atmosphere of the mass situation opens the floodgates to every illegitimate influence. Just as certain speakers can talk only when surrounded by this atmosphere and perform like a *prima donna* only in front of a mass, so too the listener is infected by his surroundings. There is an uncontrollable urge to imitate; the cheaper a slogan and the baser its appeal, the more receptive will the mass be to it.

Enthusiasm without an objective basis, unfounded indignation, and cheap emotion can all be found here. The same slogans, the same pseudo-pathos, the same dynamic effects which leave a person unaffected when he is alone in his accustomed surroundings, can "trigger" him if they are presented to him when he is in a mass gathering of people.

Genuine community is completely different. Here the individual retains his customary critical distance vis-à-vis all ideas and thoughts that are presented to him, and the community milieu makes him even more conscious and responsible. The principle of unity on which the community is based appeals—and the higher the community, the stronger the appeal—to the human being as a spiritual person and orients him in a special way to certain issues and realms. Through his membership in a community, his spiritual eye takes particular note of everything which belongs to the theme of that community. But this does not make him more predisposed to illegitimate influences, to being captured by the power of suggestion, or to being dynamically "swept along." His consciousness as a member of a family, as a citizen, and so on makes him even more aware and more critical with regard to every question that touches on the theme of the respective community.

Communities are a beneficial spiritual help because they provide a spiritual space in which individuals can gain better insight and achieve greater clarity in matters that would have been more difficult to grasp on their own. This is not to be confused with the illegitimate, uncritical attitude that goes hand in hand with being taken over by a mass. A community unites human beings as spiritual persons in an ordered, meaningful way and is a great support and help for its individual members in forming resolutions, in developing a readiness to perform heroic deeds, and in holding fast to one's convictions. The support of the community does not make individuals immature, nor does it rob them of their responsibility, nor does it function as a substitute for legitimate conviction. Instead, it creates a spiritual space which facilitates insight into ideas, because this space is itself shaped and formed by these very ideas, helping one to draw the consequences that flow from them. Objectifying a certain spiritual content which lives, for example, in a family or religious order serves to strengthen the individual and gives him special support.

It would be entirely wrong to take the influence of a milieu which operates on an intuitive level (rather than on the level of intellectual cognition) and equate it with the illegitimate, sub-rational element of suggestion. The antithesis that concerns us here is not between intellectual insight and intuitive experiencing or between explicit insight and gradual, unconscious absorption, but between the legitimate understanding of something (in whatever fashion) and being illegitimately, dynamically "swept along" by a sub-rational suggestion or "succumbing" to it when only a momentary, superficial influence has been exerted.

The higher a community's realm of meaning is, the more will it be concerned with the ultimate meaning and authentic destiny of the individual. In the supernatural community of the *corpus Christi mysticum*, the ultimate meaning of the community coincides with that of the human being. In general, the person comes into his full personality only in a community; hence in this highest of all communities, he fulfils his ultimate meaning as an individual person to the degree that he is fully a member of it. This community constitutes the utmost antithesis to a mass. But as we have seen, even the communities which are based on lower realms of meaning are also entirely distinct from a mass.

As soon as a community attempts to be more than its realm of meaning objectively permits—as soon as totalitarian tendencies begin to take hold in a state or nation, or their significance is exaggerated by being deified—the danger of the individual being taken over by a mass inevitably arises. What a community, given its particular essence, cannot achieve is replaced by the individual sinking into a mass.

Today there is a special danger that the individual may be absorbed into a mass, since the longing to overcome individualism, the desire for something which we ourselves do not produce but discover, something that is greater than ourselves, leads to the view that being "caught up" in the exhilarating atmosphere of a mass or being "swept away" by something intangible is a great suprapersonal experience. Just as the sub-rational, vital sphere has been deified, likewise here the sub-personal has been confused with the suprapersonal.

These people know so little about genuine objectivity that they fail to grasp that real growth beyond one's own subjective narrowness and arbitrariness is bestowed by every real insight into an objective truth and all behavior that conforms to it. They stretch out their hands, therefore, for a substitute that consists in some kind of power which comes to them from outside their own selves and is independent of their own arbitrariness and decision-making, whether it be mass movements or certain so-called "modern" currents in the air today. In reality, however, they do not grow beyond their own person, but slide down to the sub-personal level. They think that they have been caught up by something great and superior; but their feeling rests on a delusion.

Similarly, our desire for the legitimate support and enhancement of our subjectivity which genuine community provides, and our need to be embedded in a unity that does not stem from our arbitrary choice, can go terribly astray when we seek these things by being dissolved into a mass. The fleeting, sensational intoxication of the exhilarating atmosphere of a mass, which is quickly followed by an awareness of coming to one's senses—for every person of any depth has a guilty conscience over letting himself be "swept along" by illegitimate influences and yielding to his lower instincts—is worlds apart from the noble elevation that is granted to an individual living in a genuine community.

Here too, as with most contemporary aberrations, we encounter anti-personalism as a primary root of all the evil that has arisen in our times. We must once and for all stop elevating the community at the expense of the individual. We must grasp that the community cannot be pitted against the person. Individual and community are ordered to one another in such a way that we will never be able to understand genuine community if we do not clearly acknowledge the human being as a spiritual person made in the image of God. At the same time, we will never do justice to the essence of the person and the fullness of his being if we do not fully understand the nature of community.

As I have often affirmed in these pages, the modern anti-personalism which we encounter in Bolshevism and National Socialism represents, not a victory over liberal individualism, but its ultimate and most radical consequence. Only the rehabilitation of the human being as a spiritual person, as a being with an immortal soul destined to eternal community with God, can save us from being dissolved into a mass and lead us to genuine community.

INDIVIDUAL AND COMMUNITY

Der christliche Ständestaat
November 18, 1934

In this excerpt von Hildebrand brings more philosophical precision to the critique of collectivism. Drawing on his investigations in The Metaphysics of Community *(1930) he charts a course between "liberal individualism," which asserts the individual at the expense of deep bonds of community, and collectivism, which asserts the community at the expense of the individual person. He makes a particular point of saying—and this is very characteristic for his personalism—that liberal individualism fails really to understand the individual person, and that collectivism fails to understand community. One main target of this essay is the Austrian philosopher Othmar Spann (1878–1950), who said: "It is the fundamental truth of all social science . . . that not individuals are the truly real, but the social whole, and that the individuals have reality and existence only so far as they are members of the whole." Von Hildebrand thought that this way of exaggerating community played right into the hands of Nazi collectivism.*

In this essay, he summarizes the major themes of his social philosophy in sixteen theses.

1. The fundamental mistake of individualism is its failure to acknowledge that the human being is a spiritual person endowed with "intentionality" [the capacity to understand reality]. This failure isolates the human person from the world of objective meaning, values, and ultimately from God, due to its anthropocentric deformation of the world. Paradoxical as it may seem, it disfigures the human person very severely and effaces his true dignity.

2. Community can never be understood if the individual person is not grasped in the full depth of his being, nor can the individual person ever be fully understood if his capacity for sustaining communities and his fundamental orientation to community are not grasped. Every attempt to degrade the individual in his ontological dignity and value takes its toll on community. And any degradation of community that views it merely as an association which is indispensable for the achievement of certain external purposes but completely lacks a being and value of its own also entails a trivialization and mutilation of the person.

3. The individual person is a substance; natural communities such as mankind, family, state, nation, class, and so on, are not substances. No natural community exists as substance. Accordingly, the individual is ontologically superior to all natural communities.

4. The individual person is not just one substance among others. As a person, he is much more authentically a substance than an inanimate object or an organism. As a person, he is incomparably superior to all that is non-personal, and therefore also to natural communities, which have no personal being.

5. The individual person is incomparably more than a mere member of a natural community. As an individual person, he is ontologically antecedent not only to his function as a member of a community, but also to the communities themselves. With respect to the ontological relationship between an individual and a totality, the comparison between the organism and its members is applicable to natural communities only in part. (The case is different, however, with the supernatural community.) This is because natural communities (such as mankind, nation, state, and class) are not the ontological foundation of the being of the individual person; individual persons "sustain" the being of communities. Thus, the form of a totality differs in principle from that of an organism.

6. Although non-artificial communities (such as mankind, the family, the state, the nation, and the class) are not "organisms" in the full sense of the term, they are organic "wholes" that encompass individual persons as members. They do not simply unite them as an aggregation of individuals.

7. Communities are ontologically antecedent to individual persons insofar as individual persons are members of a community—that is to say, insofar as they enter into a community as its members. It is true that individuals sustain the community (though not *vice versa*). However, the community sustains the function of membership which the individual person exercises. This is why the *bonum commune* in the community—for example, in the state—is superior to the *bonum* of the individual citizen, whereas it is greatly inferior to the *bonum* of the individual person, to his meaning as a spiritual person, and, above all, to his salvation.

8. The individual person is superior in value to all natural communities not only in an ontological sense, but also because only he can become the bearer of moral values and (more importantly) a vessel of grace, albeit only through a completely gratuitous gift of God. Natural communities other than mankind—the state, the nation, the class, etc.—have a longer lifespan than the individual, but they are, in the last analysis, merely mortal, whereas the individual person is immortal. God is glorified more by a single saint than by any state *qua* state, or any other natural community, no matter how perfect it may be. It follows that we must utterly reject every instrumentalization of the individual person which measures his value according to his usefulness to a natural community such as the state—such as we find, for example, in every form of Spartanism. This is also the basic mistake of every form of nationalism.

9. On the other hand, communities possess a value of their own. They are valuable not only because of their importance for the individual; they also glorify God directly by their own perfection. But their own unique value is less than the intrinsic value of the individual person.

10. In questions or situations in which the *bonum commune* and the *bonum* of the individual come into contact with each other on the same level—for example, the economic situation of the individual in relation to that of the state or class—the *bonum commune* has the higher status and takes priority over the *bonum* of the individual.

11. The individual is objectively placed by God in communities such as mankind, the state, and the nation, wherein he discovers already

existing obligations toward these communities; but such obligations do not bind him on the basis of his own decision to become a member of these communities, as is the case with one's obligations to a club.

12. Another basic mistake of liberal individualism is the idea that the more peripheral a good is, the more it is addressed only to communities and not to individuals. According to this view, the goods of civilization are addressed to communities, but the higher goods are reserved only for individuals. This is the source of the well-known slogan that religion is a private matter.

For liberal individualism, the human being becomes lonelier in proportion to the increasing sublimity of the realm of values to which he relates. In his depths, he is alone. From the Catholic point of view, however, the opposite is true. The higher the realm of values is, and the deeper the level in the person to which it appeals, the more does it address not only the individual, but the community as well. God is the most intimate concern of every individual person and at the same time the most widely shared concern addressed to humanity as a whole—in other words, each individual responds to God out of the "we." Therefore, the more elevated the good that constitutes a community's realm of meaning, the more closely knit and authentic that community will be.

13. The higher the good that constitutes a community's realm of meaning, the greater will be the conformity between that community's realm of meaning and the authentic meaning of the individual person. In the Church as *corpus Christi mysticum,* the meaning of the community totally coincides with the supernatural, ultimate meaning of the individual person. Similarly, the meaning of mankind and the natural meaning of the individual person largely coincide. Hence, every attempt to instrumentalize the individual person in his relation to the community collapses, for here being an individual person and being a member of a community overlap. The more perfect the individual person is as such, the more perfect will he be as a member of the community; conversely, the more perfect he is as member of the community, the more perfect will he be as an individual person. However, in communities whose realm of meaning is not identical with the meaning of the individual, and in which the given realm of meaning encompasses

only a fragment of the individual—for example, in the state, the nation, the class—there is a very great danger of instrumentalizing the person, once his function as a member is considered to be more important than his being as an individual person.

14. The central foundation for every living consciousness of community, and for a new awakening of life out of a "we" (such as we find in the Church's liturgy), is a very profound respect for the individual person, his eternal worth, and his inalienable rights, together with a clear insight into the terrible sin that lies in every instrumentalization of the person and his being, which occurs when the person is seen primarily as a mere means for the production of non-personal goods.

15. Every form of anti-personalism (which is seen most clearly in Bolshevism and National Socialism) is a logical consequence of liberalism's failure to recognize the true essence and value of the person. But such anti-personalism goes far beyond what existed in liberalism, since it intensifies the individualistic error and disvalue. Anti-personalism is the great and terrible danger of our times. Irrespective of the guise under which it presents itself, this poison must not be allowed a role in the construction of genuine community.

16. No less important than the revitalization of the consciousness of community is a renewed understanding of the objective hierarchy of communities: first the Church as *corpus Christi mysticum (Mystical Body of Christ)*, then mankind, then the nation, then the state, and so on. The due consideration of this objective hierarchy is more important than all the autonomy of the individual natural communities. The idolization of a community, which permits its autonomy to run rampant and is typical of all forms of nationalism and all idolatry of the state, demolishes the real spirit of community—that is, of genuine and objective community. Such idolatry is every bit as egocentric as the individualism of a single person.

Today it seems more necessary than ever to keep these various elements clearly in mind as we undertake a fundamental clarification of the errors of individualism and collectivism. There can be no doubt that the hallmark of the present epoch is an "anti-personalism"—one of the most terrible aberrations of the human spirit—and that it is not only non-Catholic, but (whether consciously or not) extremely anti-Catholic. This anti-personalism, which finds its dreadful and unambiguously consistent expression in Bolshevism and National Socialism, is also present in a hidden and implicit form in many other contemporary attitudes: in the cult of the unconscious, in the idol of the "new objectivity," in nationalism's deification of the nation, in the idolization of the state, and so on.

The more we grasp the whole greatness and depth of the human being as a spiritual person who is ordered to God and possesses an eternal destiny, and the more we overcome the great danger of our times— the objectification and effacing of personal being—the more we will be able to bring about the revitalization of the authentic spirit of community. The correct starting point for the victory of the true and Christian idea of corporative community lies here, in a reawakening to the entire fullness of personal being. But the path to this goal is also indicated by the perennial admonition in the words of the Gospel: "For what will it profit a man, if he gains the whole world and forfeits his soul?"

Dietrich von Hildebrand went on to have a second life in America. He taught at Fordham University in New York until 1960, but even in retirement his philosophical energies never abandoned him. He continued to write voluminously until his death on January 26, 1977. There is a rich vision of individual and communal flourishing that informs his work as a whole; a vision that is waiting to be discovered by a new generation.

ACKNOWLEDGMENTS

We wish to thank our many collaborators whose dedication has made this book possible. We thank in a special way Mary Seifert, Michael Wenisch, and Fr. Brian McNeil, all of whom worked on the translation of the essays. Justin Keena did two complete meticulous reviews of the essays, which greatly improved their readability. Warmest thanks go to David Mills, who read and reviewed the entire manuscript and aided in crafting the editorial bridges that make the memoirs accessible to a general audience, and to William Doino, whose knowledge of Austrian and German history during the 1920s and 1930s is extraordinary and who helped craft explanatory notes on sensitive historical questions requiring great nuance.

We thank Christopher T. Haley for his review of the entire text, notably the introductory materials, which are greatly improved thanks to his fine sense for the craft of writing. John Connelly, Denis Kitzinger, and Rabbi Mark Gottlieb each provided crucial advice at critical moments. Enzo Tatasciore provided perspective and mirth when the work became overwhelming. Last but not least, a word of thanks, also, to Dylan Naegele, for transcribing some of von Hildebrand's notes and for visiting the National Archives in Washington, DC, in search of Nazi-era documents.

Our work began thanks to the Earhart Foundation, which funded the translation of the memoirs and essays with a generous grant in 2005. Additional funding from Earhart allowed John F. Crosby to write a study of the essays, of which a shortened version appeared in *First Things* ("The Witness of Dietrich von Hildebrand, 2006). Further major support came from Robert Luddy, the Cushman Foundation, Sean Fieler, Rita Benson LeBlanc, Peter Lawrence, and Charles Scribner III.

We must acknowledge a special group of benefactors who not only supported this volume but who have sustained the overall work of the Hildebrand Project. Without these generous men and women, there would be no Project, and this volume would not exist today. We thank Madeline Leblanc Cottrell, Rose-Marie Fox-Shanahan, Mary G. Georgopulos, Robert D. Hurt, Edward and Alice Ann Grayson, Nicholas and Jane Healy, Paul and Barbara Henkels, Roy and Elizabeth Heyne, Robert Kreppel, H. Kimberly Lukens, Patricia C. Lynch, Franco Madan, Jeffrey and Mary Petrino, Robert and Joan Smith, Jules and Katie van Schaijik, Alice von Hildebrand, and Gregory C. Woodward.

The Project could not have expanded in our earliest years were it not for Lee and Margaret Matherne, whose generous and faithful support enabled us to gain momentum. We thank Michael W. Doherty, who contributed the very first money we ever received. We express our deepest gratitude to Howard and Roberta Ahmanson, whose generosity is only outmatched by their friendship. And finally, words simply cannot express our immense gratitude to Robert Luddy, our dear friend, who for years has proven his faith in our mission with financial support both momentous and unceasing. To all our donors, our deepest thanks.

Perhaps no single group of friends has done more to make this book a reality than the Hildebrand Project's board of trustees. Here we must particularly single out Stephen Klimczuk-Massion, a senior member of our board, who more than anyone encouraged our hope of securing a major national publisher and "presenting Dietrich von Hildebrand to the world." We warmly thank Duncan C. Sahner, chairman of our board, who has advanced our work with wisdom and prudence. We owe an immense debt of gratitude to William Rooney who, with support from his colleagues at the firm of Willkie Farr & Gallagher LLP, provided countless hours of *pro bono* legal services during the contract negotiations with Random House.

A special word of gratitude is due to our literary agent, Loretta A. Barrett, for helping open the door at Random House. and we warmly thank Gary Jansen, our editor at Random House, who has become a great friend. No writer could ever hope to have a more faithful champion than Gary when it comes to ensuring that a book really becomes what it is destined to be.

We are deeply in Alice von Hildebrand's debt for her trust in allowing us to consult not only the original text of the memoirs but also the countless files and precious documents in her possession.

If I may speak individually in these final lines: This book has been a work of nine years. Through these years no single person has done more to support me than my beloved wife, Robin-Marie Crosby. She has faithfully fed the hungry and caffeinated the weary, but I am most deeply grateful for the way her love and her smile always manage to restore my hope, even in the most difficult of moments.

John Henry Crosby with John F. Crosby

NOTES

Who Was This Man Who Fought Hitler?

1. Dietrich von Hildebrand, "Selbstdarstellung" in *Philosophie in Selbstdarstellungen II*. ed. von Ludwig J. Pongratz (Hamburg: Felix Meiner, 1975), 107. All excerpts from this text translated by John Henry Crosby.
2. Von Hildebrand, "Selbstdarstellung," 77.
3. Balduin Schwarz, "Errinerungen an das Wirken Dietrich von Hildebrands in Deutschland und in Österreich," in *Memoiren und Aufsätze gegen den Nationalsozialismus*, ed. Ernst Wenisch (Mainz: Matthias-Grünewald Verlag, 1994), 362.
4. Quoted by Paul Stöcklein, "Dietrich von Hildebrand: Errinerungen an die Persönlichkeit und ihre Zeit (Vornehmlich 1933–1938)," in Wenisch, 368.
5. Stöcklein, "Dietrich von Hildebrand," in Wenisch, 366–67.
6. Christiane Kuller and Maximilian Schreiber, *Das Hildebrandhaus* (Munich: Allitera Verlag, 2006), 21.
7. *Die Metaphysik der Gemeinschaft* (Augsburg: Haas & Grabherr, 1930), untranslated into English.
8. *Reinheit und Jungfräulichkeit* (Köln, München, Wien: Oratoriums Verlag, 1927), English translation: *In Defense of Purity* (London: Sheed & Ward, 1931).
9. John Noonan, *Contraception: A History of Its Treatment by the Catholic Theologians and Canonists* (Cambridge, Mass.: Harvard University Press, 1965), 494–95.
10. *Gaudium et spes*, sec. 47–52.
11. Dietrich von Hildebrand, "The Jews and the Christian West," in *Logos* (2006), 145–72. An excerpt appears in this volume, 270ff.
12. John Connelly, *From Enemy to Brother: The Revolution in Catholic Teaching on the Jews, 1933–65* (Cambridge, Mass.: Harvard University Press, 2012). Connelly argues that von Hildebrand is one of the forerunners of the Church's teaching on the Jews promulgated at Vatican II. See especially chapter 4.
13. Stöcklein, "Dietrich von Hildebrand," in Wenisch, 366.

A Note on the Text

1. *Memoiren und Aufsätze gegen den Nationalsozialismus* (Mainz: Matthias-Grünewald-Verlag, 1994).

1921

1. The encyclical in question is *Au milieu de Sollicitudes* (On the Church and State in France), 1892.
2. Von Hildebrand was active in the Association, serving as chairman of the "Committee for Cordial German-American Relations" and as a member of the "Society of the Friends of Argentina in Germany."

1932

1. *Die Metaphysik der Gemeinschaft* (Augsburg: Haas & Grabherr, 1930), untranslated into English.
2. This text, published in German as *Der Sinn philosophischen Fragens und Erkennens* (Bonn: Peter Hanstein, 1950), was later incorporated by von Hildebrand into his major work in epistemology, *What Is Philosophy?* (Milwaukee: Bruce Publishing Co., 1960).

1933

1. *Liturgie und Persönlichkeit* (Salzburg: Anton Pustet, 1933). English translation: *Liturgy and Personality* (New York-Toronto: Longmans, Green, 1943).
2. *Satan at Work* (St. Paul, Minn.: The Remnant Press, no date), 41.
3. Robert Leiber, SJ, "Pius XII," in *The Storm Over the Deputy*, ed. Eric Bentley (New York: Grove Press, 1964), 190–91.
4. "Österreichs Grosse Deutsche Stunde" (Austria's Great German Hour), in *Die Reichspost*, no. 231 (August 20, 1933).
5. *Sittliche Grundhaltungen* (Mainz: Matthias Grünewald Verlag, 1933). English translation: *Fundamental Moral Attitudes* (New York, Toronto: Longmans, Green, 1950). Later incorporated into *The Art of Living* (Chicago: Franciscan Herald Press, 1965).
6. *Zeitliches im Lichte des Ewigen* (Regensburg: Josef Habbel, 1932). Incorporated into the significantly enlarged collection of essays, *Die Menschheit am Scheideweg* (*Humanity at the Crossroads*) (Regensburg: Josef Habbel, 1955). Only some essays in *Menschheit* have been translated into English.

1934

1. The three essays published in the *Ständestaat* were: "Das Chaos der Zeit und die Rangordnung der Werte" (no. 5, January 1, 1934); "Der Kampt um die Person" (no. 6, January 14, 1934); and "Der Sklavenaufstand gegen den Geist" (no. 7, January 21, 1934), reprinted in Wenisch.
2. In fact, von Hildebrand is referring here not to his essay "Ceterum Censeo . . . !" (no. 45, October 14, 1934), but to "Die letzte Maske fällt!!" (The Last Mask has Fallen) (no. 31, July 8, 1934), which concludes with the words, "ceterum censeo."
3. "Die neue Welt des Christentum" in von Hildebrand, *Die Menscheit am Scheidegweg*, 481–95, untranslated into English.
4. *Liturgie und Persönlichkeit* (Salzburg: Anton Pustet, 1933). English translation: *Liturgy and Personality* (New York-Toronto: Longmans, Green, 1943).
5. *Engelbert Dollfuss: Ein katholischer Staatsmann* (A Catholic Statesman) (Salzburg: Anton Pustet, 1934), untranslated into English.

1935

1. "Wer ist ein Emigrant?" in *Ständestaat* (no. 47, November 24, 1935), reprinted in Wenisch, 295ff.
2. "Wahres Deutschtum" in *Ständestaat* (no. 48, December 1, 1935), reprinted in Wenisch, 304ff.

1936

1. Anton Stonner, *Germanentum und Christentum. Bilder aus der deutschen Frühzeit zur Erkenntnis deutschen Wesens* (Regensburg, 1934).

1937

1. Dietrich von Hildebrand wrote a review of Hudal's book, "Zu Bischof Hudals neuem Buch" (on Bishop Hudal's new book), *in Ständestaat*, no. 46 (November 15, 1936).

Escape from Vienna

1. In Rudolf Ebneth, *Die Österreichische Wochenschrift "Der christliche Ständestaat"* (Mainz: Matthias-Grünewald-Verlag, 1976).
2. Ebneth, 263–64.
3. From a copy of the dispatch retrieved from the National Archives in Washington, DC.
4. The FBI located this memorandum in response to a request for documents mentioning Dietrich von Hildebrand made under the Freedom of Information Act.
5. Ebneth, see especially 217ff.
6. *The Soul of a Lion* (San Francisco: Ignatius Press, 2001).
7. Ebneth, 253.
8. Hellmut Laun, *So bin ich Gott begegnet* (Eichstätt: Franz-Sales-Verlag, 2004), 121ff. The English translation, *How I Met God* (Chicago: Franciscan Herald Press, 1983), is based on an earlier edition of the German which does not contain as much detail on von Hildebrand. Excerpts translated by John Henry Crosby and John F. Crosby.
9. Letter of Michael Braunfels to Alice von Hildebrand, May 26, 1986. Translated by John Henry Crosby.

PHOTO INSERT CREDITS

All photos and documents are reproduced with permission:

1. Alice von Hildebrand
2. Marc Sangnier with students. By permission of the Institut Marc Sangnier
3. "Hitler-Putsch, München, Marienplatz" [Beer Hall Putsch], Bundesarchiv, Bild 119-1486, licensed under CC-BY-SA
4. "Reichskabinett Adolf Hitler" [Hitler's first cabinet], Bundesarchiv, Bild 102-15348, licensed under CC-BY-SA
5. Alice von Hildebrand
6. Alice von Hildebrand
7. Austrian chancellor Engelbert Dollfuss in Geneva 1933, French National Library, public domain
8. Alice von Hildebrand
9. Questionnaire on Aryan status, Universitätsarchiv München, (UAM), E-II-1733, by permission of the Universitätsarchiv
10. Klaus Dohrn. By permission of Dr. Matthias Brandi-Dohrn
11. "Konkordatsunterzeichnung in Rom" [Signing of the Concordat in Rome], Bundesarchiv, Bild 183-R24391, licensed under CC-BY-SA 3.0
12. Kurt von Schuschnigg in 1936, copyright holder has granted blanket permission for any use
13. Franz von Papen, Bundesarchiv, Bild 183-S00017, licensed under CC-BY-SA
14. Alice von Hildebrand
15. Bishop Alois Hudal, public domain
16. Moritz Schlick in 1930, public domain
17. Franz von Papen to Adolf Hitler, April 30, 1937, composite image based on original with English translation; classified documents of the German embassy in Vienna, 4949 H Bd. 3; National Archives, Microfilm Publication T120, Roll No. 2500, frames E272603-605
18. Alice von Hildebrand
19. Hellmut Laun. By permission of Andreas Laun
20. "Anschluss Österreich" [Hitler's arrival in Vienna], Bundesarchiv, Bild 146-1972-028-14, licensed under CC-BY-SA
21. Alice von Hildebrand
22. Alice von Hildebrand
23. Alice von Hildebrand
24. Alice von Hildebrand
25. Alice von Hildebrand

ABOUT THE
HILDEBRAND PROJECT

The Hildebrand Project is the world's leading organization dedicated to the presentation and exploration of the thought and witness of Dietrich von Hildebrand. An original philosopher, ardent Christian, fierce foe of Nazism, and fervent champion of beauty, von Hildebrand defends the timeless truths of our Western patrimony while at the same time eagerly receiving and enriching the insights of modernity.

At the heart of our mission is the promotion of the religious, political, and especially the philosophical writings of Dietrich von Hildebrand and other personalist thinkers, such as Karol Wojtyla and Max Scheler. We believe that these authors offer fresh insights into perennial questions about human flourishing and the moral life, the nature of love, the demands of moral witness, Christian faith and practice, and the transformative power of beauty. We seek to bring these ideas into dialogue with contemporary currents of thought, infusing them into the intellectual, artistic, and spiritual bloodstream of our culture.

We fulfill our mission through a portfolio of distinct but complimentary initiatives: (1) we translate and publish the works of Dietrich von Hildebrand; (2) we introduce new students and teachers to his writings through educational events and student fellowships; (3) we support and promote new and established scholars working on von Hildebrand and personalist philosophy; (4) we invite our audience to become collaborators in our work through our unique *Partner Grants* program; (5) and we maintain a dynamic website that serves as the international locus for the study of Dietrich von Hildebrand and personalist philosophy.

For more information, visit: www.hildebrandlegacy.org.